C000085751

PEOPLE I HAVE SHOT

People I Have Shot

My Life as a News Cameraman

SEBASTIAN RICH
and
LISE MAYER

Foreword by Jon Snow

LONDON
VICTOR GOLLANCZ LTD
1990

This book is dedicated
to the memory of
John Hoagland (photographer)
who showed me how

and to Scrumblebumpkin
who will never know how much

First published in Great Britain 1990
by Victor Gollancz Ltd,
14 Henrietta Street, London WC2E 8QJ

© Sebastian Rich and Lise Mayer 1990

The right of Sebastian Rich and Lise Mayer to be
identified as authors of this work has been asserted by
them in accordance with the Copyright, Designs and
Patents Act 1988.

British Library Cataloguing in Publication Data
Rich, Sebastian
  People I have shot.
  1. Foreign news. Reporting by British
  news media, Biographies
  I. Title II. Mayer, Lise
  070.433092

ISBN 0-575-04673-2

Photoset in Great Britain by
Rowland Phototypesetting Ltd, Bury St Edmunds, Suffolk
and printed by St Edmundsbury Press Ltd,
Bury St Edmunds, Suffolk
Illustrations printed by Ancient House Press plc,
Ipswich and London

Contents

List of Illustrations

Photographs not otherwise credited on the page
are by Sebastian Rich

Foreword
by Jon Snow

The relationship between a cameraman and a reporter is perhaps one of the strangest working partnerships around. Suddenly you are thrown together for days, weeks, sometimes months at a time – working, eating, sleeping together. Then, as suddenly, you may not come across each other for a year or more. Yet upon the success of the relationship hangs the success of the entire endeavour. It's a chemical combination in which the cameraman has to try to conceptualise what's going on in the reporter's mind, and the reporter has to interpret what's passing through the cameraman's viewfinder.

When in 1981 ITN decided to send me to El Salvador, I waited with some anxiety to see who my cameraman would be. To travel to a country for the first time; to travel into the midst of civil war in which we would be novices; to try to unravel what was happening and make it meaningful for people at home, was bound to be a severe test indeed. On the brink of any of these adventures I am filled with self-doubt about whether I can actually do it, or whether I shall expose my ignorance, lose my nerve and fail. 'You're going with Sebastian Rich' they said . . . and with a wave of the hand the foreign editor identified him across the newsroom. What I saw filled me with gloom. Shoulder-length blond hair, bronzed chest and Rolex wrist-watch moving menacingly between the desks . . . from his broad smile to his designer jeans and cowboy boots, I thought this guy's not cut out for El Salvador. How wrong I was to prove to be.

Externally Sebastian suggests a complete disregard for anyone else's feelings, yet his camera-work is amongst the most sensitive I have ever witnessed. Thrown together with him in El Salvador I discovered that whilst philosophically we had little in common, he was able to translate precisely what I wanted into pictures. He always knew what I was after and was forever providing more than I ever dreamt of. And Sebastian is as tough as they come. He has walked many, many miles with me without complaint, and even at the end of the longest of forced marches I have known him, under fire, exasperating us all whilst he inserted a new set of filters into his camera to obtain the best of sunsets.

His book reads very much as he would like to be perceived – brash, four-letter strewn. Cameramen don't often write of their thoughts; I'm glad Sebastian has done something to remedy this. The interesting thing is that there is a dimension of sensitivity that appears to defy the written word and only finds expression in pictures. You have been warned: If you don't like the words, wallow in the pictures!

— 1 —

Life before ITN

On August 17th 1953 the staff of St George's hospital, Hyde Park Corner, informed my mother that she had just given birth to the longest baby born there for fifty years. In a childhood spent, or rather misspent, traipsing around Europe, this was for years the only way in which I distinguished myself.

My mother, née Melody Wendy Florence North Squires, was born and raised in Rangoon. Her grandfather had been the British High Commissioner to Burma, where his activities as a circuit judge had earned him a reputation as a hangman. Her grandmother – Gaga – was a matriarchal Burmese lady who graciously performed her role as hostess at the many state banquets it was the High Commissioner's duty to hold. These dinners, held in honour of all manner of visiting dignitaries and even royalty, were sumptuous affairs, and sometimes the food was even garnished with a thin covering of gold leaf.

Gaga was not a woman to be trifled with. She once found two cobras in the house, shot them with a revolver, and had a pair of slippers made out of the skins. Her marriage to my great-grandfather was always beset with a certain amount of tension (which increased dramatically after she caught him in a compromising position with the male punkawallah) and lasted till his death in 1937.

When the Japanese invaded Burma, Gaga grabbed her daughter, her young granddaughter and a small handful of family jewels and set off for the nearest airfield. There she held a pilot at gunpoint and ordered him to fly them to a British airfield. In England the jewels were valued by Lloyds at about £250,000 – in 1941 a vast sum. Unfortunately, the family fortunes took a dramatic dive when my grandmother married a no-good radio operator on a Greek tanker who managed to swindle the family out of their entire savings. Great-grandmother spent the remainder of her life in a tiny two up, two down in Chiswick, which she inexplicably but romantically named 'Longchamps' after the French racecourse.

My mother was sent to Roedean where she showed a great flair for music, playing her first solo at the Wigmore Hall at the age of fifteen. After school she went on to study at the Royal College of Music and became a concert pianist and cellist.

My father, Dennis, came from a traditional English working-class background. The Riches lived in Dorking where Dad's father was an aircraft engineer for Hawker Siddeley. Father, however, had 'artistic leanings' and managed to get a place at Kingston Art School and La Grande Chaumière in Paris. He went on to dabble in many things, working variously as a painter, storyboard artist, production designer and film director. My father and mother met quite by chance on a Piccadilly line tube train and they were married three years later.

Partly because of my parents' strange variety of jobs and partly because of their stormy relationship, I spent my early childhood wandering all over Europe, staying with various friends and relatives. Between the ages of one and eleven we moved from Madrid, to Paris, on to Mykonos, to London, then back again to Paris. I was often required to appear in one or other of my father's avant-garde film epics, usually not a very pleasant experience. At the age of six he gave me the lead role in a film he was making on Mykonos about a young boy who is stoned to death. He put fake blood on my head and told me to cry as I emerged from the sea. I wasn't enough of an actor to cry at will and I can remember vividly Father shouting and screaming at me till I obliged him by bursting into tears.

Back in England I was embarrassed to bring schoolfriends home because there were so many weird sculptures and paintings in the house. Another source of embarrassment was having a poncy name like Sebastian, and I told everyone at school I was called Steve. But the thing I dreaded most of all was my mother, the original hippy, coming to the school gates – barefoot – to meet me. My afternoons were punctuated by silent prayers: please God let Mum be wearing shoes today.

I went to Holland Park Comprehensive when it first opened, still a few years before it became so fashionable amongst middle-class trendies. In a class of thirty-three children I found it easy to mess around unnoticed for four years. Probably the only things I learned were in a photographic course which I took for a whole year. Although the course was taught in a dry and regimented fashion – the teacher talked more about converging verticals and parallax error than light, or composition, or choosing a subject – it stimulated my interest. Probably because of my father's influence, I had a great dislike for the conventional, so I'd photograph feet and coils of rope and experiment with film and different types of paper in the darkroom. Our teacher hated my work and my constant 'subversive' questions, and used to use me as an example of what not to do. He once made me stand up in front of the whole class and then said: 'Do you see this boy? This boy will never be anything in photography.'

When I won the Cameraman of the Year award in 1985, I stayed up all night celebrating with friends and in the morning drunkenly rang up my old teacher to gloat. I can't remember exactly what I said to him, but I do recall that he didn't even have the good grace to remember the child he had so continually attempted to discourage.

In his defence, to say that I wasn't exactly a model pupil is an understatement. A lot of my days were spent not at school, but hanging around the station with the bike and scooter gangs. One particular night I had a go on a scooter a friend had stolen. I was driving past Chelsea football ground when I heard the ding-a-ling of a Wolseley police car, and I was pulled over. The policeman asked me if it was mine and, in the true schoolboy spirit of owning up, I immediately admitted that I'd stolen it. I was charged with TDA (taking and driving away), which for a first offence usually carried a small fine and conditional discharge. Unfortunately, the judge presiding over my case was determined to use me as an example, and in his wisdom sent me to Borstal for three whole months. When he pronounced sentence there was a moment of silence, and then my mother leapt to her feet and shouted in her clear, upper-class tones: 'But Your Honour, he's a good boy really.'

In those days Borstal was simply a juvenile prison and we were locked up in our cells for twenty hours a day. Fighting was pretty mandatory if you wanted to survive, and I emerged from Ashford Remand Centre a hard little bastard. A few months later I was again arrested, this time for possession of speed, but I escaped with a six months' conditional discharge.

I left school a year early, without my mother's knowledge, and did a series of odd jobs at Pinewood studios, in a butcher's shop and as an apprentice sofa upholsterer. At the same time many of my friends were busy preparing for a life of crime, something which still held a fair amount of appeal for me. One day they asked me to be lookout and driver on a post office job they were planning, and I agreed.

This would no doubt have been the start of a different sort of career, but for the fact that on the very same day I was offered a job in a stills colour laboratory as a darkroom assistant and I decided to go for the latter option. My interest in photography was rekindled by this job, although my employment was prematurely terminated when I refused the boss's offer of an extra fifty quid for the privilege of letting him bugger me. Luckily those were still the days when there were plenty of jobs about, even for young, untrained reprobates like me, and I soon got more work, first doing microfilm processing, and subsequently as a maintenance spark at Lee Electric. Once again I got fired, this time after an evening which involved getting very drunk, stealing an HGV generator truck from work and turning it upside down in Park Royal underground station.

I was lucky to get off with nothing worse than the sack, and I decided to start taking things a little more seriously. 'Sixties London was a boom time for photography, and I managed to get fairly steady work as a freelance assistant to fashion photographers like Barry Lattigan and Lester Bookbinder.

Eventually I took a job as a general dogsbody at Camera Effects, an optical house creating special effects for motion pictures. Once we had to shoot a scene which involved David Niven changing into a vampire bat. A fruit bat had been hired for the occasion, but no matter how we lit it we couldn't get it to look scary enough. Eventually someone noticed that when it ate grapes it looked more vicious, so the bat handler was instructed to keep on feeding it more and more grapes. As the poor creature got fuller and fuller it started to expand until finally it was so full of liquid that it released a great shower of bat piss all over the crew.

Thanks to the interest of one of the company partners, Sheldon Elbourne, who both trained and encouraged me, I was promoted to assistant cameraman and eventually camera operator. Working at Camera Effects gave me my first contact with film cameras, but although I loved working there I was desperate to work with live action, so after a while I left to go freelance again.

Owing to the good grounding the Camera Effects job had given me, I managed to go from clapper loader, to focus puller, to camera operator and finally to lighting cameraman in just five years – a progression which could easily take someone twenty.

I met Penny in 1974 and we married a year later. My own parents were by now divorced and Penny and I lived with my mother and twelve-year-old little brother, Tallus, in her house in Chiswick. When our daughter, Polly, was born the three of us moved to a highrise council flat in Bow. Penny was teaching art in a tough school in Bethnal Green and I worked on commercials, documentaries, and second unit feature films. Eventually I was promoted to Director of Photography on a couple of rather bad B movies. One of them, *How Sleep the Brave*, was a Vietnam war epic shot entirely on location in Epping Forest.

My first contact with news coverage came out of the blue when I received a call from Ulster TV who asked me to do a week's holiday cover. I prepared myself for the worst. Limbless bomb victims, soldiers and civilians riddled with bullet wounds or torn by shrapnel. I knew it was only a matter of time before I saw dead bodies and I was determined to conduct myself with the necessary cool.

I arrived in Northern Ireland a few days before Christmas 1977 and joined up with the rest of the crew. After a couple of days had passed uneventfully I began to relax. On Christmas Eve we were travelling back from location in Londonderry in torrential, stairrod rain, chatting aimlessly, when through the wall of rain and gloom, brake-lights smeared into sight. The motorway traffic slowed to a snail's pace; on the road ahead blue lights flashed and weary policemen directed cars with ridiculously underpowered torches.

'Oh Christ, not another vehicle checkpoint.'

The sound of sirens pierced through some ghastly Val Doonican number which was playing on the radio. We started getting the camera equipment together, just in case.

We came to a halt and I wound down the window just enough for a rain-sodden policeman to poke his torch through and not get us soaked in the process.

'Driving licence please, sir.'

I had forgotten my driving licence, so I handed him my Press pass.

'What's all the fuss about?'

'Just a road accident, sir. On your way.'

At the time UTV were running a campaign about drunken driving. I thought it might be an idea to furnish them with some Christmas footage of motorway carnage. We slipped out of our lane and parked on the hard shoulder.

The rain was still lashing down and I almost changed my mind about getting out of our nice dry Granada. Following the blue lights along the hard shoulder we saw that there had been three cars involved in the accident. I shot a general view, working quickly to finish and get back to the warmth of the camera car. I was pleased that we had decided to stop – the rain and the twilight and the blue flashing lights made good, evocative pictures. Then I saw that one of the cars was on its own, halfway up the motorway banking, surrounded by Christmas presents spilt in the collision. I scrambled up the grass verge to reach it and brashly wrenched open the door. I was not prepared for what I saw. The two occupants were still sitting totally upright in the front seats, but minus their heads. Why was his tie still done up? A grotesque fascination riveted me to the ground. They looked almost cosy sitting there, the man at the wheel and the woman in the passenger seat, her hands neatly folded in her lap. My first dead bodies were supposed to be victims of some terrorist outrage, definitely not somebody's middle-aged mum and dad delivering Christmas presents to their grandchildren. They were not going to get a mention on anybody's news. A beam of light from a policeman's torch lit up the grisly stumps of their necks.

'What the fuck are you doing in here you fucking vultures? Piss off out of it.'

The first of a million vulture remarks. I stared into the police-

16

Above: Sebastian Rich and Iranian guard in press compound outside
American Embassy, Teheran, during 1979 Hostage Crisis
Below: One of the demonstrators outside the American Embassy,
Teheran

Above: A baby suffering from dysentery in a Salvadorian hospital
Below: One of the refugees of La Bamuda, El Salvador

man's face, not seeing him at all, then turned and lost the contents of my stomach.

Despite this introduction to standard news coverage, I loved the work immediately. Not only was every day different, but you had to be good all the time. Any kudos you might gain only lasted as long as the next bulletin, and as a novice news cameraman I was constantly striving to prove myself.

I accepted eagerly when Ulster Television asked me to cover the first Jumbo Jet flight into Aldergrove Airport. UTV teamed me with the then junior reporter, now Head-of-Just-About-Everything-At-UTV, Michael Beatty, and together with sound recordist Paul Erwin, we set off for the airport.

To our dismay the army, which uses Aldergrove's facilities for its helicopters and VIP flights, would not allow us to film there. They helpfully suggested that we film the Jumbo's flight over the city centre instead – thanks a bunch! Without decent runway pictures we knew the story would be pulled. We had already set up an interview with the 747's pilot, and while we were doing this we moaned to him about our predicament. The captain had a brilliant idea. His aircraft was stopping at Dublin airport to pick up more passengers, before heading on to New York. Why didn't we join them, at Aer Lingus' expense, on the trip to Dublin, and then film the beast take off from the runway there? After all, no one would be able to spot the difference.

At Dublin we carefully planned the take-off shot with the pilot and airport officials. We were to be approximately a hundred yards from the end of the runway, straddling the central yellow line. The captain was then going to take off a safe, but visually dramatic, distance away from us. That was the plan anyway. I tried to act nonchalant, as if I had been standing in the flight path of a Jumbo Jet all my life, but I was full of nerves. I only got one hit at this shot and I was determined not to screw it up.

Spreading the tripod as low as it would go, I peered through the viewfinder. At the long end of my zoom lens, the enormous 747 was taxiing down the runway as the crew went through their final checks. She looked fabulous to me, shimmering in her own engine heat. A thousand cameramen might have filmed this a thousand times, but to me it was the first time in the history of cinematography. At the far end of the runway, engines revved. I kept the Jumbo centred, wing tips on either side of the frame, and as she accelerated towards us I slowly zoomed back to fit the entire extraordinary aircraft into the frame area. All of a sudden the zoom handle came to an abrupt stop. I could go no wider on this lens.

A lightning quick calculation told me that if I was on the wide end of the zoom and the aircraft was still wholly in frame, it was very close indeed. By this time the aircraft was almost at its take-off speed and the black radar nose was looking awfully large. I chanced a glance away from the viewfinder and realised, for the first time in my career as a news cameraman, the invulnerability one feels behind the camera. My eye shot back to the tiny piece of glass that I was to hide behind so many times in the future.

'Why hasn't he taken off yet?' asked a somewhat nervous reporter.

'Jesus Christ!' Paul said.

Something had gone horribly wrong with someone's calculations. The aircraft was now travelling directly towards us at about two hundred miles an hour. The nose wheel lifted about fifty yards in front of us, but the two main bogie wheels were still on the ground. The noise was phenomenal. A terrified security man who was watching all this from the side of the runway later estimated that the Jumbo's tail had cleared the top of the camera by no more than two feet. As the plane passed over us, the blast and backwash of its engines sent us sprawling down the runway. I came to rest some fifty feet from our original position, still clutching the camera. We slowly picked ourselves up from the tarmac, bruised, cut and battered, but otherwise in one piece.

'Fuck me that was close!'

'That wasn't close – that was taking us to New York!'

The adrenaline hit us all at the same time.

'Are you boys all right?' The frightened security man who had rushed over to help us couldn't understand why we all seemed as happy as pigs in shit.

We were driven from the runway to the control tower where we reassured a very worried pilot. Seconds after take-off he had apparently radioed the tower to hand in his resignation, convinced he had killed us all.

'Belfast, as quick as you can please.'

The hundred-odd mile fare was going to make an astonished cabby's day. At the first off-licence that came into sight we stopped and bought a bottle of Blackbush whiskey to celebrate our journalistic coup. As the journey crawled on the whiskey started to replace our adrenaline high with a more mellow frame of mind.

'Christ, what did it look like through the viewfinder, Seb?'

'Fantastic.'

I couldn't really remember the end of the take-off that clearly, but it must have been fantastic, mustn't it? A terrible cloud of self-doubt swept over me. Did I have the right exposure? Had I laced the film up properly? I even had some doubts now as to whether the camera was ever switched on.

I had gone from such high spirits to such a low ebb in a very short space of time that the whiskey was making me feel slightly sick. Back in Ormea Road the forty minutes processing time was sheer, unadulterated agony. I watched every stage, and even sat in the two-foot-square darkroom with Ronnie, a very large and very patient lab technician, while he unloaded my precious footage into the various bits and bobs that would take it through the magical mystery tour of rollers and basins of coloured water.

Eventually a somewhat flushed Ronnie handed me the two-hundred-foot roll of tightly bound film, still warm. Astonishingly, there was no fanfare as it came off the final rollers.

I dived straight into the nearest toilet and went into the first available cubicle. Inch by inch I unravelled my Holy Grail. Holding up the reversal film, I could see an image. It was the correct exposure, and as far as I could tell, it was even in focus. As I burst excitedly into the newsroom all heads turned quizzically. Be cool, I thought. Catching my breath I asked if anyone had seen Michael or Paul.

'Sorry, haven't. Oh, by the way, how was the Jumbo thing?'

Jumbo *thing*, I thought. How dare you.

'Oh fine, not too bad . . . Quite good actually.' I thought I was going to burst.

'I think they're both in edit booth one waiting for you,' remarked one of the scriptwriters.

I handed over my treasure to the editor, who in my mind laced it up far too roughly in the claws and cogs of the viewing machine.

'How did it look coming off the lab, Seb?' Paul asked.

'Dunno,' I said casually. 'Went for my tea in the canteen.'

'Oh?' Paul gave me an odd look.

The screen flashed into life and there she was sitting at the end of the runway. Closer and closer she came until she almost leapt out of the screen.

'Fuck me!' the editor shouted.

It was the greatest compliment anyone had ever paid me. To end a perfect day Ulster TV had offered up the pictures to ITN, who ran them at length as an 'And finally . . .' piece on *News at Ten*, crediting a mad Irish team.

The mad Irish team decided to go to the evil Max's to celebrate our triumph. As we passed the canteen on our way down, Paul nudged me. 'Enjoy your tea, Seb?' A sign on the door read: Closed all day for redecoration.

I continued to accept more and more freelance news work for Ulster TV and for the American networks NBC and ABC. In those days they would send their cameramen away for months at a stretch, but at a time when Penny and I were living on beans, the money was both good and constant.

Three of the most hideously boring months of my life were spent in Iran during the autumn of 1979 at the height of the American Hostage Crisis. This assignment was for ABC News who sent me, a sound man, and a succession of neatly coiffured reporters to cover the story from Teheran.

Every morning our driver would pick us up from our base at the Intercontinental Hotel and transport us and our equipment to the US embassy where we were deposited at a tiny Press enclosure outside the gates. There, from nine o'clock in the morning to nine o'clock at night when the relief shift arrived, the news crews would stand huddled together in freezing temperatures while hundreds of Iranian women, whom we dubbed 'changing bags' after the thick, black, light-proof cloth bags we used to change reels of film, shouted abuse at us and chanted slogans like 'Bye Bye America' or, following an 'unfavourable' news bulletin, the more ominous 'Bye Bye ABC, Bye Bye BBC.'

In this situation it became a constant and almost impossible challenge to find ways to alleviate the boredom. The press corps's usual antidote to long periods of hanging around is to get drunk. Although Iran was now a dry country, there was a flourishing black market, and we had managed to buy some bottles of a locally distilled alcohol which was made from almonds and tasted like aviation fuel. Unfortunately, under the constant scrutiny of the antagonistic crowd outside the embassy, it was too dangerous to risk drinking it openly. One way round this problem was to start drinking at breakfast, but no matter how much you managed to swallow before you left the hotel at eight-thirty in the morning, it wouldn't last for the whole twelve-hour shift and you'd invariably find yourself with a throbbing head, a bursting bladder and several hours of work still to go.

Eventually I hit upon a solution. I made a long tube by taping a number of straws together and fixed it into the neck of a bottle of the almond vodka with a lump of plasticine. The bottle went into the pocket of my thick padded jacket and the straw passed up the inside of the jacket lining and emerged at the lapel. Pretending to be cold, I could then stamp my feet, rub my hands together and pull my collar tightly about my face while I seized the opportunity to take a huge slurp of Iranian paint-stripper. This system became widely adopted and it was not unknown for the demonstrators to be treated to the sight of the world's press dancing around wearing Mickey Mouse ears and smiling broadly at them, warm in the knowledge that we were as pissed as journalists.

The American network crews have a reputation for being far more into drugs than their more boozy British counterparts, and at the Intercontinental they always seemed to be surrounded by an entourage of strange people who would appear out of the wood-work and offer to procure anything in the general area of wine, women or controlled substances that might be desired. One night, more out of boredom than anything else, I asked a particularly persistent hanger-on what the chances of getting some really good cocaine were. 'No problem,' was his reply, which alone should have been enough to raise our suspicions. The very next day he appeared carrying a Gucci briefcase and announced that he had an entire kilo of cocaine. Our suspicions should have been aroused even further when he offered to sell us what would have probably been worth about eighty thousand pounds for a mere five hundred dollars, but everyone was already fantasising about having sufficient drugs to keep the entire unit brainless for the rest of the winter. Unfortunately, when he finally opened his case and produced a bag of the fabled cocaine, we saw that it was bright purple. None of us had much experience of drugs and we all looked at each other, wondering who was going to be the one to find out whether this violet powder was narcotic, hallucinogenic or merely poisonous. Eventually I plucked up the courage to try it and discovered that unfortunately, or possibly extremely fortunately, whatever it was, it bore no resemblance to any known controlled substance.

Flying back to London two days before Christmas, I treated myself to an entire bottle of champagne. I had left Iran with an unreasonable loathing for the country and almost everyone in it. However, only two weeks later ABC rang and asked me to return to Teheran, and tempted by what were in those days considered vast sums of money, I somewhat reluctantly agreed.

I arrived despondently at Mehab airport two days later, but as soon as I showed my passport they declared my visa unacceptable and ordered me to leave the country. The revolutionary guard couldn't understand why I looked so happy as they marched me at gunpoint to the first available plane and made me climb on board. This happened to be an Air India jet which was already on the runway waiting for clearance to take off. Once we were airborne I asked the stewardess where the plane was going and discovered to my delight that our destination was Bombay, a place I had always wanted to visit. Upon arrival I checked into the Taj Mahal hotel, sent a telex to ABC New York explaining the situation, and proceeded to spend an enjoyable week being driven around the local film studios and generally seeing the town at ABC's expense before they finally gave up hope of rectifying the situation and flew me back to London.

My first contact with ITN came while I was covering the Queen's Silver Jubilee visit to Northern Ireland for UTV, and a small bomb was found in the university grounds at Coleraine. I was the only cameraman to film the device being detonated by the army and ITN picked up the footage from Ulster. They asked who the cameraman was and this led to a number of freelance jobs for ITN. On two occasions they offered me a staff job, but both times I turned them down. Even though I thoroughly enjoyed the work, I still wanted to be a lighting cameraman in feature films.

One day I found myself working as the lighting cameraman for a milk campaign commercial. I was in the process of lighting a Yorkshire pudding rising, when the client came over and said he wanted the Yorkshire pud lit 'with pure drama'.

I laughed and we lost the account. The third time ITN offered me a permanent job, I accepted.

— 2 —

El Salvador

(1981–83)

BODY COUNTS

When I first went out to El Salvador in January 1981 neither British TV viewers nor the journalists themselves knew much about either the country or the situation there.

The Nicaraguan revolution had taken place in 1979, and after Reagan came to power in 1980 Central America became an increasingly big issue in the United States, especially when Reagan mentioned El Salvador in his inaugural address to the nation. The assassination of Archbishop Romero, who was gunned down by an army officer as he led mass in San Salvador's cathedral, and the subsequent army massacre of mourners at his funeral, increased international interest in the war. For several months Jon Snow put pressure on ITN to send him out there, and eventually they agreed.

And so one night I found myself sitting in a Miami hotel room waiting for a connecting flight to San Salvador the following day. I had never been to a real war before, and the pictures CBS were broadcasting on the set in my room filled me with such terror that I seriously considered running away. It didn't help that I was being sent out as a replacement for a WTN cameraman called Ian Mates, who had just had his head blown off by a landmine.

When we arrived in San Salvador we booked into the Camino Real, the base for most foreign journalists and crews. The capital itself appeared largely untouched by the guerrilla war which was being waged in the mountains in the north of the country. Since none of us then spoke more than a few words of Spanish, our lifeline in El Salvador was our fixer, an Italian by the name of Marcello Zanini. Zanini, who now works as a cameraman for WTN, then lived in El Salvador where he had been a columnist on a recently

24

banned newspaper. He acted as our guide, interpreter and general factotum, and on many occasions got us out of nasty situations unscathed. Marcello somehow managed simultaneously to be highly efficient and scrupulously elegant. Even when we had been sleeping on the jungle floor or crouching in the dust under fire, the razor creases on his silk trousers would be immaculate.

On our third day there we drove out of the capital, still completely ignorant about what was really going on in the country. About twenty kilometres out on the Pan American Highway we reached Sichitoto, a town straight out of a Graham Greene novel with its white stuccoed church and dusty roads where the direct vertical sun beat down on big brimmed hats and old men slumped in chairs. As we entered the central square we heard the sound of wailing, and there, laid out in a row, were fourteen coffins, lids off, and inside them the corpses of the army's latest victims – old men, women and children. This was our introduction to everyday life in El Salvador in which the extreme beauty of the landscape and the natural exuberance of the people contrasted so sharply with the horror and suffering you were constantly witnessing.

Washington had convinced the world that the troubles in El Salvador were caused by Communist infiltrators and Cubans and had hidden the fact that this was a guerrilla war fought by the peasants of El Salvador over issues like land reform.

Even within the local populace there was a great deal of confusion about the situation and some of the campesinos even believed the American propaganda and claimed there were Chinese in the hills.

When ITN first saw Snow's sympathetic reports about these unfortunate people and their suffering, they thought he had gone mad. They decided we were cutting Cubans out of our footage and sent a stern telex telling us to go off with the guerrillas and find the Cubans and Russian arms. In fact this was one of the few Kalashnikov-less wars in recent history; almost all the weapons on both sides were M16s bought in the arms bazaar in Miami and both right-wing junta and leftist guerrillas were running around with western-made weapons.

The Gulf of Fonseca is a coastal inlet between El Salvador and Nicaragua which, according to Washington propaganda, was awash with Communist-supplied arms for the guerrillas.

We decided to investigate these claims and got a facility with the Salvadorian navy. The Salvadorian naval base was in a town called San Francisco at the other end of the country. We went down with an Argentinian photographer, Beth Nissen, a *Newsweek* correspondent who travelled everywhere with her cello, and John Hoagland. John was a mad, stop-at-nothing photographer who had married a Salvadorian air hostess from Taca airways and settled in the country. He was eventually killed in crossfire while photographing a skirmish between army and guerrillas.

We didn't reach San Francisco till evening. When we booked into the one hotel in town we received some curious looks, but it wasn't until a young woman leapt into the shower with me, grabbed me by the bollocks and asked what she could do for me that I realised we were staying in a brothel.

The next day we met up with the commander-in-chief of the Salvadorian navy, who was appropriately called Nelson. This was particularly apt as the President, Duarte, was named Napoleon. Nelson was chuffed to have a TV crew on board. He denied any knowledge of arms coming in by sea. The navy was completely on the sidelines in this war, as was obvious when he took us out on patrol. Out of the navy's five patrol boats, only two were working, and one had been cannibalised for spare parts.

Even out at sea the sun was scorching. We stopped and searched only one boat, a small fishing vessel, and in general spent a pleasant day in the company of naval personnel who appeared almost totally untouched by the war. As for the boatloads of Russian and Cuban arms coming in by sea there was not a sign.

This was the sort of garbage on which Reagan had convinced Congress to go to war in Central America. Alone we were witnessing that Reagan had just been lying, and this made us very unpopular both at home and in the US where ABC were carrying our reports. Nevertheless there seemed to be an insatiable appetite for our stories. Even in the days before video and satellite when it was necessary to ship the film, we were getting a story on every night.

It was a great life, shooting by day, shipping by night. Evenings spent sitting at a whorehouse table while Snow typed his stories by candlelight. This sort of experience is dying out now – whereas in those days we would go on an assignment for weeks and sometimes months at a time, it's now rare to stay with a story for more than two or three weeks.

Our daily newsgathering outings, usually in the company of a stills photographer or one of the scribes, like *The Times* correspondent Michael Leapman, got us quite a reputation. Every night in the Camino Real we would be besieged by less adventurous journalists who'd try to find out what we had been doing. The media in general were very slow to treat El Salvador as an important news story. The BBC didn't bother to send anyone out for ages while in America word spread that it was a highly dangerous place for journalists. The result was that they didn't come, or if they did, their visits were extremely cursory. One evening when we were desperate to ship film out we drove to the airport to see if we could find a plane to transport our film. When we arrived the airfield was deserted. We were about to head back into town when suddenly a small executive jet landed. Snow rushed over to find ABC's State Department correspondent and his cameraman preparing to do a stand-upper about the situation in El Salvador without budging more than a few metres from his plane. Snow tried to persuade him at least to come in and have dinner at the hotel but he wouldn't, and minutes later he jumped back into his Lear, wiping the sweat from his forehead (and clutching our film).

The thing about El Salvador was that as long as you were with one side or the other you felt reasonably safe. Even after seeing what the army were capable of, when you were attached to them you didn't feel personally threatened.

One very real danger that you faced was that you might trigger a landmine – and quite a few journalists went that way. When you were passing through an area where the guerrillas were active it was customary to walk in front of the car carrying a white flag and keeping your eyes peeled for mines, which were sometimes just the lid of a biscuit tin. Some mines were detonated by a wire which watching guerrillas would pull when troops passed. If they saw who you were they would probably let you through. Ian Mates, the cameraman whom I replaced, had the side of his head blown off when a nervous child acting as a lookout accidentally pulled the trip wire on a mine.

The most frightening aspect of all was the right-wing Death Squads. This faction of the army was the equivalent of Papa Doc's infamous secret police, the *Tontons Macoute*. The Death Squads were responsible for the brutal murders of supporters of the guerrillas, intellectuals, known leftist sympathisers, and sometimes just people who had dared to voice dissent. Some of the victims – the *Desaparecidos* – vanished without trace, usually when the government didn't want an enquiry; others were unceremoniously dumped in the streets after the seven p.m. curfew.

During our first few weeks in El Salvador we would spend an hour or so every morning driving around the streets of the capital filming the dead bodies which had been dumped there during the previous night. This body-count run always took place before breakfast, partly so that we could film the corpses before they'd been taken away to mortuaries or their families had claimed them, but also to minimise the risk of bringing up our *huevos revueltos* all over the Paseo del Gracia.

On an average day we found about a dozen Death Squad victims, usually men between the ages of fifteen and forty. Like most people who live in relatively safe places and have watched a lot of Westerns, I had always believed that bullets make nice neat holes in people's bodies. After viewing the work of the Salvadorian Death Squads I realised that Sam Peckinpah was a master of understatement and good taste.

If someone has been shot in the head with a revolver, approximately seventy per cent of their head will be missing; if the bullet comes from a high velocity rifle, approximately a hundred per cent of their head will be missing. In fact the *least* gruesome of the corpses we saw had gunshot wounds. Some had been hacked to death with machetes, while to save ammunition others had been held in the middle of the road and run over several times with a truck.

So that no one was left in any doubt as to who was responsible for these brutal killings, the Death Squads' special signature was to leave the corpses barefoot. Sometimes they garnished their work by horribly mutilating the bodies – it was not uncommon to find corpses with their testicles chopped off and stuffed in their mouths.

*

After a few weeks we gave up our early morning jaunt. London wouldn't show any of the pictures, which they deemed too gruesome, and my colleagues were sick of getting up at six in the morning. I have always been an early riser and since at the time I was still obsessively doing my Marathon training, I started using the now vacant early morning period for regular training runs. One day, in the middle of a particularly good run, I rounded a corner to find two new corpses splayed out in my path. To the right of the bodies stood a small group of onlookers, blocking the road. I couldn't tell whether they were friends of the murderers or the murdered and I wasn't very keen on the idea of pushing through their midst – besides I didn't want to break my stride – so I simply kept going and did a neat hop, skip and jump over the two bodies. Unfortunately the percussive thud of my feet on the pavement alerted the congregation of flies which had already gathered on the bodies, and as I passed they rose up, swarming into my eyes, into my hair and straight into my open mouth and down my throat.

In 1982 an entire Dutch crew was killed by one of the Death Squads. They were caught out because their reporter used the telephone at the Camino Real to call guerrilla contacts and these were intercepted by secret police. When the crew went to make their arranged rendezvous with the *muchachos* they were followed and knocked off. I was out of the country when this happened, but the next day Snow and his crew went up to the spot where they had been murdered to investigate. A few minutes after they arrived at the scene an open-backed truck pulled up and about fourteen men carrying guns jumped down and surrounded them. From the men's threats it appeared that this was the same group who had killed the Dutchmen, and they were terrified. Eventually Zanini somehow managed to sweet-talk them down, and loaded up with watches, money, and their prize haul – a John Lewis beach towel – they left.

Snow later told me how pleased he was that I hadn't been with them. One night a few months before, he and I were stopped on the Litoral road by a fifteen-year-old boy armed with a grenade and a gun. Snow had tried to make me give the boy my new and expensive watch, and in foolhardy stubbornness I had refused.

The murder of the Dutch journalists made us realise that our British passports and press cards wouldn't save us if we came to be on the wrong side of Duarte's regime. Even in the comparative haven of the Camino Real most of us would push a few bits of furniture against the door before we went to sleep. One night at about four a.m. there was an earthquake and Jon woke up screaming and shouting, convinced some nasty had broken into his room and was trying to shake him out of bed.

His imagined scenario would not have been too farfetched. At an official press conference a couple of weeks before, the assembled journalists had gasped in awe and horror as Snow publicly asked some army generals why they always dumped the bodies of murdered civilians in the street. Later that night there was a Tannoy announcement in the Camino Real ordering the representatives of the British press to go to the hotel carpark. We nervously obeyed and arrived in the parking lot just in time to see an entire car-load of bodies dumped on to the tarmac in front of us. Jon's question had been answered.

Sitting around in the bar of the Camino Real, we often heard talk of the volcano of San Salvador or Quezaltepec Picacho, which was rumoured to be one of the Death Squad's favourite dumping grounds for the corpses of their many victims. We listened sceptically – such reports abounded in El Salvador and many were invented or at least vastly exaggerated. None of the other journalists we talked to had actually seen these bodies and the drive out there was known to be particularly unsafe.

Eventually we decided to investigate it ourselves so Jon, Don, Marcello and I loaded our equipment into our car, and with 'PRENSA' and 'TV' spelled in camera tape on the windscreens and our white cloth waving out of the window, set out of town on the road that headed for the base of the volcano.

Quezaltepec looks like a drawing of a volcano in a children's book – a perfect black triangle with the point snipped off. When we reached the foot of the volcano we pulled over to the side of the road. A gully separated us from the slopes which were made of black volcanic rock. In bright sunlight it seemed as though the whole of this black landscape was quivering and shimmering. We got out of the car and looked at the surrounding area, but we could see no sign of bodies on the undulating bare rock. Marcello was the first one of us to realise what we were actually looking at.

He shouted and waved his arms at the gully and some of the black rocks lifted into the air. What we had taken to be sunshine reflecting on lava was actually the backs of countless vultures which were busy feasting on the remains of literally hundreds of murdered people. As soon as our minds adjusted to what our eyes had been looking at it was impossible to believe that a minute before we had been unable to see anything at all. I have never before or since seen so many dead bodies in one place. It instantly reminded me of a book of Hieronymus Bosch paintings which had terrified me as a child. It belonged to my father who kept it in his study and I used to dare myself to creep in and look at the pictures.

There were hundreds and hundreds of corpses, many of them those of women and children. Some had obviously been there for months, while others looked about five minutes old.

It seemed like a particularly sick joke on the part of the killers to choose to dump bodies in a spot where the chemical content of the soil actually preserved the evidence of their crimes. It was only the greed of the vultures which gradually stripped the flesh from the corpses and when they were reduced to skeletons, the black background exaggerated the white of the bare bones.

Suddenly we all felt terrible fear that these evil people would come back and kill us for filming this evidence of their murders, and we quickly set about filming our report.

It doesn't take long to get used to grisly things if you're exposed to them often enough, but even though the sight of mutilated bodies no longer made any of us flinch, we would suddenly find ourselves retching and gagging when a surprise breeze wafted the smell of viscera and open bowels to our nostrils. At one point I was filming a corpse when a huge vulture suddenly landed on the dead man's chest cavity and unceremoniously ripped his cobblers off. We arrived back at the Camino Real with award-winning footage, but our faith in humanity shattered.

Meanwhile political momentum outside El Salvador was beginning to grow – Reagan was demanding more armies and more aid. The situation held more than a few shades of Vietnam and people expected American troops to start marching in. All this kept interest going at the London office so they kept sending crews.

For a newsman, working in El Salvador was like breathing pure oxygen; we never went to bed without having sent at least one good story. We were sitting in the Camino Real one day when lots of aid workers rushed into the hotel. They were looking for members of the international press, and when they spotted us they came over and implored us to go with them. They feared that hundreds of innocent people living in a refugee camp were about to be slaughtered by the army.

We jumped into our car and zoomed off in convoy with the Green Cross ambulances to a La Bamuda – a small settlement about forty kilometres outside San Salvador on the Sichitoto road. The village was in the middle of a very hotly contested area and there were soldiers everywhere. We stuck white flags on poles out of the car window as we drove along, hoping that these and the accompanying ambulances would lessen our chances of becoming casualties ourselves. On the road we passed the burning remains of an ambushed truck, and as we drew closer we could hear the fire of the advancing armies. We eventually rolled straight into the central square at La Bamuda where we found hundreds of very frightened *campesinos* huddled together outside the church. Of the 900 or so people there, 780 were children, mostly orphans, and about 100 were women. Although there were only a handful of men there, the army claimed it was a settlement of *subversivos*, who had been supplying food to the guerrillas. The unit commander had given them an hour to clear the camp – and said they would kill anyone who remained after that deadline. This was clearly impossible for them to meet – these people had no means of transport, and many were too weak or injured even to stand.

We accompanied some of the Green Cross workers to the local army camp, where they pleaded with the commander to extend the evacuation deadline at La Bamuda to give them time to organise some transport for the inhabitants. The commander refused their request out of hand and told them to go away. It was only when they pointed out that he was being filmed by a foreign TV crew that he grudgingly agreed to give them more time. The Green Cross workers later told us that on this occasion it was only the presence of our cameras that had stopped the massacre of hundreds of innocent people. They knew of several other settlements, where without the

Right: Army
captain,
Peñas Blancas,
El Salvador

Far right: Guerrilla
leader,
Peñas Blancas,
El Salvador

Left: Jon Snow with guerrillas in El Salvador. He was given a donkey to ride, but his long legs touched the ground on either side of the animal

Below: Sound recordist Don Warren teaching a small boy to read. Peñas Blancas, El Salvador

threat of international publicity, men, women and children had been unceremoniously slaughtered.

PEÑAS BLANCAS: IN THE HILLS WITH GUERRILLAS; IN THE HILLS WITH THE ARMY

Early in 1982 we again visited El Salvador on a filming expedition which through sheer luck was to win us every news award going. The first part of the trip had been fixed up outside the country, and involved sneaking into El Salvador over the Honduran border to join up with a group of FNLS guerrillas and film their activities. We flew down to Honduras from Miami and there hitched a lift on a single engine Cessna aircraft belonging to the French aid agency Aviation Sans Frontières. The pilot was a French Concorde pilot who flew these relief flights to refugee camps in his spare time. He was taking a great risk in allowing us to accompany him since we were planning to cross the border illegally, and if we were caught he would be held responsible. From our point of view this was a good method of entry into El Salvador because the flight cut off at least five days' march through the bush.

We crammed ourselves into the Cessna's hold along with its cargo of bags of salt and grain which were destined for a camp set up for Salvadorian refugees just inside the Honduran border. The plane took off into low cloud and flew low over the mountains. Our destination was a runway on a grassy slope, where you landed going up hill and prayed you could stop, because otherwise you shot off the other side and crashed. After a safe but bumpy landing we had to sneak off the plane without being spotted by Honduran security and hide out in the village until nightfall.

This time Jon Snow, Don Warren and I were accompanied not by Marcello but by another mad Italian fixer named Renato. This extremely erudite man was a Marxist-Leninist philosopher who had, amongst other prestigious academic qualifications, a doctorate in Middle Italian. When the going grew really tough, or on an evening when the stars seemed particularly bright, he was apt to reel off long passages of Dante, in the original fourteenth-century Italian, from memory.

When it was dark enough, Renato guided us to a rendezvous point. We left the road and walked directly into the bush for about forty metres until we came upon a small group of about a dozen armed guerrillas, calmly smoking as they waited for us. The guerrilla leader was an educated man who had been sent from higher command to escort us and act as an information officer.

The border between Honduras and El Salvador is demarcated by the course of the wide, fast-flowing River Lempa, which runs through a range of mountains. It was too dangerous to attempt the crossing at night, so we camped in the jungle, sleeping on the ground. We were sick of eating refried beans and the ubiquitous tortillas which so closely resembled heavily used face flannels, so when they pulled up fish traps full of langoustes out of the river we licked our lips in anticipation. Unfortunately our delight turned out to be premature. After they had boiled the lobsters for a couple of hours their flesh was as tasteless and rubbery as any tortilla.

At daylight the guerrillas loaded us one by one into steel petrol drums, which they had specially adapted to serve as mini canoes, and swam us across to the other bank. For several weeks we marched into the bush. Every morning when we awoke there seemed to be several more men with us. These 'anti-government terrorists' were just local peasant boys in makeshift uniforms, very friendly and cheerful, utterly committed to their cause.

The going was pretty tough. We were marching over hills covered by fairly thick jungle and sometimes when the path petered out we had to hack our way through the undergrowth with machetes. We marched all the daylight hours and sometimes for twenty-four hours at a time. Whenever we asked how much further it was they replied 'Just another couple of hours'. I think they secretly enjoyed seeing how far we could march.

Sleeping on the ground proved surprisingly easy after these long days of marching, especially with the added help of half of one of the morphine tablets we carried in our first-aid kits. One morning Don woke up on his resting place on the jungle floor to find every exposed part of his body had been bitten in the night and was covered with welts.

Breakfast always consisted of coffee and maize tortillas, lunch was a five- or ten-minute halt for more of the same. Whenever we stopped at a peasant village on the route the inhabitants would take care to see that we were well fed. Unfortunately that usually meant an even larger helping of tortillas.

As the days wore on we learned how to get into a marching rhythm by watching the heels of the man in front, but our own feet still became badly blistered. Chewing the leaves of the coca plants which grew on the hillsides helped us to combat exhaustion and the effects of the high altitude. Sometimes after hours of marching we would suddenly notice that the sun was now behind instead of in front of us and realise that we had come round in a huge circle, presumably to avoid an army patrol. Once we emerged from the cover of the trees on to an open stretch about a mile across. We had to dive for cover under small bushes on three occasions as army spotter planes made several passes overhead.

When we finally reached their camp in the Peñas Blancas village we were exhausted. A hut had been rigged up with hammocks especially for us and we unceremoniously collapsed into them, to awake banana-shaped, but restored, a good seventeen hours later. We again breakfasted on tortillas and coffee before brushing our teeth and showering. This feat was achieved by splitting a piece of cane and driving it into the mountainside. Water running down the rocky slopes collected in the gutter-shaped groove and spilled over the end which formed a spout.

For the next couple of days we stayed in Peñas Blancas filming village life. It was a sizeable village. As well as the guerrilla soldiers there were about 200 women and children and the village even boasted a school, an operating theatre and a uniform 'factory'. The village of Peñas was grouped around a clearing in the centre of which grew a spreading mango tree. This was the scene of political meetings and group singalongs, either one of which invariably seemed to lead to the other.

We had been warned not to stray from the boundaries of the village, but one day in search of a good view and a slightly more private spot where he might evacuate his bowels, Jon wandered off into the surrounding jungle. He was making his way along one of the paths which led to and from the village when some fortunate instinct caused him to glance down at his feet. There was a small dark patch in the leaves just beyond his toes and looking closely he

35

could just discern the point of a protruding spike. He was literally on the brink of a man-trap – a deep pit covered over by a camouflage of leaves and branches in which sharpened spikes covered with human excrement were set. He had stumbled upon, and almost into one of the guerrillas' own man-traps and narrowly avoided an unpleasant death, for even if he had survived the wounds caused by the spikes, the faeces would have quickly poisoned his blood. He was badly shaken by the experience, and the desire for a crap long forgotten, he took to his hammock where he stayed white and silent for hours.

A few days later, as we made the return journey through the jungle, we came upon a woman and her child treating a guerrilla who had accidentally slipped and fallen back into a man-trap of the same type which he had himself constructed. The unfortunate man had severe puncture wounds in his arms, legs and stomach. We gave the woman half of our supply of morphine – there was nothing to do but lessen his pain, in these conditions it would have been a miracle if he had survived.

Another time we walked into a village to be greeted by a young boy who stood in the middle of the path silently holding up his right hand on which all the fingers had been blown off. A small puppy ran out of a village hut wagging his tail and barking playfully. One of the guerrillas unceremoniously raised his rifle and shot the little dog through the head. That night we had meat for the first time in days.

Back in the capital we rested for a while in our four-star hotel before once again venturing into the Salvadorian bush. This time it was with the government forces, who had granted us a facility to accompany them on an expedition up country.

We set out in three helicopters with open doors, flying in V-formation over the same jungle terrain we had just marched through. We suddenly realised that we were in fact flying over almost the exact path we had taken on foot with the guerrillas, and in twenty minutes we had covered the same distance that had taken us many long days of marching. This discovery excited us considerably and I filmed Jon doing a piece to camera as he hung out of the open door of the helicopter. He had to shout at the top of his voice to be heard over the noise of the rotors and we had to pray that none of the soldiers near enough to hear could understand what he was saying.

When the helicopters finally landed our excitement grew even greater, for we recognised the spot as a small clearing just outside the very guerrilla village where we had just been staying. Without thinking I started to lead the way up the path towards the village, before a violent hiss from Jon stopped me. The young captain gave us an extremely odd glance.

Instead of the familiar Peñas Blancas village of a few days before, we were confronted by the sight of a few smouldering huts and some dead cattle, bloated and swarming with flies as they rotted in the sun. There was no sign of the guerrilla soldiers or the 200 women and children who had been living there. The army's official story was that this was the former site of a training camp for 500 well-armed guerrillas, which they had captured and razed to the ground. There was no mention of any women and children.

For the next five hours we toured the surrounding area on foot, witnessing similar scenes of destruction as we passed through a series of burnt and deserted villages. At one point we passed through an orange grove and we halted our march as one of the soldiers shinned up a tree, descending a few moments later with an orange in one hand and a honeycomb in the other – a delicious treat after the unrelentingly monotonous diet of tortillas.

Back in Peñas Blancas village before the return flight home the young captain proudly posed for a photograph under the mango tree, at his foot the bell of the captured village. Apart from his uniform there was nothing to distinguish him from the young guerrilla fighters who had stood there the previous week.

He gave us another of his peculiar glances.

'Journalists have been here, I know.'

I started to feel sick. 'What makes you think that?'

'Look!' The captain bent down and picked up a brightly coloured plastic tube from the ground. I instantly recognised it as a core from one of our film spools which I had got in the habit of giving to the small children of the village to play with.

'Of course, when we find out who they are we will kill them.'

'Of course.'

— 3 —

The Barcelona Bank Siege and Shopping with Colonel Qadhafi

(May 1981)

There is enormous competition between crews from different stations – in ITN's case our particular rivals have always been the BBC. Sometimes you succeed in beating them to the best pictures through skill, charm, experience, intuition and hard work. Other times you just get lucky.

One afternoon I was preparing to leave Wormwood Scrubs, where we had been filming some story about prison conditions. After weeks of being away or working late I had sworn to my wife on pain of death, divorce and unanaesthetised castration that I would be home early to help with a dinner party we were having that evening. However, just as we were loading the last of the camera gear into the car my bleep went. It was the foreign desk, who told us to go straight to London airport and pick up a Lear jet for Barcelona where gunmen, demanding the release of army officers arrested in the recently attempted coup, had stormed a large city bank and were holding hostages.

Because of some mix-up at the airport our correspondent, John Suchet, had had to pay for the Lear jet with his Amex card. Also in the crew were Nigel Thompson and John Holland. John Holland was one of the most popular people ever to work at ITN – also the biggest practical joker. When a few years later he tragically died of cancer, the whole of ITN gathered at his graveside to pay their last respects. Several of us stood by the grave giggling nervously, for so renowned was John for his often extremely sick jokes that we were secretly convinced that at the last moment he was suddenly going to pop out of the coffin. It was only when I saw them begin to shovel earth on to the casket that I could accept that John was really gone.

Needless to say, in terms of sophisticated behaviour and displays of intellectual maturity, our journey to Barcelona was on a par with a school outing. Suchet decided that the fact that he had paid for the plane gave him the right to pilot it, and I came away with several rolls of film, now hopefully lost, showing everyone including the pilot running around the cockpit half-dressed.

In Barcelona we went straight to the site of the siege. The twelve armed men had taken over a bank in the centre of town and were holding thirty-six people hostage. The street outside had been cordoned off by the *guardia civil*, who had ringed the bank with marksmen. Within the cordon was a special area for the press. It was a real bunfight – as well as journalists from all over Spain, several foreign TV crews had been attracted by the story. We managed to get ourselves a prime position in the street outside, and set up our equipment.

A couple of days passed. We were sleeping on the pavement next to the white tape and waiting for something to happen. What happened was: we got hungry. And then *very* hungry. Unfortunately none of us could speak Spanish and our attempts to negotiate with local passers-by for food had met with almost no success. We began to get peevish and watched jealously as other journalists tucked carelessly into their *bocadillos* and *cervesas*. We were getting desperate when John spotted an English tourist amongst the crowd of curious onlookers beyond the cordon. We pounced on him, dragged him over and begged him to save our place for about a quarter of an hour while we went out to get some provisions.

This accomplished, we returned, much restored, to reclaim our ringside patch. Unfortunately the *guardia civil* officer who was now standing guard by the cordon decided, for reasons of his own, not to let us back through to the press area. This irritated us and we started arguing with him. This annoyed him and he started pushing us back. Then he grabbed hold of my camera. I shouted 'Let go of my fucking camera' and wrenched it back. Unhappily, I didn't realise that the policeman had stuck his finger into the microphone socket at the front of the camera. As I pulled it away his finger snapped and he fell to the ground, writhing with pain.

Hearing a commotion, a few of his colleagues looked across and saw what they took to be a British camera crew waging a four-man assault on one of their *muchachos*. Before I even had time to wish I knew the Spanish for 'Just a minute officer I think there's been some terrible misunderstanding', several of them threw me to the ground, piled on top of me, picked me up again and threw me in a van along with the rest of the crew.

At the station the Spanish police gave us what was a first-class bollocking in any language, before starting to ask us hundreds of questions. All we could think about was how ITN had gone to huge expense to fly us over to Spain and we were missing the story. We kept pleading with the police to allow us back to the bank. This was a big mistake. Once they had cottoned on to the fact that the best punishment they could possibly inflict on us was to keep us as far away from the story as possible, we'd lost the battle.

We weren't registered anywhere since we'd been sleeping outside the bank since we arrived, so the police themselves rang up a hotel and booked us a room. They put us back in the van, drove us to the hotel, marched us up to the room under guard and locked us in.

Inside the room we were all going mad. Suchet and I were pacing manically while Nigel and John sat dejectedly on the bed trying to think up stories for the office about how the camera didn't work, and wondering whether we could get a feed from someone else. Eventually, and with much regret, we decided to tell London the truth. A shamefaced John Suchet phoned ITN and was just being put through to the foreign desk when we heard what sounded exactly like a rapid burst of machine-gun fire outside in the street. Everyone had been so fed up that no one had done more than casually glance out but now we all rushed to the window and looked out. We realised that we were in a first-floor room overlooking the Ramblas – the long avenue which runs through central Barcelona and is famous for its gardens, its bookstalls, its transvestite prostitutes, or in this case, its besieged banks. What the police had unwittingly done was to book us a hotel room directly overlooking the bank under siege, and giving us a far better view of the scene than we could have ever got down below on the street. The sound we heard, which so closely resembled gunfire, was gunfire. From our window we had what was probably the only unobstructed view of all the hostages lying flat on the ground while two of the gunmen sprayed the street with machine-gun fire. I grabbed my camera and started to film. A few seconds away from confessing all to the editor of the day, Suchet was now doing a piece to camera hanging out of the window.

The other crews were furious. There had been more than a little bit of gloating as we were dragged away by the not-so-civil *guardia*. Now they were being shouted at by their editors for missing all the best pictures while we went home heroes.

A few years later a young WPC, Yvonne Fletcher, had been shot dead as she routinely patrolled an anti-Qadhafi demonstration outside the Libyan embassy in London. Her killer, protected by diplomatic privilege, was allowed to fly back to Libya without even being questioned. In the midst of the ensuing furore I was despatched with Suchet and sound recordist Sean Gilmartin to cover the Libyan end of the story.

We flew to Zurich where we joined forces with an ABC crew to charter (again at vast expense) a private Lear jet to take us to Tripoli. We hadn't had time to get any official clearance, and as soon as the plane entered Libyan airspace their air traffic control radioed us to leave immediately. Our pilot, who looked as though he'd seen a few dodgy situations in his time, calmly identified our flight. Again the voice on the radio ordered us to leave Libyan airspace or suffer the consequences. Supercool Chuck Jaeger merely continued to repeat our identity over his radio while keeping his course set for Tripoli. Eventually two MiG fighters appeared out of the sky on either side of us. They flew so close that it was tempting to wave or make faces at the pilots. The MiGs escorted us all the way to the airport.

We landed at dusk and were instantly hustled off by armed guards to explain ourselves to the airport officials. The officials in question decided to dismiss us as harmless lunatics when we told them we'd come to interview President Qadhafi. For some reason they all seemed to find this idea hysterically funny.

Two days later we were beginning to understand the joke if not to share it. We were staying at the Hotel El Kabir, the press's regular haunt in dusty downtown Tripoli, but the few journalists who had managed to make it out to Libya at all found ourselves reduced to hanging around the foyer getting nothing at all in the way of hard news. We couldn't even discover where Qadhafi was, much less get an interview with him. Reactions were therefore pretty sceptical when a government spokesman turned up at the hotel at breakfast time and announced that if any of the press corps were interested, the Colonel was planning to go on a shopping expedition in a particular street in Tripoli later that morning.

We didn't hold out much hope, but sure as eggs is eggs when the appointed time came a big black limousine drew up at the street corner the government official had specified and out stepped the Colonel, only a few feet away. What a scoop. I swung my camera up on to my shoulder, focused and pressed the small start button. Nothing happened. I wiggled it again – it's all too easy for a cameraman to get over-excited and accidentally hit the delicate start button twice, only to discover when he comes to turn it off that it has been off all the time. But still nothing.

It had worked fine the day before when I shot some general views of Tripoli, it had worked that morning when we tested it in the hotel room, but now it was completely, utterly and absolutely dead. Being a mechanically minded person my immediate response was to start hitting it.

'Is the fucking camera working yet?'

'No it's fucking not.'

I kicked it a few more times, but to no avail. John was noisily going bananas, jumping up and down and squealing like a bobby-soxer at an Elvis concert. While all this was going on we were walking backwards in front of Colonel Qadhafi who was striding in and out of the local shops, while all the other reporters fired questions at him. Out of pure habit Suchet himself kept chiming in.

'The fucking camera's fucking broken John – shut up.'

We were saved from total disgrace by the ABC cameraman, who, when he had eventually got the footage he required, lent me his camera (and later some of his film of the walkabout). Suchet was finally able to interview the Colonel, and I nearly had heart failure a second time around when he made up for lost time by baldly accusing Qadhafi of being a terrorist and murderous killer (accusations which the accomplished politician coolly brushed off).

The camera of course had some minor fault rectified by a technician in a couple of hours. Such is the habit of news cameras. They always work when you're filming something stationary, but fail as soon as you're in the middle of a riot or have just spent hundreds of pounds hiring a helicopter.

— 4 —

Woolly Pully: Riots in Derry
(April 1981)

My regular sound recordist had gone sick and I had been assigned one Mr Michael Parkin as a replacement. This guy had got the job as an on-the-road sound recordist through ITN's policy of promoting from within. Michael had been a studio sound-mixer – a highly technical job, but looked down upon by us self-appointed Kings of the Road. A rather quiet, normal man with normal brown trousers, normal white shirt and even a brown tie. To round it off he wore a sweet little tank-top pullover.

The day started off quietly at Westminster. We were doing all the usual boring talking-head interviews – politicians jerking off on the sound of their own voices and political correspondents making their questions longer and more boring than their interviewees' answers.

At lunchtime I ambled to the newsroom feeling sorry for myself, and having a whinge about how bored I was.

'Okay you – Belfast now.'

Newsdesk had requested a crew to go to Northern Ireland immediately as the rioting in the charmingly named Bogside area of Londonderry was getting a little hotter than usual.

'Who's my sound man?'

I didn't think for a moment they would send Mike to somewhere like Northern Ireland. That was reserved for 'The Boys', 'The Chaps', 'The Young Lions', as some of us were referred to by Bobby, a matriarchal assignments manager.

'Mike Parkin's assigned to you today.'

'Bloody hell. You don't want to go to Derry do you Mike?'

There is a rule at ITN that if anybody feels that they don't want to go to a war zone or an area of conflict they don't have to, and I felt sure that the boffin in the woolly pully would definitely turn down this assignment.

'On the contrary – I'd love to go – I've never been to Ireland before.'

On the aircraft over to Belfast, I played the role of the well-seasoned traveller, slipping my boots off and nonchalantly reading my newspaper on take-off. To my amusement I saw Mike pick up the air safety card from the pouch in front of him and study it intently as the stewardess went through her well-rehearsed monologue of safety procedures. It dawned on me that Mike had never flown before.

We approached Aldergrove airport on a standard Belfast afternoon, grey and drizzling. The aircraft buffeted gently on its final approach and I was tickled at the sight of Mike's knuckles protruding from his tightly clenched fists. I started to read my newspaper again. We hired a car at Aldergrove and without stopping at UTV went straight to Derry.

The rain stopped long enough for us to appreciate the scenery between Belfast and Derry – a gentle pink velvet sunset was just settling into its rightful place as we sped through the Glenshane Pass.

By the time we had checked into the Everglades – a motel on the outskirts of Derry incongruously decorated in the style of its Florida namesake, there were already reports of sporadic violence in the Bogside area. But it was early yet – the pubs were still open, *Match of the Day* was still on, and the boyos were just warming up.

After dinner we drove to The Diamond, a memorial in the town's centre, and parked the car. It was a longish walk from there to the Bogside, but I didn't want the camera car hijacked and burnt – not because I had any loyalty to Avis Cars – it was just a long walk back to the hotel. Having filled Mike's brain to bursting point with horror stories of death and destruction over dinner, and revelled in watching his eyes turn into saucers, I now led Woolly Pully into the breach.

The main library was ablaze – lighting up the night sky and creating frenzied shadows of soldiers and RUC as they struggled to hold their positions at the end of the street. We eased ourselves cautiously along a wall trying to make ourselves as small as possible.

'Look out!' Mike shouted.

A petrol bomb was hurtling in our direction. We reached the other side of the road just in time to avoid being set alight. Bottles and stones rained down on us and an empty bottle hit the camera square on the lens. At this a roar of approval went up from the boyos.

'That's right you's bastards – you's hide behind the Peelers,' someone shouted.

I noticed that even with all this going on the cable between the camera and the recorder had never once tightened or become in any way a nuisance. This is an art usually attributed only to a well-seasoned player and can make all the difference in the world. A nervous or inexperienced sound man at the end of the cable – tugging or not watching where he is going – is annoying enough on an ordinary shoot, and even more so in a full-scale riot, where he has to be the eyes and ears of his cameraman.

Another petrol bomb exploded just yards away from us. With the camera still running we ran for better cover. As we were crossing the street Mike shoved me firmly in the back and I fell forward into the gutter.

'What the fuck do you think you're doing?' I shouted.

A housebrick bounced off the pavement where I had just been standing.

When we finally arrived behind the line of soldiers and police-men, we could see that the mass of rioters were just some sixteen metres away. Someone shouted 'Blast bomb!' This is a particularly nasty device – a pound or so of explosives wrapped up with six-inch nails, ball-bearings and any other kind of junk at hand. This piece of nastiness is finished off with several contact detonators which make it explode on impact. I looked up to see something flying through the air. Instinctively Mike and I flattened ourselves against the nearest brick wall. The bomb landed with an ear-shattering ex-plosion only a metre or so away. I turned to see a policeman writhing on the floor with a long steel nail firmly embedded in his throat, red foam bubbling from his lips. I stuck my camera lens into his face.

We decided to leave the police lines and try to get some pictures from the other side. As we made our way over some wasteland, I took a bottle of Scotch out of my jacket pocket and took a long pull. It was promising to be a long, fun night. In a derelict house we found a group of balaclava'd youths busy making petrol bombs. I asked if we could film from their position. 'No problem,' was the reply. Huddled behind a metre-high wall I wondered if these youths were the makers of the Molotov cocktails that had been thrown at us a few moments earlier.

'Have you's got a light?'

'Yeah sure – hang on a minute.' I ferreted around in my jacket pockets to find some matches. I turned round to light the boy's cigarette to find an unlit petrol bomb under my nose. Mischievous eyes pierced at me through a balaclava.

'Come on – give us a light.'

Fortunately, Fate and the Ulster weather saved me from what could have been an interesting moral dilemma about the impartiality of the press. My book of matches had been soaked through by an earlier downpour and was utterly useless. Mike threw me a withering glance.

About fifty metres away to our left the main bulk of the rioters had now switched their attentions to a burning RUC Land-Rover next to a row of terraced houses. We reached them just as the police started firing rubber bullets into the crowd. Great pictures as the blasts from the riot guns momentarily lit up their owners' determined faces. A terrible scream went up above the din of the riot. A young boy had been hit in the side of the face.

'Come on you's bastards – film this – see what them fuckers have done.'

His lower jaw was so much raw meat. Friends dragged him into a doorway where an old woman tried to shoo them away. The crowd suddenly turned in the opposite direction. We had been filming the injured boy and had not noticed half a dozen or so RUC who had dropped to their knees ready to fire a volley of rubber bullets into the crowd. Running from the impending salvo the panicking rioters bowled us over. This was actually a bit of luck for us as all shots went straight over our heads into the retreating mob.

By now we had it all – burning cars, bleeding boys, blazing buildings, a critically wounded policeman. It was time to call it a night and get our tapes back to the editor. We picked our way back to The Diamond through broken glass and smouldering cars. By now my whole body was shaking with pent-up adrenaline, so I took another swig of Scotch, and offered the bottle to Mike. He declined, and with steady hands continued calmly loading our equipment into the back of the Granada.

— 5 —

The Falklands: Thatcher's 'Surprise' Visit

It was that time of night when the first ring of the telephone makes your heart miss a beat, and you are out of bed and half dressed by the time you lift the receiver on the third. Tonight, however, it was only my ITN assignments manager who as usual had had a drink or two. After a lot of mumbling and heavy breathing I managed to pick out the words

'Sebastian . . . go to Falklands . . . right now . . .'

Half an hour later he had called me five times, and five times I had replied, 'Fuck off – ring me when you're sober,' before slamming the receiver down. I naturally had a few moments of wondering if he was serious, but since it was so soon after the end of the war, it was almost impossible for the press to fly to the Falklands, much less in the middle of the night. The sixth time the phone rang the joke was wearing thin and I told him so. It was only when I ran out of breath and insulting adjectives that I discovered I was in fact talking to the news editor.

The news editor assured me that there was indeed a plane leaving for Port Stanley in only a few hours' time. The Prime Minister was intending to visit the islands and had invited a small group of journalists to accompany her. Security was given as the reason for the hurried and secretive nature of the departure, as apparently there was still some fear of her plane being knocked out of the sky.

I reached the designated meeting place in Whitehall and joined up with the rest of the ITN crew – political correspondent David 'Muppet' Walter and sound recordist Roger Lorenz. We climbed on to the waiting bus which was filling up with sleepy, dishevelled journalists who, like us, had been dragged from their beds only half an hour before. Most of them were political writers and lobby correspondents who were unused to venturing further than the

Commons bar. In fact a few of them looked as though they had come directly from that very venue.

When we were all aboard and settled the coach set off for the airfield. I stretched my legs out and attempted to go to sleep. A few minutes later a sudden lurch of the bus roused me, and looking down I noticed that my boots were resting in a small pool of water. This puddle was fed by a tributary of liquid which could be traced all the way up the centre aisle of the coach till it reached its source at the trouser leg of a certain journalist. This tiny, beetroot-nosed man, who was the senior political correspondent for an international news agency, was so drunk that he had pissed himself.

The RAF seem to possess the knack of looking smart at any time. The men who met us as we pulled into Brize Norton just before four a.m. were a sharp contrast to the busload of weary journalists, which included one urine-soaked man who was so insensible from drink that he had to be carried. In the departures hall we were informed that we would be travelling all the way to Port Stanley in a CI30 Hercules. A Hercules is one of the most uncomfortable aircraft in the world, and the thought of a thirty-six-hour flight with only webbing seats was not tempting. We cheered up considerably when we were told that we would be joining up with Mrs Thatcher in Ascension Island and from there to the Falklands she and her entourage would be travelling in the same plane; we were confident that for her benefit the RAF would have jazzed up the on-board facilities.

It was just beginning to get light as we were led across the tarmac to the waiting plane, still carrying our drunken colleague. The back of the CI30 was open and as we peered into the cavernous hold I knew there was something horribly wrong. As our eyes grew accustomed to the darkness, we realised that the bulk of the hold was filled by a single, large, solid object. On closer inspection it turned out to be an enormous caravan, containing the quarters of the Prime Minister and her staff. The remaining hold space was allocated to the press corps, but, unfortunately for us, they had totally gutted the Hercules' interior to make room for the caravan, and not even the webbing seats remained. It was a nightmare journey. We couldn't talk over the noise of the four engines – what's more the syncophaser was broken, so each engine was vibrating at a different pitch – and the only place to sit was on petrol tanks.

The person who suffered the most was of course our unconscious companion, who eventually awoke to the dawning realisation that for thirty-six hours he couldn't wash, eat, or get another drink.

The only thing that alleviated the tedium of the flight was watching the Hercules refuel in mid-air. When this happened we'd clamber up to the cockpit and watch as a huge aircraft flew first alongside, then above and slightly in front of us. When it reached the correct position the back would slide open and a long hose with a shuttlecock-like attachment would drop out. It was into this that our pilot had to manoeuvre the nose of the Hercules before refuelling could take place.

After what seemed like an eternity we arrived at Ascension Island – a barren lump of volcanic rock which serves as a US and RAF base in the middle of the Atlantic. There was a six-hour stopover before our connecting flight to Port Stanley, so the RAF press officer led everyone off to the terminus for some food and sleep. I thought I would rather go for a run, so I set off on my own along the nearest road. On either side of me stretched acres and acres of crusty black volcanic rock which were completely devoid of any vegetation. It was like running across the set of *Lost in Space*. After about fifteen minutes I still felt lousy. The landscape seemed to be getting weirder and weirder and I began imagining prehistoric monsters about to jump out on me from behind the twisted towers of lava. The tarmac road I had started out on had petered out and for the last five minutes or so I had been running along a dusty track. Suddenly the track finished. By now I was completely spooked and I decided that the best thing I could do was to retrace my steps.

I must have been slightly disorientated however, because, although I thought I was going back the way I came, I suddenly realised I was running on the smoothest tarmac I'd ever seen. What was especially strange was that, unlike a road, I couldn't see the edges of it – it just seemed to stretch to the horizon in every direction. I kept running, my head hanging down with tiredness, hoping I'd come to something at the end.

At first the noise of the aircraft didn't even register – after all the island was an airbase so it was hardly an unexpected sound. It was only when I looked up to see a huge American Starlifter (at five times the size of a Jumbo Jet, the biggest aeroplane in the world) thundering towards me that I realised that I was jogging along the main runway of Ascension Island. I belted over to one side and sat down to watch it take off. After a few minutes some MPs arrived, and after a brisk reprimand drove me back to the Portakabin and the rest of the journalists.

After another ten hours in the hold of the C130 we arrived in Port Stanley. The wooden buildings with their roofs of corrugated iron, the greenness of the grass and the grey, drizzly weather give it the appearance of a village in the Hebrides and make it hard to imagine that you are just off the coast of South America. In the aftermath of the war the military greatly outnumbered the rather bemused islanders, whom the troops had unkindly dubbed 'Bennys', after a particularly stupid character from the TV series *Crossroads*. Everywhere you looked there were abandoned or crashed Argentinian helicopters and Pucara fighters, and the ground was littered with ordnance of every description, much of it still live.

Our hotel was a wooden shed with a tin roof. Argentinian officers had been billeted there during the war and the owner had obviously made quite a tidy profit out of the conflict. For the next five days we accompanied Thatcher in her Chinook helicopter as she flew around the islands talking to a few crofters and shaking hands with everyone in sight. Roger Lorenz, a staunch socialist, amused himself by sticking a CND badge on the end of the microphone so that everywhere she went this badge was a few centimetres from her nose.

On one occasion her press advisers saw and seized upon a fantastic photo-opportunity when the army asked her to try out an anti-aircraft gun. She was duly seated upon it, given goggles and earmuffs and warned by the gunner to be careful of the recoil. At this she turned and called to Denis, who was lurking somewhere in the background, 'Denis – do you think this thing will jerk me off?' When she looked back the entire press corps were sniggering helplessly.

During our brief sojourn in the Falklands my running once again got me into trouble. On my first morning in Port Stanley I ran down to the quayside then turned left along the shore and headed towards

Tumbledown Mountain. There was a track bearing off to the left and I ran along this for a while, before jumping over a small barbed wire fence into a field. I assumed the fence had been put there to keep some sheep in. This was a bad mistake. I had run about two hundred yards into the field when a huge voice suddenly bellowed 'STOP'. The owner of the voice, a sergeant in Her Majesty's armed forces, proceeded to inform me that I had run into the middle of a minefield. He and a few soldiers in a jeep watched from the other side of the fence as under his instructions I attempted to retrace my steps. Since I had been zigzagging and jumping over the chalky patches in the grass it was almost impossible to see the route I had taken. For a while I inched my way back, extremely scared and expecting to be blown to bits every time I put my foot down. After I had covered about twenty yards in this manner I could stand it no longer and just started to run hell for leather. I finally collapsed in relief on the other side of the fence and was treated by the sergeant to a large slug of Scotch and one of the worst bollockings of my life.

— 6 —

Lebanon
(1982–3)

KHALDI

Total pandemonium reigns at Beirut international airport. It is controlled by the Lebanese army and whatever faction happens to be in favour on that particular day, so every security guard is his own boss, and bribery is about the only way to achieve anything. I arrived there early in the afternoon of June 24th with Des Hamill, sound recordist Nigel Thompson and editor Peter Read to cover the reported escalation of hostilities by Israel against the Lebanon. No sooner had we cleared immigration when an armed official pounced on our equipment and refused to give it back to us until we'd paid him the correct 'duty'. Several hours and several hundred dollars later we finally cleared customs and caught a cab to the hotel.

Like any newly arrived crew we were anxious to get some decent footage in the can as quickly as possible. Even if you aren't working towards a particular bulletin or feed time, there is always an urgent need to establish yourself on the ground, and it is not uncommon for a unit to do more work in the first four or five hours after arriving in a place than in the entire remainder of the trip. Thus after only a brief stop-off at the Commodore Hotel, a four-star concrete tower in downtown Beirut used almost exclusively by journalists, we went out to get some pictures.

Our usual driver, Ahbed, wasn't available, so instead we hired one of the young men who were always hanging around outside the hotel in the hope of getting a fare. With his racy black Golf GTI and blue jeans, this driver looked incongruous even in a city full of bizarre sights. Although he had had no experience of working with news crews, he seemed extremely enthusiastic, and spoke reasonable English. So while Peter went up to his room to sort out the editing gear, Des, Nigel and I squeezed into the car and went straight out into the streets of Beirut.

It was immediately apparent that the bombing was much heavier than at the time of my last visit only a couple of months earlier. Although we didn't know it yet, the Israeli invasion of the Lebanon was imminent, and they were paving the way with frequent air attacks on suspected PLO positions.

In our quest for newsworthy pictures, we developed a slightly crazy *modus operandi* which involved cruising around the streets of Beirut watching the Israeli bombers come in. As soon as we saw where they had dropped their loads, we would speed over there in the Golf and film the ensuing carnage. Since this system enabled us to arrive at a place literally a minute or a minute and a half after it had just been bombed, we were getting dramatic footage of blazing fires, shattered buildings, and dying people – all the stuff a news editor's dreams are made of.

After about two hours of this grisly ambulance-chasing, we noticed that a squadron of Israeli Kfir fighters were now heavily strafing the little seaside suburb of Beirut called Khaldi. From our vantage point at the top of the coast road we had an extraordinary view as the planes swept along the beach and dropped their cargoes of cluster bombs and rockets, sending up huge fireballs and clouds of smoke.

Like many boys I had become enthralled by aircraft at an early age, and from several miles away the destruction of Khaldi was a romantic sight. I felt as though I was filming an expensive and carefully orchestrated scene in a war movie, as the formations of fighter planes emerged out of the sun to bombard the houses, cafés and beach huts of this sleepy little town.

As soon as the fighters had departed we threw our equipment in the Golf and headed off down the coast road towards Khaldi to view the aftermath of the attack at close quarters. Sure enough a large proportion of the area had been destroyed. A single 1000lb bomb can leave a crater the size of a house, and the Israeli fighters had dropped dozens on the PLO unit which was encamped there. As we stopped the car a large building on the other side of the street slid gracefully to the ground.

We got out of the Golf and identified ourselves to one of the many PLO soldiers who were scattered around the area. He and his comrades were extremely cordial, perhaps pleased that a news crew was recording their plight, and we soon found ourselves standing in the midst of the smoke and rubble, chatting and taking snapshots.

In retrospect, our naïveté was staggering, but for some crazy reason we had assumed that once the fighters had hit a target they went away. The extent of our stupidity became all too clear when a young soldier to my right suddenly called out '*Ishi ishi ishi!*' which in Arabic means 'They're coming!' or 'They're back!' I looked up and saw some rapidly growing dots in the sky. They were the Israeli jets heading straight for us at 600 miles an hour. All of the romantic, *Boys' Own* notions I had felt earlier, the excitement at the speed and power of these aircraft when viewed from a safe distance, disappeared as fast as the planes approached.

As they dived towards us the air was filled by a noise so enormous, so deafening, that it caused physical pain. Before we even had time to comprehend fully what was happening, a couple of the Palestinian soldiers grabbed hold of us and pushed us down into a trench which ran along the side of the road. As I fell, I glanced behind me, just in time to see our car and driver, a mere twenty metres away, vanish in a huge ball of flame as they received a direct hit from a bomb.

Des and Nigel had also been bundled into the trench and we huddled there with a couple of soldiers while planes screamed, bombs whistled and the force of repeated explosions shook the ground. Every time there was a blast, the resulting change in air pressure made you feel as though you were being punched in the stomach and your face and the force of the shock waves made your whole body shake. For minutes I lay there in a foetal position burying my face in the earth at the bottom of the trench, so scared I could hardly breathe.

Each time a plane came down we would hear the scream of the engines, closely followed by the whoosh of rockets and the screech of bombs, which were specially fitted with strips of metal which caused them to emit a high-pitched whistle guaranteed to induce greater panic in their victims. Each time there was a period of about seven seconds between the bombs' release and their landing, seven seconds in which you tried to bury yourself deeper and deeper into the earth and willed the bombs to kill anyone else but you. From the timing of the explosions it became apparent that the Israelis were pattern-bombing the trenches in our area and it was only a matter of time before one landed in ours.

I suddenly became aware that Nigel, who has a degree in mathematics, had adopted a half-sitting position in the trench and was holding forth to no one in particular about the odds of one of the fighters scoring a direct hit on our trench. He was busy formulating equations, taking into account the velocity of the planes, the estimated air speed of the bombs and the surface area of our ditch, in order to demonstrate that mathematically we would actually be most unlucky if a bomb landed on us.

I looked up at the Palestinian fighter on my other side; the khaki of his uniform had been visible out of the corner of my eye and for some reason this had afforded me a small measure of reassurance in the midst of this utter terror. I suppose I had somehow assumed that because he was in a uniform he would know what to do. When I looked up at his face, however, I saw an image of pure fear. His lips were drawn back over his teeth in a snarling grimace and tears poured from his eyes. There was blood dripping from his hands where he had actually buried the fingers of one hand into the flesh of the other.

As the minutes passed we began to perceive a certain pattern in the attacks. There were about three fighters which would swoop down and bomb us before peeling off to regroup and come back once more. We started having a discussion about whether to stay where we were or run for some better cover during a hiatus. It was like the sort of conversation you might have in the pub except that fear made the physical action of speaking very difficult.

Since no one could come to any decision, I asked Des if he wanted to do a piece to camera. Under the circumstances it seemed as good an idea as any other, so during one of the brief intermissions in the bombardment, I got into a kneeling position with the camera on my shoulder and Nigel crouched behind me with the boom. We had to be careful to stay below ground level as the bombs were still falling close enough for the force of the blast to tear your head off had you been foolish enough to stand. We had actually started recording and Des had said something like, 'As you can see the PLO are under very heavy aerial bombardment,' when the planes were suddenly upon us again, diving full throttle out of the sky.

The next time the planes peeled off I knew I had to get out. I reached above me with both hands and pulled myself up. As soon as I stuck my head out of the trench I realised to my horror that I had put my hands into what little remained of the stomach of one of the young soldiers we had been talking to and photographing minutes earlier. The most extraordinary thing was that although he had lost both legs and most of his entrails were hanging out, he was still alive. He was moaning softly and saying in English (Jesus, why in English?) 'Help me, help me, help me.'

We jumped out of the trench, uncertain what to do. On the ground in front of us the soldier lay dying and calling for help; above us the fighter planes were re-grouping for another attack; and all the while the little ITN computer in my brain was telling me that I was surrounded by award-winning news footage. All I felt was fear, and all I could think was that I wanted to be anywhere else but here by this trench and this dying soldier waiting for the planes to come back. Nigel appeared beside me with the recorder and we actually went through the motions of trying to link the sound cable to the camera, but we were shaking so much we couldn't do it. In the end we just ran.

We had noticed a disused café and some beach huts about a mile away, in an area where there didn't seem to be any bombing, and it was for these we headed, Des and I passing the camera back and forth between us as we ran.

At one point we were overtaken by a Red Cross ambulance travelling at tremendous speed. We flagged it down, and our spirits rose as it slowed, convinced that now we would get whisked away to safety. Our feelings of relief evaporated when the back doors flew open and a man with a Kalashnikov greeted us with a burst of machine-gun fire. To this day we have never managed to find out who he was or why he fired at us; but it further enhanced the nightmarish quality of the whole episode.

At last we made it to the café on the beach. It was a hot day and despite all the adrenaline I began to feel rather woozy. I sat down in one of the beach huts and put my hand to my head. When I brought it down it was covered with blood. Upon investigation Des found and extracted a piece of shrapnel the size of a thumbnail, which was embedded in the side of my head, just above my right ear. Under the circumstances we had got away extremely lightly.

There were about half a dozen PLO soldiers at the café and they treated us with kindness and concern. When a truck stopped on its way to the comparative safety of the city, they bundled us on to it. Sitting in the back of the truck, dangling our legs over the edge, as we bumped towards Beirut, we instantly began to feel braver. Even the sight of the Kfir fighters regrouping in the sky for another bombardment had lost its former terror. But all our new-found bravado vanished as we suddenly realised that one of the planes we had been watching was heading straight for the very truck we were travelling in. Looking up, I saw that the piece of metal protruding from the roof was not, as I had assumed from an idle glance, the arm of a pick-up truck but in fact the barrel of a gun. We were travelling in the back of a mobile anti-aircraft gun.

In Beirut the sight of journalists staggering into the foyer of a four-star hotel caked with dust and blood is not specially unusual, and the desk clerk at the Commodore greeted our Return from the Jaws of Death with a deadpan 'Afternoon Mr Hamill, Mr Rich, Mr Thompson – good day was it?' Later, watching the tape we had proudly handed over in the editor's hotel room, Peter Read was nearly throttled when his first comment on our 'genuine war footage' was 'Well that's not fucking much is it?' Eventually we too had to admit that it was one of the most boring and undramatic pieces we had seen. It was shaky, captured nothing of the atmosphere, and the phenomenal noise levels had caused the system to override so that large sections of the tape were almost mute.

KIDNAPPED

After our hair-raising adventures at Khaldi, we passed the next two days in a pleasantly low-key way, filming odds and ends around the streets of Beirut. By the third day we were even beginning to relax.

The office wasn't expecting anything so we decided to take a drive down the coast road, maybe even to have another look at Khaldi. Our editor, Peter Read, had barely left his hotel room since he arrived and was feeling cooped up, so he asked if he could join Des, Nigel and me on our little jaunt. Peter is the sort of man people always describe as a 'gentleman'. An old Etonian, he has the voice of a Shakespearian actor and the dress sense of a prep schoolmaster from Hastings. Even in the heat and dust of Beirut he was attired in tweeds and brogues. Since he is also easy-going, scrupulously polite, and not averse to the odd tipple, he was one of ITN's most popular editors, and we were pleased to have him along.

We packed up the gear and set off in an old white American Impala with no tread on the tyres. After the events of the other day, hiring a new driver had, not surprisingly, proved quite difficult, but in the end the lure of the dollar had triumphed.

Only a block away from the hotel, a car containing four or five men with pistols and Kalashnikovs appeared by our side. It's not unusual to see people carrying guns in Beirut and I automatically turned to them and smiled. As I did so they suddenly cut in front of us, blocking the road and forcing us to slam on our brakes. Three of them piled out of their car, flung open the doors of our car and leaped in. One of them jumped into the front seat with me and stuffed a Magnum against the side of my head, while two more armed men climbed into the back and commanded our driver to start driving. There was a lot of shouting and screaming in Arabic, but we didn't have a clue what was happening. We thought of all the nice options first – is there a story they want us to film? Perhaps we're being taken to see Yasser Arafat? However, we soon began to have a fair idea that things were seriously amiss. Having guns rammed against your head with the hammers back and fingers on the trigger was still definitely OTT – even in Beirut.

We rode like this for about ten minutes in total silence. Every time I tried to speak the man next to me would slam the gun against my head. After a few more minutes he took the Magnum away and someone behind me pressed a pistol into the nape of my neck. Des, sitting in the back next to him, noticed that the hammer was back and his finger was moving on the trigger every time we went over one of the many bumps on the pitted road. Despite the fact that he had a Kalashnikov pointed at him, Des in his inimitable fashion tried gently to ease the man's arm down, tugging at his elbow every time he saw a particularly large bump coming up in the road.

For the second time in three days I experienced abject terror. We still had absolutely no idea of who these men were, where we were going, or what they wanted with us, and we could see something like madness in their eyes. The full horror of our predicament only dawned on us when they ordered our driver to turn into a quiet side street. There were some women standing there chatting, and the gunmen swore at them angrily and barked at our driver to move on. As he did so the driver twisted around in his seat and screamed at us, 'They're looking for somewhere to kill you'.

We then understood why we had been driving around in circles for the last ten minutes.

Eventually we came to a halt in an empty courtyard. The gunmen got out and made the driver get out, and we knew that now they were going to kill us. They backed away to form a semi-circle around the car and took aim. Nigel and I were half in the car, half out, both vaguely wondering whether to try to run for it. Peter said something suitably Etonian like 'This is goodbye chaps', and Des – I think – made a joke. I felt a sharp stabbing pain in my stomach as though someone had jabbed a needle into me. Looking down I realised I had pissed myself. There was a click from one of the guns and they were literally just about to open fire on us, when a man from the same outfit, but obviously of higher rank, came around the corner and at the top of his voice screamed at them to stop.

Now acting under this man's orders, they bundled us back into the car and drove us to a house where they put all four of us in a small room. We were still utterly terrified and I found I was shaking uncontrollably, but for the first time we were able to talk to each other.

All of us were utterly bemused by the morning's events. It was only when one of our kidnappers asked us where the driver of the Golf was that the pieces of the puzzle finally started to click into place. 'He's dead,' Des said, and received the chilling response, 'But he's my brother'.

It transpired that the Kurdish militia (as we discovered them to be) obviously thought it very suspicious that a 'news crew' had disappeared with one of their men and returned a few hours later, unscathed, with a flimsy story about a bombing raid. They believed neither that he was really dead, nor that we were who we claimed to be. Because of my blond hair they had decided that I was an Israeli soldier, who had smuggled their comrade across the border to Israel where he was now being interrogated.

We denied all these allegations fervently, but to no avail. Eventually Peter Read managed to convince them that he had a tape at the hotel which would prove our story, and suggested they take him back there under guard to fetch it. To our joy they agreed, and drove him back to the Commodore to fetch tapes, VTR and monitor. While he was passing through the foyer under the armed escort of several Kurdish militia men, Peter spotted BBC journalist Chris Drake in the foyer and managed to tell him of our plight.

When Peter returned we played the tape to them. It was only the wobbly footage I had shot of Desmond in the trench and some general views of Khaldi – but I suppose partly because we were telling the truth, and partly because I must have looked far too wide-eyed and terrified for anyone to remain convinced I was really an Israeli soldier, they started to believe our story.

Inevitably, in a city where men with guns stand on street corners demanding hundred-dollar bills from every westerner who passes, the subject next turned to money: 'How much would your organisation pay to have you released?' This band of Kurds were quite rightly angered by the fact that although through us and our stupidity a man had been killed, we hadn't even bothered to inform anyone of his death, or to find his family and pay them compensation.

In truth, our western arrogance, coupled with the fact that so much had happened to us in the half-hour or so after the driver and his car had been hit, meant that apart from telling a few people at the hotel that the driver had been killed, we had completely forgotten about the matter.

Meanwhile, elsewhere in Beirut, there were other developments. Although it was the day on which the British embassy was pulling out, Chris Drake struggled through the ensuing chaos and eventually managed to track down the deputy ambassador. Accompanied by Chris and two plain clothes soldiers he came to the location where we were being held to begin the negotiations between ITN and the Kurdish militia. All I could think of was a recent row over expenses I had had with the man who now held my life in his chequebook.

About sixteen hours later our captors took us outside and told us we could go. All the calm I had been struggling to muster finally deserted me, when one of the men who only hours earlier had been on the point of shooting me came and put his arm around my shoulders and offered us a lift back to the hotel. This friendly gesture made tears of rage spring to my eyes and I screamed at him to get away from me.

I'm sure he found it genuinely difficult to understand why, now that they had their money and we had our freedom, we couldn't all just laugh about it and be mates.

After our ordeal ITN decided to send us to stay in Junieh, a wealthy seaside suburb of Beirut controlled by the Katib, the Christian militia, sworn enemies of our Kurdish kidnappers. In this elegant port we would have a chance to recuperate while at the same time being at hand to cover events in the Lebanon. The presence of the Katib would also hopefully keep us safe from any further trouble with the Kurds. We were welcomed at the hotel like heroes, and checked in to our rooms to find them generously stocked with fruit, flowers and liquor. Also waiting for us was a telex from the office:

'CONGRATULATIONS ON YOUR RELEASE. YOU ARE ALL WONDERFUL. PLEASE INFORM SEBASTIAN HIS HOUSE HAS BEEN BURGLED.'

I arrived back in the UK just in time for my wife's birthday. I was finding it harder than usual to adjust to life at home. My sense of time seemed to have become completely distorted. I would sit down to watch the early evening news on TV and still be staring at the screen when the National Anthem came on. Holding my concentration long enough to accomplish simple tasks like taking the children to school, or talking to the man in the corner shop started to become a challenge.

To celebrate Penny's birthday we went to dinner in an Italian restaurant around the corner from ITN. In the middle of the meal I excused myself, went to the toilet and rammed some coke up my nose. I was still battling to keep a lid on whatever it was that was trying to surface in my head. Back at the table I gulped down a couple of glasses of red wine. This made me feel slightly better. I had a great desire just to sit there and listen to Penny talk about nice, easy, sane things, but the nasty little cocktail I had just plied myself with unleashed a terrible paranoia. On the other side of the restaurant the waiters whispered and pointed and a woman with an over-painted face stared at me.

'Happy birthday darling.'

Apparently I sat at the table and started to gibber and cry.

By the time they got me home I was incapable of speech or coherent thought.

'How do you feel Sebastian?' the doctor asked me.

'How do I feel? I don't fucking know. Please don't tell me.'

The children were sent to stay with friends while for the next week Penny spoon-fed me, washed me and talked patiently to me as though I were a small boy.

Even after the worst of it had passed I couldn't return to normal. Quite ordinary things would make me anxious – sometimes it was the sound of a car back-firing in the street, or some kids letting off a firework, which would send me diving on to my belly behind the living-room sofa. Other times it was as simple as the sight of a group of men standing chatting on a street corner, or a car driving slowly down an empty street.

When some six months later I heard I was going back to Beirut, I was scared. I had pestered the office to send me back to the Lebanon, hoping that using the same principle as mounting a horse again immediately after you take a fall, the experience would remove the pangs of terror which kept surfacing whenever I thought of the place.

I arrived in Cyprus with my sound recordist Richard Rose, to discover that all flights to the Lebanon had been temporarily suspended. Since we were replacing an outgoing crew who had left their correspondent in Beirut, we had no choice but to book a passage on the next ship out, in this case a ferry bound for Junieh harbour.

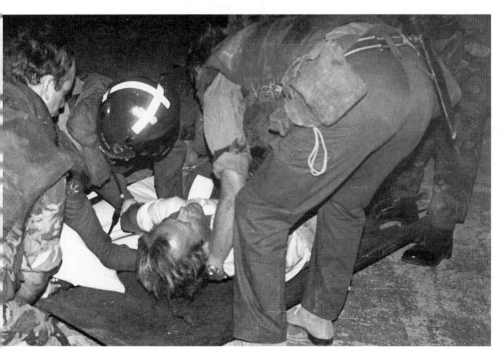

Above: Sebastian Rich running in the streets of Beirut
Below: Sebastian Rich airlifted out of Beirut after being wounded by
shrapnel *(photo: Royal Army Medical Corps)*

Above: ITN sound recordist Nigel Thompson with PLO fighter minutes
before Israeli bombers struck
Below left: Sound recordist Richard Rose returned to the Commodore
Hotel one day to find his room had been destroyed by a stray shell
Below right: Coco the parrot, at the Commodore Hotel, Beirut. The
bird's perfect imitations of gunfire and incoming shelling often caused
guests to dive for cover

During the voyage my nerves increased, but I comforted myself with the thought that at least we were arriving in a relatively safe Christian-controlled seaport. The next morning I climbed on to the deck to see the familiar sight of the old Beirut Holiday Inn, so pockmarked with shell-holes that it resembled a giant Gruyère cheese. To my horror I realised that for some unknown reason our ferry was docking not in Junieh but in Beirut's devastated port.

Richard could see how rattled I was and kept me busy helping with the unloading of our mass of equipment.

My pulse-rate had just begun to return to a reasonable level when I glanced up from the pile of steel boxes to find myself a few yards away from one of my former kidnappers, who was leaning against the side of an old Chevrolet parked on the quayside.

The man acknowledged me with a small wave and continued to stare at me as I dived into Ahbed's waiting car and cowered on the back seat. At the hotel I made a bee-line for the bar, where I attempted to recover my composure over a bottle of cold beer. But the nightmare wasn't over yet. A few minutes later I felt a tap on my shoulder and turned to see the man grinning at me from the next bar stool.

'Drink?'

It turned out that my kidnapper was now one of the regular drivers at the Commodore Hotel. As far as he was concerned all old scores had now been settled between us, and he wanted to be friendly. Beirut being what it is, and the people there being what they are, I accepted his drink and even bought him a couple in return, but every time I saw him lurking around the hotel I couldn't help feeling slightly sick with fear.

WOUNDED

Sitting in the restaurant of the Commodore Hotel you could hear the shelling over in East Beirut. Closer at hand light machine-gun fire and exploding mortars made the windows and sometimes your hands shake.

Breakfast was a ritual which could easily last up to an hour and a half. Putting off the inevitable moment when they would have to get out there and see the noise, journalists who in normal circumstances found it hard even to look at a fried egg before lunchtime would order huge platefuls of food.

'More coffee please.'

'Perhaps just one more helping of scrambled eggs.'

'Got any fruit?'

And so it would drone on. In this macho milieu, talking about the war was considered uncool. Admitting you were shit-scared was a definite no-no. On the other hand, since pouring drink down your throat and stuffing drugs up your nose were almost *de rigueur* of an evening, most mornings featured a hangover of some considerable size. After a while it was hard to tell what was making you feel so dreadful – the after-effects on their own strung you out on a sharp spiral of anxiety – as though an elephant were about to sit on your chest.

'Don't worry – you never hear the one that hits you,' was the received wisdom handed out by the Commodore crowd.

Unfortunately there was no one around who could verify this statement.

We ambled the thirty or so yards between the dining room and the waiting camera car and there was usually time for a last-minute visit to the toilet for two five-milligram Valium washed down with a little Scotch – just enough to keep the lid on Pandora's box for another Lebanese day.

On this particular Lebanese day Richard and I were looking forward to nothing more dangerous than a sleep by the swimming-pool. It was our first day off in ages. We had been on loan to ABC – an agreement which is reciprocal between the two networks. This arrangement sounds great in newsroom logistics, but it's a pain in practice and we were badly in need of a rest.

'Hi guys, how're you doing?'

Both of us visibly recoiled. The sight of Brent Sadler bounding into the foyer with a fresh face and a hungry ego was as welcome as a fart in a drysuit. Our new correspondent had just arrived on the night boat from Cyprus and he had that eager look in his eyes that I recognised and dreaded. Brent was a close and valued friend and also a very hard-working journalist, but – please God – not today.

'So . . . where's good bang bangs?'

Since at one count there were sixty-three different warring factions in the city, on an average day one could find fairly good 'bang bangs' (technical parlance for shots of people blowing the shit out of each other) in practically any side street in Beirut. If you were lucky you could film some of this street action in relative safety, and with a bit of creative cutting it would still look dramatic enough for television. It has been known for some journalists and their crews to film an entire war from their hotel balcony window and, I might add, win awards.

'Let's go.'

Too concerned with our reputations to demur, Richard and I meekly gathered our gear. Minutes later we had left the hotel and were cruising the maze of streets which is West Beirut in Ahbed's white Oldsmobile. Unfortunately, Brent had arrived on a remarkably quiet day, and after a couple of hours of nothing but a lot of bullshit dialogue about how it was all happening right here yesterday, and 'Oh what a shame it's not today,' we decided to visit our old friends, the British Peacekeeping Force, over in East Beirut. As part of the UN Peacekeeping Forces, the British army's role in Beirut was to monitor the situation, to patrol, and to be seen as an impartial observer, or as a high ranking officer stationed there described it to us: 'Here we are again, handcuffed fucking babysitters.'

The little shrine to Queen and Empire stood not all that proudly at the foothills of the Chouf mountains in the Christian sector of Beirut. A dusty old turn-of-the-century brick building surrounded a small courtyard, which housed the pride of the British presence in the Lebanon – twelve Ferret Scout patrol cars. During the day the heat inside the un-airconditioned barracks was unbearable and at night they were miserably cold. The five-storey base boasted a flat roof the size of a tennis court on which armed sentries were posted twenty-four hours a day. The four sandbagged watchtowers were superb locations for getting on-the-day general views of Beirut, and if you were lucky, and someone else was not so lucky, artillery battles from one side of the mountains to the other.

We visited the base most days to pick up information, to film, and to top up our suntans. Sometimes we drank a Budweiser or two, courtesy of the Brits' 'special guests', the American marines who often used our sundeck as a lookout. Today's artillery exchanges came from the direction of Souk el Gharb, a small town which lay about ten kilometres further east in the Chouf mountains. For several months the Druze militias had occupied positions on these rocky hills and with arms supplied by the Russian-backed Syrians engaged in fairly constant shelling of areas occupied by the Lebanese army. The Druze were well-equipped and their shells for once seemed to be well-aimed, reaching military and civilian targets within the capital itself. For this reason the last forty-eight hours had seen a government offensive to drive back the rebels and secure the hills, but after a day and night of continuous fighting, they had failed to make much headway. If anything, the rebels appeared to be gaining ground.

Brent was getting excited. Ever mindful of the early evening news bulletin slot, he decided we ought to whizz over to the village of Souk el Gharb for a closer look at the government forces positioned there. The drive was pretty hair-raising. Apart from stray shells landing on either side of the road, various militia groups used the car for a bit of sniper practice. On similar occasions we had tried the safety measure of tying a white flag to the radio aerial, but this proved less than useless and probably made us a better and more tempting target for our one-eyed friends.

When we finally arrived in Souk el Gharb it bore few traces of its former tranquil beauty. From earlier visits I remembered a lovely little village which clung to the side of a giant, bougainvillaea-covered mountain. We now stood amidst a heap of rubble and remnants of hurried evacuation. The few remaining buildings were occupied by Lebanese soldiers, and their army's one and only MASH unit, a place I should have, on reflection, taken just a little more notice of. We introduced ourselves to a small but stocky, moustachioed Lebanese army captain, who agreed to give us an interview. Despite his confident predictions of a Lebanese victory, he was obviously nervous and, as he spoke, his eyes darted anxiously from side to side. The artillery battle was clearly hotting up and incoming shells were landing near enough to shake the ground and change the air pressure.

The captain was not the only one concerned by the proximity of enemy fire. While we were filming the interview I had some- how managed to manoeuvre all of us into a small gap between an army truck and what was left of a brick wall. It was a totally illogical thing to do as neither would have offered any protec- tion if anything larger than a tennis ball had landed near us, but a tired, soggy, frightened brain does very illogical things. Richard nudged me. I turned and looked up at my giant friend who whispered in my ear, 'I think we've had enough, don't you?'

Although we were on the front line of the fighting the footage was still too tame to satisfy Brent. When you send regular reports from a war zone, the pictures that thrill them in London one day are considered ordinary the next and boring a week later. The pressure was continually growing to provide more and more action-packing footage and on his first day out Brent wanted to get something extra special.

We knew from what the captain had said in the interview that he was planning to go further up the mountain to Khaifoun, a village which lay in no-man's-land between the two rival forces. When we asked if we might tag along for the ride he turned on us saying, 'What's the matter with you fucking people? This is my country, not yours. Stay where you are and when I come back I will give you an account of what's going on.'

It wasn't that we couldn't see the sense of his words, or that any of us really wanted to go up that mountain, but years of conditioning made us instantly launch into a well-rehearsed counter-argument. We could just as easily have been trying to persuade Ian Botham to give us his views on the MCC or attempting to convince a housewife that it was all right to film out of her window and the police won't mind at all madam. Persuading people to act against their better judgement is as much part of the job as remembering to carry spare batteries or wearing a cricket box at an Orange day parade in Ulster, so despite our ever-growing desire to be back at the hotel bathing in Budweiser, we mustered every argument we could think to get us up that mountain. It took quite a while to make an intelligent and sensible man take what was, with hindsight, an extremely foolish decision.

'Come on for Christsake, and don't get in the way.' (Plus something muttered in Lebanese that I think might have meant much the same in any language.)

All fellow claustrophobics will agree that an armoured personnel carrier is a hideous vehicle in which to travel any distance. It's basically a fairly secure steel box on caterpillar tracks, rather like a tank minus the gun, designed to get fighting men from one location to another. It has one huge rear door which opens hydraulically to form a ramp. After the soldiers clamber into an area about two metres square the door shuts behind them and lightly broils everyone at regulo 8. As we climbed in with the captain and his men, we noticed with mild horror that the contents of this particular vehicle were grenades, RPG heads and mortar rounds, all rattling around on the floor in loose disarray. Since an APC is not the smoothest form of transport this was more than a little disconcerting. The door slammed shut and we set off up the mountain in our growling oven. You could hear machine-gun bullets pinging like demented wasps on the side of the APC and the occasional loud thud of a mortar. We had travelled about a kilometre when something heavy, probably a rocket, landed nearby, sending shrapnel slamming against the armour-plated sides.

'This is not a good place to be!' shouted Richard.

The level of the noise in our Lebanese limousine was not unlike the din of a helicopter at close quarters, so conversation was at a minimum. By now we had committed ourselves to a course of action we would not have been able to change even if we had wanted to, and, as adrenaline combined with the realisation that we were probably the only crew and correspondents to be getting these sort of pictures today, our weariness and anxiety began to fade. There was nothing else to do but hang on and wait for the oven door to open.

After a while the APC came to an abrupt halt and the door fell open. When my eyes adjusted to the bright sunlight I could see we were parked about twenty metres away from a small cluster of houses. On the stretch of dusty dry earth between us and the nearest building, little clouds of dust spat into the air as bursts of machine-gun fire raked the ground. We jumped out with the soldiers and, instead of weaving and rolling across the ground, just ran like hell to the nearest shelter, diving on to the veranda like bit actors in a bad B movie.

Sitting with our backs propped up against the veranda wall we caught our breath while the captain pointed out the sights like some Lebanese estate agent. The south-facing roof terrace did have genuinely breathtaking views. In front of us the mountain pitched steeply down to a valley planted with olive trees and vineyards. The house itself was set into the mountainside so, although we had parked behind it and entered at ground level, we were actually on a first-floor veranda. The occupants had obviously left in a great hurry. In the sitting room a sofa and set of armchairs covered in a brown velour material were still arranged around a now smashed and dusty coffee table, while in a blue nursery soldiers had pushed their way through discarded children's clothes and teddy bears to take up defensive positions at the windows.

On our somewhat over-dramatic arrival we found a number of Lebanese soldiers already engaged in a fierce firefight with Druze rebels who occupied hillside positions to the left and to the right of us. The target practice on our APC must have paid off because suddenly one of the Lebanese soldiers fell to the ground, a bullet straight through his head. This didn't go down well with his partner who burst out from our cover behind the veranda and seemingly went berserk, running back and forth along the balcony spraying machine-gun fire at random. This was beginning to look like award-winning stuff. Richard and Brent and I caught ourselves all grinning idiotically at each other.

When the soldier stopped firing, I turned my lens towards the hillside opposite us. Through the camera viewfinder I saw a man in white headdress stand up from his cover.

'Fuck me – I can see the enemy!'

It was the first and only time I had the opportunity to focus on the face of one man and, without cutting, pan around to show the face of the man he is trying to kill. I could scarcely control my excitement. What none of us yet realised was that the soldier's foolhardy actions on the veranda had enabled the Druze to pinpoint our location. Through the viewfinder I saw a puff of white and blue smoke rise from the back of the man in the white headdress. I was later to learn that this was the exhaust gas from a rocket-propelled grenade-launcher but at that distance the missile was on us before my thumb had time to move the centimetre between the zoom control and the on button.

The force of the impact blew me backwards through an open doorway. Someone must have dragged me to the back of the room because when I opened my eyes I was lying with my head propped up against the wall. I could see two Lebanese soldiers who were obviously dead – one of them decapitated – and a third who had lost half his leg. Brent and Richard had vanished. I suppose I just assumed they had been blown to bits too, although to be truthful I only cared about myself. To my right, half a dozen soldiers lounged on the brown velour sofa casually sharing a cigarette. If the events of the last few minutes were of any interest to them they were keeping it extremely well hidden.

Looking down I noticed that my white Lacoste T-shirt had acquired an interesting red pattern which had not been there at the time of purchase. There was a lot of blood around and there was no reason to think it was mine – after all I didn't hurt anywhere. The only thing puzzling me was that I didn't seem to be able to get up. Tentatively I lifted the corner of my T-shirt and revealed a gaping gash about fifteen centimetres long and ten centimetres wide. I screamed so hard and loud that just for an instant in all this chaos I was genuinely embarrassed. There followed a moment of grisly fascination as I peered at the pieces of metal poking out of the wound, then the pain slammed into me, and the elephant sat on my chest so hard I cried. I was sure that you died from this sort of wound, and in the tradition of many life-long atheists I began to pray.

'Dear God, I promise I will never do stupid macho things again if you get me out of this one alive. I don't want to die, not here, please not here. . . .' I thought of my little Burmese great-grandmother who after eighty-odd years of scorning religion spent the last few weeks of her life being visited by a constant stream of priests, ministers, rabbis and sufis whom she had invited over, 'Just to be on the safe side dear'.

Outside the rebel attack was gaining momentum and the sound of exploding mortar rounds and automatic gunfire was getting closer. I couldn't help feeling slightly astonished that the entire

Lebanese conflict hadn't been stopped the instant Sebastian Rich was wounded. A few feet away the bloody remains of a soldier sneered at me: If you can't take a joke you shouldn't have joined.

The soldiers still sat in a row on the sofa, staring straight ahead as if they were watching a matinée. Then in a gesture straight out of Hollywood one of them leant over and pushed a lit cigarette between my lips. This seemed like a good sign – after all, why waste a precious Marlboro on a dying man? I was so grateful that I didn't have the wherewithal to tell them I had given up some years ago.

'Come we must go.' The Lebanese captain suddenly appeared at my side.

'No.' The logic as to why we should leave the relative calm of the house for the hell outside eluded me.

'We must get back down the hill – the house will be destroyed.'

'No . . . I can't move.'

'You must.'

'I won't.'

'Then I must make you.'

He slapped me hard across the face – movietime again – and dragged me half-stumbling, half-crawling to the open doorway at the back of the house. Twenty metres away I could see the APC. As far as I was concerned it might have been twenty kilometres. The ramp was down and through the opening I could see Richard and Brent. The explosion had blown them in the opposite direction to me, away from the house, and from there they had found it easier to run for cover in the APC. Richard, who had sustained a nasty shrapnel wound in his shoulder, had somehow still managed to salvage what was left of our equipment. The captain manhandled me across the yard while Richard and Brent screamed encouragement, as though we were participants in some bizarre TV game show. We finally reached the ramp and Richard pulled me inside and made me as comfortable as he could on the floor of the APC while Brent cradled my head. When Brent saw my wound all he could say was 'Oh fuck, oh fuck.' I think for the first time in his life it dawned on him that holding a Scotland Yard press pass was not enough.

An injured soldier was unceremoniously thrown in on top of me and the remainder of the platoon clambered on board after him. The screaming soldier clutched what remained of his lower leg – there wasn't much – just a nub of bare bone. Between us all we provided an unholy chorus of screams and abuse.

It was only after the ramp had closed that the captain realised that our original driver was absent. Whether he had been killed or simply deserted we never knew but it was becoming painfully apparent that there was nobody in the APC who could drive it. The captain ordered a corporal to take the controls but his shouting and flailing arms indicated that he was as much at home in the driver's seat as in the command module of Apollo 5. It was obvious from the terrifying din outside that if we did not get down this mountain fast we were canned meat.

Richard's training as an engineer enabled him to work out at least how it started. With a push of the button the diesel burst into life, but despite the exhortations of his fellow passengers the dazed corporal continued to sit at the controls refusing to drive, get out or move in any direction.

At this point Richard, usually the most gentle of men, snatched a rifle out of a soldier's hands and rammed it into the temple of our unwilling driver. One look at Richard's face, his gums bared back over his teeth in a savage grimace, roused the corporal from his torpor. With a whiplash motion the APC leapt forward, did a half-circle at high speed and then stalled. Richard re-started the engine and with the corporal continuing his unconventional driving lesson we began to jump and lurch down the mountainside.

We were taking more incoming fire and heavy objects, probably pieces of shrapnel, kept thudding against the armour-plated sides of our vehicle. One-Leg had started screaming again. Illuminated by a single shaft of light which penetrated the APC from the upper turret hatch, his exposed bone gleamed grotesquely white.

Every bump and jolt was by now extremely painful and I was beginning to lose consciousness. A sudden jerk caused my head to snap back and I found myself staring at a large nut and bolt a few inches from my face, emblazoned with the words 'Made in the USA'. I couldn't get rid of the depressing thought that a bolt saying 'Made in the USA' might well be the last thing I ever saw.

Seconds later a thunderous bang shook the entire vehicle as a mortar round landed almost directly on top of us. We came to a sudden halt, One-Leg passed out and I head-butted the bolt. When the ramp flew down, I began to panic. I was convinced that the APC had somehow been immobilised and everyone on board was now going to run off and leave me. In fact I had just lost track of time and we had actually made it back to the town of Souk el Gharb. Soldiers and medics raced towards us and started to unload the wounded. Although his own wound was bleeding heavily, Richard swept me up into his arms as though he was about to carry me over a bridal threshold. As he lugged me towards the medical unit he kept muttering, 'You'll be all right, you'll be all right', over and over in the tone of voice people usually reserve for dogs or small children.

At the MASH unit a medic rushed towards us snapping an ampoule of morphine which was obviously destined for me. What a welcome sight, for the pain by now was unbearable. The medic had just reached us when without warning Richard worked one arm free and punched him square in the face shouting, 'Leave him alone! Leave him alone! – Can't you see he's in a bad way?'

I softly begged Richard to put me down and let the doctors attend to me but he was adamant in his refusal.

'It's all right Sebastian, I won't let them near you.'

'Please Richard, please.'

When at last my pleading convinced him that no more harm was going to come to me, Richard carried me into the makeshift MASH unit and laid me on an old blood-stained mattress. The medic reappeared and unceremoniously tore off what remained of my shirt, wincing as he caught Richard's watchful eyes. All round there were wounded men lying on every available surface. There was no sign of One-Leg and I remember thinking how odd it was to share something so frightening with someone and then to be separated. I stared at the floor, wondering why the lovely maroon carpet was gently moving and then realising it was not a carpet at all but a small lake of congealing blood. Richard was now chasing everyone with a red cross on their helmet, grabbing desperately at passing sleeves in an attempt to get someone to attend to me. Eventually he collared a doctor who had just finished treating a soldier suffering from horrific phosphorus burns. The doctor sauntered over to me and rather contemptuously peered at my stomach. As he fiddled with my wound I saw something drop off his sleeve. The 'something' was a small lump of phosphorus, and on contact with the blood in my stomach it flared like half a dozen Alka-Seltzers. The pain made my back arch like a giant crab. I wished with all my heart I could pass out, but this luxury seemed to elude me. As they fished out the last piece of bubbling phosphorus, a medic shot me full of morphine, giving instant, delicious relief. My head sank into a giant marshmallow and I smiled for the last time that day.

Ahbed leant over me stroking my hair and muttering 'Shwey-shwey', gently gently, '. . . next time shwey-shwey'. A few minutes earlier he had appeared in the MASH tent in tears, screaming: 'I knew this would happen, you go too fast all the time, you go too fast.'

Now, with my stomach packed very crudely with wadding and bandages I was loaded on to a Red Cross ambulance with a job-lot of wounded heading back to a real hospital in East Beirut. Since ITN still required its daily fix of news from the Lebanon, Ahbed and Brent hotfooted it back to the Commodore in the Oldsmobile to edit what material we had and despatch it to London. Richard had no choice but to come with me to the hospital as I still clung to his hand with a grip a tungsten monkey-wrench couldn't have loosened.

At the hospital I was X-rayed before being put on another bed to wait for a doctor. Conditions here were not much better than at the MASH unit, with a small, greatly overstretched staff attempting to treat both military and civilian casualties in appalling conditions and without sufficient supplies. Richard again went in search of a doctor, eventually returning with a surgeon, or possibly the hospital maintenance man, since he tried pulling the bigger bits of shrapnel out of my stomach without using an anaesthetic or even sterilising the forceps. I was starting to look forward to a new career as a Human Crab Impersonator. When Ahbed arrived at the hospital, having delivered Brent safely to the hotel, he found Richard wandering down a corridor with me yet again in his arms.

They laid me in the back of the camera car and we set off in the direction of the Commodore. To my delight I found a six-pack of beer and before too much protest could be raised I had drunk three.

The morphine and beer seemed to be forming a wonderful combination in my bloodstream and I cheered up considerably. I was still lovingly clutching the remaining three cans of beer as Richard carried me through the hotel foyer to the accompaniment of the mumblings and bleatings of the lobby lizards gathered by the daily news wires on the wall.

'Brent Sadler, *News at One*, The Lebanon.' Brent was still rehearsing his voice track and he gave me only a quick smile of recognition as we entered the editor's room. I had expected nothing more as even in my befuddled state I knew it must be very close to London's deadline. They laid me on the bed and, as they worked, I happily tucked in to a conveniently placed crate of Budweiser. By now I was mobile enough to get hold of the phone next to the bed. I placed a call to ITN in London and to my amazement it came through almost immediately. Vernon Mann, the foreign editor of the day, was incredulous when he heard my voice.

'Sebastian are you all right? We heard from Brent that you were in hospital.'

The booze and morphine had briefly rendered my speech diamond clear.

'No problem Vernon – give me a couple of days in Dixie and I'll be back in there.'

'Are you sure Sebastian?'

'Absolutely.' I replaced the receiver and promptly passed out.

The memories of the next few hours range from sketchy to nonexistent and many of the events were only described to me weeks later. My artificially induced alertness had completely fooled my colleagues into thinking I was okay. It was only when Brent took a look at the X-rays that the hospital had left stuffed down the front of my trousers that he discovered I was full of metal. He immediately placed a call to ITN editor-in-chief, David Nicholas, in London and informed him that he was about to have a dead cameraman on his hands. David Nicholas immediately rang Michael Heseltine, then Minister of Defence, who authorised a Chinook helicopter to pick me up at the British base in Beirut and airlift me to hospital in Cyprus.

*

DE COMMCEN AKROTIRI

FLASH

FM 7 SQN DET
TO MR S RICH TPMH
INFO ITN HQ LONDON
     OC 7 SQN DET

UNCLAS

SIC SPO/OOF

UNDERSTAND YOU ARE NOW WELL ENOUGH TO DEAL PERSONNALY WITH INVOICE
FOR SERVICES RENDERED BY 7 SQN. SETTLEMENT IN FULL OR YOUR PROPOSALS
FOR CREDIT WOULD BE APPRECIATED AT YOUR EARLIEST CONVENIENCE,
I.E. YESTERDAY

1. TO ONE CHINOOK 2-1/2 HRS FLYING £25000.00 STERLING

2. TO DANGER MONEY FOR CREW AND THE BOSS, FIVE AT £500.00 EQUALS
   £2500.00

3. TO SUCCOUR PROVIDED BY OUR CREWMAN (SUCKER) ALONG THE THE LINES
   OF QUOTE ITS ONLY A SCRATCH GUVNOR UNQUOTE, £350.00

4. TO AIRPORT TAXES PAID ON YOUR BEHALF TO HOODED GENTLEMEN WITH
   AK47 AND VERY POOR MANNERS AT BIA, £1500.00

5. TO TLC PROVIDED BY TPMH STAFF DURING THE FLIGHT WHEN THEY
   SHOULD HAVE BEEN IN THE BAR WITH US, £585.00

6. TO COPY OF VERY EXCLUSIVE SQN PRINT (ONLY 30000 PRODUCED) SHOWING
   THE AIRCRAFT YOUR FLEW IN OR ONE VERY LIKE IT, £100.00

7. TO SOBERING UP THER BOYS SUFFICIENTLY FOR THEM TO BE ABLE TO
   SIGN THE PRINT, £250.00

        TOTAL £30285.00
        VAT   £6057.00
   GRAND TOTAL £36342.00

RGDS 7 SQN

BT

COMMCEN
2 5 SEP 1983
RAF AKROTIRI

NNNN

'Have we had a little drinky sir?' I had regained a small amount of something that resembled consciousness. Momentarily I was back in that hellhole of an APC. 'No oh no.'

'How much have we had to drink then?'

Scared to open my eyes I listened hard. The engine noise was familiar but somehow different. My eyes sprang open and I tried to lift myself up, only to be firmly but gently pushed down. I felt incredibly thirsty.

'Beer.'

'How many cans of beer sir? Do try and remember.'

I opened my mouth but nothing seemed to happen.

'Is that four sir?'

Something incomprehensible once again bubbled from my lips.

'I think he said four Doctor.'

'Why can't you hear me? TWENTY-FOUR you stupid bastard.'

'Good morning Mr Rich – how are we?'

'We?' I thought. 'Are there two of us in this bed?'

My brain had conveniently forgotten the events of the last twenty-four hours and, as my eyes prised themselves half-open, thought that I was just waking up from the night before with a terrible hangover – nothing unusual in that. A few more minutes' sleep and then I'll get up and go for a nice long run. Something was tugging at my arm. It hurt me when I moved. Someone was pulling at my eyelids.

'Mr Rich, Sebastian, wake up, sir!'

I had been called 'sir' again – memories of the past twenty-four hours tumbled back, knocking some of the fog from my brain. I was not in my room at the Commodore after all. I had been picked up by a Chinook helicopter at the British army base in East Beirut and flown to the Princess Mary RAF Hospital in Akrotiri in Cyprus. And it wasn't a hangover that was making me feel so lousy. The last thing I could remember was lying on a trolley outside the operating theatre while a couple of doctors poked at my stomach.

'What a bloody mess,' I heard one say. I stared up at the ceiling and saw that for some reason it was covered with dozens of stickers bearing the insignia of various regiments of the British army. 'Got an ITN sticker?' the anaesthetist enquired cheerfully. 'I stick the needle in here and wherever you pass out your sticker goes.'

Some time had obviously passed since then. I began to be aware of the strange body in my bed – tubes extruded from its arms, its nose and its stomach from where on closer inspection a rather nasty green fluid was collecting in a plastic bag at the side of the bed. I realised I was unbearably thirsty.

'Drink.'

A warm hand cupped itself behind my neck and lifted my head, while a plastic cup of delicious, cool water was raised to my lips.

I vomited into my pillow and fell back into my drugged sleep.

'Seb . . . Seb . . . Seb. . . .'

The next time I opened my eyes, my entire field of vision was filled by the face of my foreign news editor, Mike Nolan. Inexplicably this no-bullshit-hard-bastard from Australia seemed to be crying.

I learned later that I was an extremely poor specimen at the time. My skin was bright yellow, I had lost a lot of weight and my eyes had sunk back into my head. That, combined with the effect of the various bits of plumbing attached to my body, had led Mike to believe he was looking at a candidate for the last rites.

As soon as they had received news of my airlift from Beirut to Cyprus, ITN had arranged for my wife to fly out and join me. Mike had come out with her primarily to give as much support to Penny and me as he could, but also with the directive that he was to proceed to Beirut as soon as possible to coordinate the news crews who were still out there. He admitted to me afterwards that the sight of me in my current state did little to bolster his confidence for his impending trip.

Now that the wound is healed and the whole episode has passed into the realms of after-dinner anecdote Mike remains one of the few people who understand what a nightmarish time it was for me. I had had two separate operations a few days apart from each other and the combined effects of anaesthetic and shock made me pretty befuddled. For several days I drifted in and out of sleep, while Penny sat at my bedside holding my hand and talking to me. I can't remember all the things we said to each other but it was a great comfort to know she would be there whenever I awoke.

I was the only genuinely war-wounded patient in the entire

Above: Sebastian Rich and spark Rob Bowles in the Olympic
stadium, Los Angeles
Below: David Walter, Roger Lorenz and Sebastian Rich
interviewing the Prime Minister on her tour of the Falklands
shortly after the end of the war

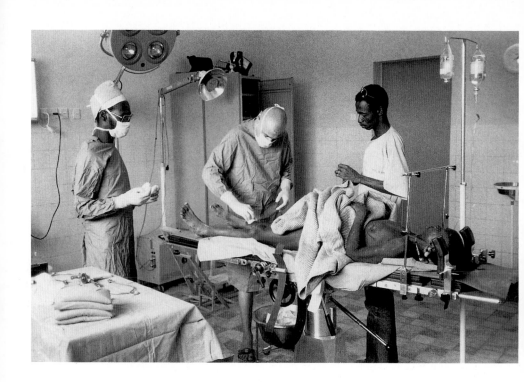

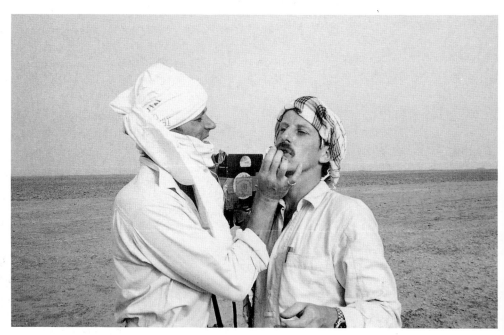

Above: Italian doctors and aid workers treat a woman with a badly
broken leg in a refugee camp near Timbuktu, Mali
Below: A less serious operation. Sebastian Rich applies lipsalve to sound
recordist Jon Hunt, Mali

military hospital. Two young soldiers in the neighbouring beds were suffering from concussion and a badly broken arm, but they thought that I was an officer and had decided in the circumstances that it wasn't prudent to discuss their injuries with me. I later found out that they had come to grief while leering at a well-built Cypriot girl from a hotel balcony. Rather the worse for drink they had lost their footing and tumbled thirty feet on to a concrete pavement.

By the fourth or fifth day I was beginning to feel somewhat better, when a grinning doctor approached me clutching a glass bottle.

'Thought you'd like some souvenirs old man.'

Rattling around in the bottom of the glass jar were seven pieces of jagged metal – the former contents of my stomach, now cleaned with surgical spirit and jingling against each other as he waved the jar in his hand.

It must have been obvious that I was utterly appalled by the idea, because before I could speak he said, 'Well perhaps not old chap – pop by to see you later,' and vanished with my shrapnel.

I later discovered that there were actually eight large fragments of shrapnel in my stomach, but one proved too difficult to extract and was left embedded in the muscle of my abdominal wall. They assured me that it would do no harm and to date they are thankfully right. There were also hundreds of tiny slivers of metal sticking into the skin of my hands and legs which I pulled out myself in the weeks to come. It was as though I had fallen into a huge cactus or stuffed my limbs into unbonded fibreglass.

The relative peace of breakfast time in the hospital was shattered one morning with cries of, 'Where the fuck are you Rich? Come on you bloody toad, where are you you bastard?' These unwelcoming comments turned out to be emanating from a sound recordist named Nick Fellows who was with one of the American news crews in Beirut. His news editor had been so impressed with the pictures we had brought back from our disastrous outing to the Chouf mountains that he had ordered his crew in the following day. Like us, they had got some spectacular pictures of close-range combat, also like us it had been a stupidly dangerous thing to do. The crew had been caught in an almost identical Druze attack and Nick had had his elbow blown away by shrapnel. He too had been flown into Cyprus for emergency treatment at the Princess Mary.

Although we had been wounded in almost identical circumstances we had each reacted in such opposite ways that I found it almost impossible to talk to him about the experience. Whereas Nick loved the romance of what he saw as an exciting escapade, and proudly displayed his glass bottle full of 'Frag' to anyone who enquired, I felt that the whole affair had been ugly, stupid and unnecessary. I was embarrassed at having been injured, relieved but guilty to have been in the privileged position of being air-lifted out, and deeply pissed off at being incapacitated at a time when I was particularly obsessive about being physically fit.

This same obsession got me into big trouble and set my recovery back by at least a week. I was growing impatient with the slowness of my recuperation, so, when I discovered that the hospital had its own gymnasium, I resolved to get myself strong again as fast as possible. When no one was looking I propelled my wheelchair into the main lift and descended to the ground floor where I found a small but well-equipped gym. I lowered myself from the chair to the sit-up board where I proceeded to burst virtually all of my stitches before being carried screaming back to the ward by an orderly. The RAF physio who was in charge of me was furious and I'm sure was responsible for my being fitted out with a new stomach drain that hurt like hell whenever I so much as tried to reach for a bedside grape.

The plot by the hospital staff to keep me immobile paid off. On September 26th I was declared fit enough to transfer from the hospital to a local hotel where Penny and Mike would babysit me until I was allowed to fly back to England. Mike Nolan had managed to book us an entire suite in the Churchill, one of the grandest hotels in Larnaca. This was quite a feat at a time when virtually every wealthy Lebanese was holed up in Cyprus to avoid the fighting back at home. They wheeled me up to our rooms, where a couple of celebratory bottles of chilled champagne, also courtesy of my foreign editor, were waiting. This was the first alcohol I had had since my orgy of lager-drinking in Ahbed's Oldsmobile, and after only two small glasses I was sitting on the balcony giggling like a child and feeling very happy to be alive. Mike, mindful of the fact that Penny and I hadn't been totally alone together for a very long time, said goodnight and departed to his own room. I had one more glass of champagne as Penny helped me on to the bed and tucked me up. After the hospital it was great to be in a hotel and I fell asleep instantly.

Halfway through the night I awoke feeling dreadful. I was burning with fever, parched, and my arms and legs were itching like crazy. I turned on the light and threw back the bedclothes to see that my body was covered with huge welts, my fingers were swollen to the size of plump pork sausages, and most disconcerting of all, my willy now closely resembled an Ogen melon.

Penny immediately called the hotel doctor. When his knock finally came she threw open the door of our suite to reveal a man who could only have been Omar Sharif's twin brother. Expensive jacket casually thrown over one shoulder and a Louis Vuitton doctor's bag in his hand, he had the kind of smile you can't look at directly without a pair of Ray-Bans. Omar apologised for the delay – he had been in the middle of a winning streak at the roulette table when our call came.

The doctor examined me, then turning to Penny took her hand and together they sat down at the foot of our bed. Completely ignoring me, he explained to her that my latest deformities were the result of an allergic reaction between the champagne and the medication I had been taking over the past few weeks and I should be back to normal within the next couple of days. Looking across the expanse of my naked misshapen body, complete with welts, sutures, a stomach drip and grotesque penis to the foot of my bed, where the handsome bastard was chatting up my wife, I felt at a distinct disadvantage. He wrote her out a prescription and they glided to the door, occasionally looking back at me and laughing. When he had gone I looked accusingly at Penny.

'What was all that about?'

'Oh nothing. I just asked him if he could make all the swelling go down, but leave the melon as it is.'

The following week Mike caught a Beirut-bound ferry, while we hobbled back to Heathrow. It was an odd experience to be the objective of the newshounds and camera crews gathered at the airport, instead of one of their number. Back in London there was a long, slow period of recovery aided by my own family and extended family at ITN, who bombarded me with telegrams, flowers and, when I was well enough, phone calls and visits.

— 7 —

L A Olympics

In the summer of 1984 the circus came to Los Angeles in a very big way, and I came with it. The trip had been given to me as a sort of compensation for my injuries in the Lebanon. In the five years or so I had worked in news I had almost exclusively covered war stories and my then head of assignments, Ronnie Hubbard, thought it would do me good to have a dip into the world of razmataz and nonsense.

The flight to the USA started as the rest of the trip would continue, with the executive producer drinking the plane's entire menu of liquors from the top down to the bottom, and after recovering starting from the bottom and working upwards again.

The first story we covered was the terrible pollution of Los Angeles – would it be a hazard to our finely-honed athletes? As luck would have it there was a huge forest fire raging in the Hollywood hills the day we arrived, so in true journalistic tradition we linked pollution and the fire together. The hills were burning beautifully; fire department helicopters water-bombed the scorching ground. This made for fantastic pictures. We lined Jeremy Thompson up under where we thought the next 20,000 gallons of water would land. A thought struck me as I started the camera rolling. If we were too accurate, would we be filming the drowning of a British journalist in the forest fires of the Hollywood hills in August?

We had about a week before the games officially started, and the newsdesk was eager for games-related stories. This gave us the opportunity to get rid of some *Starsky and Hutch* fantasies. One of our first stories was to do a piece on the Los Angeles police force – the peg was loosely connected with the danger to our athletes from

American criminal elements. This meant spending the night in one of LAPD's black and whites. We could hardly wait.

We cruised some of the seediest and least up-market areas of L A. Our call sign went up: 'Brawl in a downtown club, proceed with caution, man armed with machete.' Great, great. We were literally fizzing with excitement as our tyres screeched to the scene, lights blazing and sirens wailing. The police car slammed to a halt outside a sleazy-looking club. A young Mexican was lying on the ground outside covered in blood. On closer inspection we found that his right arm was hanging on by a thread of flesh and tendon, the result of a vicious knife-wound. One of the policemen called for medical back-up while his partner looked around for the man's assailant. Another policeman bent over the unfortunate Mexican.

'What happened to you?'

Silence. A few gentle slaps on the face from the cop brought him round slightly and, through the man's spluttering and broken English, we began to patch together his simple tale. A man in the club had asked him for a cigarette. He had refused. The man had therefore produced a machete and tried to hack his arms off. What alarmed us most was the Mexican's own attitude to the incident.

'It was all my fault. I should have given the peeeg the fucking cigarette,' he kept saying. When we got back to the police car we had great pictures but a slightly jaundiced view of the city.

The night sparkled and crackled with our enthusiasm. We were children with new toys and we were having a ball. Our black and white slowed down to curb-crawling speed to check out a street walker. She was a stunner with legs up to her armpits and a figure like an hourglass. The car drew up slowly from behind. She knew we were there, but chose to ignore the somewhat lurid remarks of the two officers caterwauling from the windows. 'God they get prettier every day' one of the cops remarked. The police-car moved in front of the street walker and gave one quick squirt of the siren. She bent down and leered into the window, 'And just what can I do for you boys tonight?'

A lot of incomprehensible slang was exchanged and we went on our way. Sean asked how much a girl like that charged for the night. Both policemen broke out into hysterical laughter and could not be silenced for a good two minutes. 'A girl like that,' one of them said through gulps of air. The driver slammed on the brakes and reversed at high speed back towards the hooker. We came to a screeching halt by the now fed-up lady of the night. The driver leaned over his mate and called her over. 'What is it now for Chrissake? You're frightening customers away.'

'These boys in the back here are from British TV and would like to know how much a girl like you would charge a night.'

She laughed and reached into the car to stroke Sean's chin, then quick as a flash she grabbed both ends of her extremely short mini-skirt and lifted it above her waist to reveal a handsome set of male genitalia. The policemen by this time were in no state for anything, and tears of laughter dribbled down their cheeks as we lurched away from the curb.

With only two hours' sleep we found ourselves heading at seven o'clock on a bright and sunny morning to LAPD's police helicopter base, where such movies as *Blue Thunder* had been shot. It was situated on top of a huge skyscraper and choppers took off and landed every minute or so. We were to join a chopper squad patrolling the Hollywood hills and their environs. Wearing regulation caps and bomber jackets Sean and I boarded our craft to be greeted by Butch Cassidy and the Sundance Kid, or was it Robert Redford and Paul Newman. These guys couldn't be for real, chewing gum and saying things like welcome to death from the skies. What came first, the TV series or the real thing? We took off and instantly did a testicle-sucking steep turn to the west of the city with the sunlight directly behind us. L A's skyscrapers glinted like vast jewels in the early morning sun. We flew between the great buildings, pulling faces at pretty office girls as we hovered by. We had one thing we had to film for an opening sequence for *News at Ten*, which was the world-famous Hollywood lettering stuck in the Hollywood hills like some unfinished game of Scrabble.

'Yeah sure, no problem.'

My testicles once again whizzed into my pelvic cavity for protection. On arrival at the giant lettering we hovered for a while to give me time to work out the best angle to film the things. I couldn't make up my mind which would look better – to pan left to right or right to left or possibly from above or below. The radio blared into life – a man had just robbed a grocery store and had got away on a motorbike. He was also armed with a handgun. It was a call for all available units. 'Sorry guys – art will have to wait for another day,' our pilot said as he put maximum powers to the rotors and headed in the direction of the incident.

We swooped low and fast above the freeways looking for the man on the motorbike. A call came in from a police car and pinpointed his location. He was just two blocks away from us. My adrenaline pumped into an all-time high. 'Shit!' I had forgotten to turn the camera off from the last shot and the battery was flat. My fingers were like jelly fumbling for the spare battery. The faster I tried to put wires into finnicky little holes in the camera the faster they would jump out.

'There he is,' the co-pilot shouted.

Flaring the rotors to slow us down, we hovered about a hundred feet above the speeding motorbike, the robber looked up. I zoomed in, he lifted his right hand off the handlebars and pointed a revolver at us. The gun looked enormous in my viewfinder. Before I had time to think the pilot spun the helicopter steeply to the right and the G-forces tried to embed the camera into the back of my skull. The robber fired. Luckily the shot was a million miles from us. We came back on to our original course to find two police cars in pursuit. The robber took a right turn into a dead-end street. From the air it looked an incredibly stupid thing to do and for a moment I found myself wishing him down another street. After all the hullabaloo of the chase, he seemed to give himself up very quietly. Someone on the helicopter radio said, 'Everything under control', so we left the scene and went to protect L A from evildoers for the rest of the day.

The opening ceremony of the Olympics was beyond belief. The Games were only a stone's throw from Hollywood, and nothing was going to stop the Americans showing that they could still produce the most lavish spectacles in the world. Musicians playing grand pianos appeared from behind the giant pillars of the stadium, men on jet-packs flew down from the clouds, dancing girls formed into a map of the USA in the centre of the arena, and thousands upon thousands of balloons were let loose into the smoggy Hollywood skies.

And so the Games started in earnest, including every sporting event from the Decathlon to synchronised swimming. One of our camera positions was just behind the announcers' box and we had fun listening to the different commentators reporting back to their countries about how their athletes were faring in the Games. We could hear with great clarity the particularly biased reports of the British correspondents.

'Our boy did superbly well – thirty-first position!'

'Well what a good effort. If she hadn't fallen over the second hurdle, she might very well have qualified for the finals.'

'It matters not you win or lose but how you play the game' was an adage which no longer applied in the modern world of aggressive sport, but it seemed to be taking Britain a long time to recognise it.

The Americans, who were winning the lion's share of medals in the Games, particularly after the Soviet bloc boycott, went to the other extreme. They exploded into a jingoistic, flag-waving fervour, and President Reagan made a special speech to the nation announcing the birth of 'The New Patriotism'.

A strike at ITV coincided with the Games and this meant that ITN was now the only outlet for the Olympics on ITV. For the first two weeks we were the only ITN crew out there, and we rushed from trackside to swimming pool and shooting range to equestrian ring in order to cover every conceivable event. We had one free hour in the early morning during which spark Rob Bowles and I would run from our hotel up to the 'H' of the Hollywood sign and back again, and two free hours in the late afternoon. The round trip to Santa Monica Beach took an hour and a half in the car, and most days we would speed up there, flatten ourselves on the sand for half an hour and then zoom back to the Olympic village.

With the exception of athletes like Daley Thompson, Steve Cram, Sebastian Coe and Fatima Whitbread, there was a noticeable dearth of British sporting laurels, and interest at home centred around events like the sudden collapse of Ovett on the track, and Mary Dekker's famous mid-race collision with the barefoot British-passport-holding South African Zola Budd. This latter event caused a tremendous furore worldwide. Mary Dekker, an American and the favourite to win the 3,000 metres, collapsed in apparent agony by the trackside after tangling with Britain's new young hope in the inside lane. Dekker later alleged at a press conference, into which she was tearfully carried by her fiancé Richard Slaney, that Budd had deliberately elbowed her out of the way. I don't know what happened out there on the track, but I did happen to stroll behind the press tent a minute before the famous presser (press conference) just in time to catch a glimpse of Mary Dekker. She was walking quite capably, with no sign of even a limp.

Occasionally we would be called from the Games to cover other news stories. One night a man mounted the curb with his Buick and drove for a hundred yards along the sidewalk in an attempt to hit some pedestrians. Another time we caught a flight down to San Ysidro on the Mexican border where, following a row with his wife, a man named Oliver Huberty had entered a McDonald's and gunned down thirty-six people, killing twenty. This was the largest death toll by a single gunman in a single day in America. Before police marksmen succeeded in felling him he was heard to explain, 'I don't like Mondays'.

— 8 —

Drought in Mali
(May 1985)

The drought in West Africa was the worst for many years, devastating crops and livestock alike. I was sent with sound recordist Jon Hunt and reporter Jane Corbin to spend several weeks in Mali and the Ivory Coast, filming a Channel Four News special report on the situation.

Our first stop was Abidjan, the capital of the Ivory Coast, to cover a preliminary story on the economic situation in West Africa. This consisted mainly of interviews with ministers, administrators and other bureaucrats, all of whom thought they were very important, and loved to chunter on about how well their individual department was doing, even though they were almost entirely dependent on foreign aid and the IMF. They seemed oblivious to anybody outside the comfort of their offices. In the evenings we were bombarded with invitations to dine with British diplomats and other expatriates, all of whom seemed to live in luxurious re-creations of Kentish country homes.

It was only when we left the city and set off across country in a Land-Rover, that we saw the tragedy that was overwhelming so many African nations. Mali, which had once been the bread basket of France, was now one of the poorest countries in the African continent. With a drought that had been searing the fertile soil for many years, the whole country was now so much unyielding dust. The land that had been the mother and provider for the once proud nomadic tribes was all but exhausted and people had been reduced to scraping a living on the outskirts of the major towns, and accepting handouts from the aid agencies. The distended tummies of starving children were everywhere. Usually the children were too weak to move and too tired to care. They spent the days in the relentless heat cradled in their mothers' arms, sucking from flat and withered breasts that had long since ceased lactating, but afforded a little comfort.

Built on a hill and surrounded by a vast lake, Timbuktu must have once been a fantastic sight. But, over the decades, the water had gradually dried up, and now this fabled city was no more than a collection of mud huts on a hillock in the middle of a huge dustbowl. We had come to a refugee camp just outside Timbuktu, to film the plight of about two thousand men, women and children, who, for one reason or another, were now 'displaced persons'.

As I sank another full-bodied glass of Valpolicella, I wondered how much longer people like me would be filming these harrowing scenes. It was the end of our stay, and we were the guests of a group of Italian doctors and nurses who had cooked us a farewell dinner. This was much appreciated, although it seemed more than a little incongruous to be eating delicious pasta and sampling fine Italian wine in the middle of the African desert in the heart of all this human suffering. One of the doctors saw me staring incredulously at the food on the dinner table. 'We may live in shit, but you tell me where it says we have to eat shit. Just because the people you are treating are in a terrible condition, it doesn't mean you have to suffer to do your best work for them, and you should not feel guilty in looking after yourself.' The aid workers had concocted this sumptuous spread with supplies sent by their families to their agency's headquarters, then on to Mali with the rest of the medical equipment. A very sensible procedure, I thought, as I stuck my face into a second helping of excellent fettuccine.

Jon Hunt, who was recovering from a mild dose of cholera, was not eyeing the culinary delights with the same vigour. He had woken up a few days before with foul, infected water quite literally gushing from all orifices. Cholera dehydrates you very quickly and in this heat the chances of survival without medical attention are non-existent. In our brief stay in West Africa we had already seen scores of victims of the fatal disease.

The same Italian doctors with whom we were now feasting had scooped Jon up from the mud-hut floor we had been calling home for the last few days and put him on a makeshift hospital bed; no sheets or mattress just the bare springs. Before he could protest, two enormous syringes were plunged into his thighs, and a drip into his left arm. The powerful antibiotics and the glucose solution kept infection and dehydration at bay, and after a short while he stopped looking like a wrung-out flannel and even gave me something that resembled a smile.

Unfortunately the full complement of doctors had been leaving that morning to inspect another refugee camp further up country and were not coming back until evening. I had eyed Jon's drip suspiciously.

'Don't worry, one of the locals will change it,' one of the doctors had said as he left the hut.

'Like fuck he will,' Jon had croaked, somewhat undiplomatically and within earshot of a 'local'. 'Sebastian can do it.'

'Bloody hell, Jon.' I had sat on the edge of his bed listening to the diminishing engine noise of the doctors' truck and at the same time watching the life-giving fluids decrease.

'You help me,' I said in the most confident voice I could muster. Jon had held on to the needle that was buried up to its hilt in his arm while I disengaged the dangerously low bottle and replaced it with another. I knew that no air bubbles must be allowed into his bloodstream, but at that time that was as far as my medical knowledge extended. Nevertheless he had survived to stare a plateful of unwanted fettuccine in the face.

On that trip the casualties amongst the crew were high. The doctors had informed us that because of Jon's condition the rest of us would have to have booster tablets as it was obvious that the jabs we had been given in London were proving inadequate. As bad luck would have it, Jane Corbin happened to be the one person in a million who was allergic to the booster tablets and her entire body erupted almost instantly with the most awful tender, red welts. On their return from the bush the doctors administered an antidote and Jane recovered, albeit painfully, in twenty-four hours.

I too had not escaped the delights that Mali had to offer. While filming knee-deep in the river Niger, one of the world's most polluted stretches of water, I scratched my leg. This in itself was nothing to cry about, but a nasty little amoeba had dived straight into the wound and within days I had a running sore that was in danger of becoming a very real problem. One of the doctors spotted me limping across the compound and dragged me off to the surgery where I was subjected to the delights of field surgery without local anaesthetic. My leg was now cured, but the final legacy of Mali did not rear its ugly head until three months later, when a doctor at the Manchester Royal Infirmary informed me that I was the proud owner of a seven-foot tapeworm. It was a vicious circle. The humans shat on the ground, the cattle ate the shit, you ate the cattle and hey presto – one of the most disgusting ailments you could ever contract; to this day I am still unable to eat beef.

Through all this Mali offered up some of the saddest and most poignant pictures I have ever shot. I won the Cameraman of the Year award that year and Mali was part of the portfolio. It was disconcerting sitting in a dinner suit in the Dorchester Hotel, watching those images on a big screen and knowing that most of the people who appeared in the film were probably dead.

— 9 —

The Year I Wore a Suit: On Tour with The Prince and Princess of Wales

(1985–86)

Buckingham Palace had approached ITN to make a fly-on-the-wall documentary about The Prince and Princess of Wales* and, much to my surprise, I was the one chosen to capture every Royal sniffle and blink. It was an odd choice on ITN's part as I had not even covered a Royal photocall or a Royal Tour never mind a whole documentary on the *World's Most Famous Couple*. The company logic was that ITN wanted a fresh look at the Royals and didn't want the standard coverage. (Was that a compliment or not?)

On a practical level, the first thing I had to do was put on a suit. I told ITN I didn't have anything that even resembled matching top and bottoms. 'No problem,' was their answer, they were going to throw the book out of the window on this one. So, without a twitch, or a guilty conscience, I stopped off at a little French tailors I had heard about in Bond Street, Yves somebody or other, and spent an entire month's mortgage. And with sound recordist Jonathan Hunt and lighting man Neil Hamilton all this was times three.

Our first location was Kensington Palace where we were to shoot a general piece with Princes William and Harry playing in the living-room. On arrival the butler showed us first to a waiting-room, then into the living-room to set up our lights. At first it was all a little bit awkward. This was the first time the crew had met any of the Royal family, and this was to be the tester. If this shoot didn't go well, I am sure another cameraman and crew would have been allocated to the job.

There was a piano in the room, so I got the two Princes to goof

---

* Eventually called *In Public In Private*.

around on it for a while. All this was very alien to me and I was struggling like crazy to figure out what would make good footage. All the pictures of Royal kids I had ever seen made them look as though butter wouldn't melt in their mouths, so I decided that my challenge would be to show the Princes as normal children, fighting, tantrums, the lot. Whether it would ever get used in the film was another matter, and for once I was glad that the decision was not mine.

I was filming Prince Harry playing with some toy cars on the floor when I became aware of a constant tugging at my ankle. It was becoming distracting to the point of annoyance. I left the camera running on my shoulder and peeped behind me to see Prince William running a toy car up and down my trousers. Without thinking, I removed the future King of England from my leg with a small cuff on the bottom. For a moment the room froze and I suddenly realised what I had done. But all was well. Like any other mother, the Princess scooped William up in her arms, mildly scolded him and told him to leave the cameraman alone.

After the initial shoot of the small Princes at Kensington Palace, the go-ahead to carry on with the rest of the production was given, and all fears of ITN crew members being sent to the Tower were temporarily allayed.

Our next task was to film, in its entirety, the workings of a Royal Tour. Over the coming year we would be accompanying The Prince and Princess of Wales on official visits to Japan, Australia, America, the Fiji Islands, and many other destinations. We were to be given unprecedented access to the Royal couple, and although we were not made to sign the Official Secrets Act, the entire production was an act of trust on both sides and there was an unspoken agreement that we would act in an honourable and discreet fashion, especially where the popular press were concerned.

It was with a small swarm of butterflies that we arrived at Heathrow to board the Royal aircraft, bound for Melbourne. The Royal Australian Airforce Boeing 707, one of the world's most reliable aircraft, was to be our home for the next thirty-six hours. I suppose I had expected the plane to be kitted out like something out of *Dynasty*, but it was surprisingly normal. The configuration of the cabin was the same as on a conventional aircraft, except that

Above: Sebastian Rich, The Princess of Wales, Jon Hunt and Neil Hamilton on the deck of nuclear-powered submarine HMS *Trafalgar* *(photo: Tim Graham)*
Below: ITN crew with The Princess of Wales outside the Governor's Residence, Canberra, Australia *(photo: Tim Graham)*

By kind permission of HRH The Princess of Wales

Above: Flooding in the Sudan. This man has constructed a tiny dam to keep his feet dry

Left: Desmond Hamill and Sebastian Rich wading through a lake of sewage in the outskirts of Khartoum, Sudan *(photo: Stuart Nicholl)*

everything was of first-class standard and there were fewer seats. The front section of the aircraft had been sectioned off for the Royal couple, complete with beds and showers. Throughout the flight the hairdressers and the valets would dive behind the curtains that separated the oily rags from the Royals to tend to their every need.

As well as an equerry, a lady in waiting, a valet, a hairdresser, and secretaries, we were accompanied by detectives from the Royal Protection Squad, who were permanently assigned to the Prince and Princess.

En route to Oz we made a brief, informal stop-off on the island of Fiji. David Roycroft and the Press Secretary, Victor Chapman, were responsible for planning every aspect of the forthcoming visit to the tiny island, right down to the exact landing position of the aircraft so that the red carpet could be laid in the right place, and they needed to reconnoitre for the official visit later in the tour. This gave us all a great opportunity to stretch our legs and The Prince of Wales went for a brisk walk along the side of the runway.

With just one hour away from Melbourne a flurry of activity erupted on board the aircraft. There were clothes to be sorted out by the Valet and the Dresser, ceremonial swords to be polished, and the hairdresser Richard Dalton went forward to perform his best work behind the curtain. We touched down to a brilliant cloudless day in Melbourne. Even the Royal aircraft was not exempt from the man from the Department of Agriculture, who fumigated the whole aircraft with two large aerosol cans of insecticide, just in case we had brought any nasty creepy-crawlies with us.

By this time the Prince and Princess were suited and booted and ready to leave the aircraft, but there was a delay in the final positioning of the plane on the runway, and the Princess was becoming more and more agitated, pacing up and down like a caged tiger and clicking her fingers, while the Prince relaxed reading a newspaper and trying to spot familiar faces in the waiting crowd. As the aircraft door opened, an unaccustomed heat blew in, taking our breath away. We had to position ourselves in such a way at the exit that we could film without spoiling the shots of the massed TV and press waiting on the outside.

The Prince and Princess spent ten days in Australia, visiting Melbourne and Canberra. It was ten days packed with walk-abouts, embassy dinners, polo matches, charity telethons, more walk-abouts, more official dinners, and even a day at the races for the Melbourne Gold Cup.

And so the tour continued across the globe. The next stop was Fiji, then Honolulu where Jon and I, in a brief respite from a seemingly never-ending workload, stood on Waikiki beach for half an hour before heading off to Washington with the sand still between our toes. In America the Prince and Princess were welcomed like a pop group, even down to the screaming and hair-pulling crowds which had greeted the Beatles in the early Sixties. From embassies to drug stores to presidential banquets, we followed the Heir Apparent and his wife like bulky shadows, attempting to capture the essence of their public and private lives.

Next stop Japan, where the Royal couple visited the cities of Kyoto and Tokyo, met heads of state, watched Sumo wrestling, attended banquets, visited temples and tea-rooms, and toured the famous Imperial Palace and its spectacular gardens. The welcome the Prince and Princess received here was not unlike the reception they had had in America. The Royal couple seemed to be the idols of every young Japanese and they lined the streets in their tens of thousands to get a glimpse of the Royal party. The big bonus for us as a camera crew was that we could see over the heads of everybody else, so there were no problems in a bunfight. Even the larger Japanese cameramen and photographers were frighteningly polite when you asked them to shift out of a camera position that they had been saving for hours, and our stream of obscenities would invariably be met with a woeful tilt of the head and a polite shrug of the shoulders. Several times the Royal party walked slowly past one of our camera positions, blissfully unaware that while they were busy cementing East-West relations, we were re-enacting the battle of the Midway.

At other times our privileged position with the Royals had its downfalls as well as its perks. On the odd occasions that we needed to work with the rest of the press pack to get a different perspective on the tour, we were usually treated as lepers by our former colleagues. Sour grapes on the part of the *Daily Gotcha* and other paparazzi didn't bother us, except in that at times it made it difficult to get a decent shot. At a fixed camera position for a photo opportunity, shoulders would suddenly pop up in front of the lens and our feet would get stamped on 'by mistake' – all that sort of annoying stuff you can do without when you're trying to get a decent snap.

Concorde was a pleasant change from the Australian Royal Airforce Boeing 707 – although it was a lot smaller, it had a definite style of its own. We were off to Vienna with The Prince and Princess of Wales to press the flesh and see the sights on yet another Royal visit. We had been on tour for some months now and had become a more accepted part of the Royal entourage. The paparazzi realised that we weren't going to spill the beans, the security staff knew who we were, and the Royal couple were by now used to the idea of a TV crew following them about. Life was dropping into a relaxed but tight routine.

On the Vienna leg of the tour the Prince and Princess were to be the guests of honour at an important fashion show. As well as the Royal couple and members of the household, we were travelling with over a hundred of the world's most famous high-fashion models, who were all part of Britain's contribution to the fashion show. This was a sheer delight and the waft of expensive perfumes flooded every nook and cranny of the cabin.

The setting for the fashion show was one of Vienna's beautiful Baroque buildings – if the Prince did not want to gawp at Bruce Oldfield's or Jeff Banks' latest creations, he could lift his gaze and marvel at the incredibly ornate ceiling. As a crew, our only problem was that the Royal Household did not want the world's press to see the Princess's reaction to the various garments that passed her by on the catwalk, possibly because a smile or a frown from the Royal visage might make or break the sales of any one of the exhibiting designers. There were howls of protest from the press when The Princess of Wales' decision was announced, and we joined in the general whingeing. The press secretary did not want to aggravate the paparazzi further with a flagrant display of favouritism towards us by slapping us in a better camera position, but the shot we needed for the film was the Princess looking at the garments, not the back of her head.

While filming the rehearsals a very stupid idea struck me. What if

I became part of the show itself? The plan was still germinating when Jon and I went in search of the show's choreographer and explained our predicament to him. My jaw fell open as I listened to his proposal; in his mind's eye he saw me as a fashion photographer walking backwards in time to music down the catwalk while filming the models. It might then be possible to get a quick grab-shot of The Princess of Wales at the same time. I reluctantly agreed that it was a very good idea, but I was already getting cold feet at the thought of mincing down the catwalk in front of thousands of people including the dreaded ratpack.

'Are you absolutely sure this is a good idea?' was Jon's only none-too-encouraging comment.

We decided to keep our plan from the Royal press officer and wear any flak afterwards. The next burning question was what I was to wear. The choreographer asked me who my favourite men's designer was, and since the only two names that sprang to mind were Yves Saint Laurent and Paul Smith and I already had my Yves Saint Laurent suit, I opted to be dressed head to toe in the latest Paul Smith creations. This turned out to be old-style brogue shoes, chino trousers, and a tweed jacket, topped off with a yellow silk waist-coat. The next step was for me to be choreographed into the show. Willing models were found and we rehearsed my début on the catwalk: as the lights went up I was to appear on the platform alone, dramatically drop to one knee, and wait for the model to come out from backstage. On cue from the music, we would then both dance to the end of the catwalk, circle and return. While Jon was rolling his eyes in utter disbelief at the sight of this outright poser wiggling down the catwalk, I was secretly starting to enjoy myself but, in the absence of any audience, I think I was getting just a little over-confident. We had had to hire a one-man-band camera, as it was physically impractical for both Jon and me to make fools of ourselves at the same time. I also don't think there was enough money in all the banks in Vienna to induce Jon to come and join me on the catwalk.

As the auditorium started to fill with the doyens of the fashion world, I suddenly had an extremely bad attack of the collywobbles. I would have felt much more at home in the middle of a riot in the Falls Road, wearing a Union Jack T-shirt, than standing backstage dressed up to the nines, facing the prospect of dancing in front of thousands of people including The Prince and Princess of Wales. I was terrified.

The newscaster Martyn Lewis, who had joined us as the executive producer on this section of the film, could quite clearly see that I was getting into a terrible state, my hands were sweating and shaking, my mouth was bone dry and my chest felt as though I was about to have a heart attack. Martyn, who had spent a great part of his life in front of the public gaze, sat me down backstage and gave me a thorough pep talk, a cross between psyching up an American football player and persuading a fourth-former to play Widow Twanky in the school panto.

The lights went up and there was the music that I was supposed to do my thing to. All I had to do now was to wait for the right beat and I was away. The models joined me in the wings and made nice cooing noises in my ears and this, combined with Martyn's expert advice, seemed to do the trick. I jumped on to the catwalk and assumed my opening stance, 'Don't fall over you prat,' being the one thought tearing through my head. The models glided on and we bumped and ground our way along the catwalk. As we approached the middle section of what seemed like an endless runway, I turned my camera on an unsuspecting Prince and Princess. They had recognised me from the moment I had hit the catwalk. The Princess of Wales had her hand over her mouth trying not to laugh and Prince Charles gave me that sort of look that said 'You utter wally'. But we had the pictures. As far as taking stick was concerned, I got off very lightly, and, apart from a few 'You old puff' remarks from the Royal Protection unit, and a couple of gentle digs from The Prince of Wales, I came out relatively unscathed.

As well as the banquets, the fashion shows, the galas and the flag-waving walk-abouts, we accompanied the Prince and Princess as they carried out many less glamorous duties. The Princess of Wales was particularly interested in combating drug abuse, and we filmed her visiting patients at a Cardiff drug rehabilitation centre and meeting customs men at Heathrow airport. While Prince Charles toured some of Britain's inner city areas, Her Royal Highness carried out solo engagements, including a visit to Dr Barnardo's orphanage in Northern Ireland, and visits to a hospital for spinal injuries in Sheffield and St Joseph's Hospice in Hackney. We also filmed her on board HMS *Trafalgar*, a nuclear-powered submarine, off the West coast of Scotland. Specially kitted out for the cold weather and slippery deck in a windcheater and denim dungarees, the Princess met the crew and was given a tour of the vessel before we dived to a depth of a hundred and fifty metres. On a less official note, we filmed the Royal couple at home at Highgrove, where we shot reams of footage of The Princess of Wales playing with her children and Prince Charles pottering around in his beloved garden.

It was all great fun and in many ways one of the most interesting assignments I had ever had, but, when I hung up my suit at the end of the year, I was surprised to find how eager I was to get back to the gritty and distinctly unmagical world of hard news.

— 10 —

The Kowloon Bridge
(November 1986)

One of the assignments that gave me the greatest joy and satisfaction was the story of a stricken oil tanker called the *Kowloon Bridge*. This huge beast had somehow gone aground just a few hundred yards off the coast of County Cork, and the pounding of very high seas was threatening to break its back and spill millions of tons of crude oil into the sea.

I was doing routine cover in Northern Ireland at the time that the vessel ran aground. For logistical reasons at ITN, the original crew who had been sent to cover the *Kowloon Bridge* story were called back to London after only a day, and we were despatched to take over the story from them. Our instructions were to meet reporter David Chater on location in the afternoon and have material ready to feed to London for the five forty-five bulletin. We arrived on the coast with just a couple of hours' daylight left in which to film. The tanker was listing badly to port, and every wave threatened to tear it in half. The sight of a 400-metre-long ship foundering on the rocks was awesome and made great pictures. We kept it simple, and with the combination of the outgoing crew's pictures and a stand-upper from David, we were able to send a fairly lively piece back to London for the early bulletin.

We spent the rest of the evening with some fairly dubious local characters trying to organise a boat to get out to the *Kowloon Bridge* for some close-up footage. Meanwhile a helicopter was being organised from London – the BBC had been flying overhead all day long and we had been very envious of the aerial pictures on their six o'clock bulletin.

Next morning, we arrived at the jetty to be confronted by a rust bucket of a trawler that was to take us to the *Kowloon Bridge*. David, who had had a few light ales the night before, eyed this sailing toilet with some horror. Our captain seemed extraordinarily well-informed both about the circumstances in which the *Kowloon Bridge* had grounded, and the contents of its numerous holds. Thoughts of old-time wreckers sprang into my head. Surely not.

The weather was not being kind to us and, by the time we had reached the bows of the tanker, the swell was up to eleven metres, and it was proving nearly impossible to stand still long enough to get a decent shot. With every swell we would be shot along the deck from bow to stern – usually on our arses. The wind had also changed drastically and now I had a drenched camera and recorder to contend with. Normally one drop of water on the recorder would render it totally useless, but luckily both recorder and camera were holding up well. A helicopter flew low, just above our heads, not the BBC's but one of ours. A local crew and chopper had been hired out of Cork to get us some aerial shots, and, God, how I envied them in that nice warm machine. As if in answer to my thoughts, another wave smacked me straight in the face.

Our skipper was trying hard to get us as close as he could to the lee side of the tanker, so that we could get some respite from the elements and also obtain some more stable footage. As we lurched and puked our way round the stern, we could see some of the external damage – a gaping hole with ripped girders poking into the sea. David started shouting and screaming. I could not understand what he was on about, over the noise of the sea. He grabbed me by the arm and pointed to the side of the ship. I could now see the reason for his great excitement, for hanging over the side of the tanker, blowing in the wind, was a rope-ladder. We looked at each other with childish grins, not believing our good fortune. We knew it was very foolish to attempt the climb on to the tanker, even without the added hindrance of the camera and all the paraphernalia that went with it. Another small problem was that the ladder reached only half-way down the hull – but with the giant swell we might just make it.

The skipper of what, next to the enormous tanker, now seemed the most minuscule of trawlers, edged his way to the bottom of the ladder – no mean feat, as the sea seemed to want to push us in every way but the direction of the tanker. With a metallic thud, we hit the hull and all collapsed in unison on the deck of the trawler.

It was becoming increasingly apparent that we were going to have very little time in which to attempt this hare-brained scheme, as the weather was growing worse by the minute. In addition, the closer we came to the stricken tanker, the more forbidding it looked. We were all going off the idea a little.

The captain shouted, 'If you're going to go, go now for Christ's sake!'

We were at the top of the swell and the rope-ladder was staring me straight in the face. Without thinking, I slung the camera over my shoulder and jumped at the rope. It was at this point that I decided that there must be a good technique for boarding ships in high seas, and this was not one of them. My nose slammed into the side of the hull and my feet slithered about on sodden rungs while with my one free hand I tried to nurse a swollen proboscis. David was close behind me screaming obscenities, and trying to hurry me up as Jon Hunt, the sound recordist, carrying the most awkward piece of kit, was getting ready to do his Batman impersonation on the rope. I fell headlong on to the deserted deck. The crew of the *Kowloon Bridge* had been airlifted to safety the previous day. David sprang on to the deck with a jaunty hop that said, 'I have been at sea all my life', while Jon struggled up behind us carrying the BVU 50, a terribly awkward device which recorded the videotape and dislocated your whole body at the same time. This piece of equipment was cumbersome at the best of times, never mind when you're trying to wrestle with a wet rope-ladder in high seas.

It was one of the fastest stand-uppers we had ever done. The tanker was threatening to capsize and sink at any moment. Luckily the waves did not reach the high deck, so we were dry, albeit very unstable. The entire boat was rocking quite violently from side to side, and we had to wait for a lull in the swell before we could film. On the deck everything looked quite normal, nothing visibly broken or crushed, just the whole thing listing very badly to port, and the occasional loud crack and groan of metal warning us that we were on an extremely dangerous floating nightmare. David had to grab hold of the handrail to steady himself. He looked down at the sea, held his breath and looked straight to camera. Thankfully he did the piece in one take and we were clambering down the rope-ladder before he could say *News at Ten*. The skipper of the trawler timed it perfectly – he rode the sea, picking us up one by one on the crest of every swell. We bopped and lurched back to the harbour feeling quite exhilarated. We were sure that we were the only ones to have actual footage from the deck of the stricken ship.

We were editing our pictures in a Portakabin just outside the main offices of RTE, the Southern Irish television network. Space being at a premium meant that we had to share the cabin with the Broken Biscuit Company, not an ideal situation, as neither network fancied the idea of the other being able to see and hear each other's stories before they went on air. We knew they had been up in a chopper for the last two days, but to our knowledge their correspondent John Thorn had not set foot on the deck. If that was the case, this would stitch him up quite nicely.

We fell into the Portakabin dripping water everywhere.

'Hello chaps, and what have you been up to?' John Thorn said as we squelched our way over to our edit consoles. Why did he have that smirk on his face? A gentle but serious probing started from both correspondents.

'Been back long, John?' David said.

'Oh, a little while,' replied John.

This verbal jousting went on for about ten minutes, with neither hack scoring any points at all.

'David, for Christ's sake let's play the bloody rushes back and see what we've got,' I said, as I wrung a litre of sea water from my trousers. The cassette rattled into the player and the pictures sprang up on two of the monitors. I looked round to see John Thorn peering over his own monitor. As he caught my eye he ducked down very quickly. Something about that one furtive glance told me that we had scooped him. I whispered in the editor's ear, 'Run on to the footage of David on the deck of the ship,' and tweaked the volume up just enough for it to be heard in Timbuktu.

'David Chater, *News at Ten*, on board the oil tanker *Kowloon Bridge*.'

I had not been watching the pictures, but had turned my chair to watch the reaction from Mr Thorn. The words 'on board' had provoked the required reaction. John shot up from behind his screens, eyes like organstops as he absorbed our sound and pictures. I asked our editor to run the pictures again. I knew the feelings he was experiencing only too well – a tight fist in the stomach and an overwhelming desire to ask, 'How the fuck did you get those bloody pictures?' But, like all of us, he was far too cool to ask.

John dashed into a nearby office and grabbed the nearest telephone. I have no idea whom he rang, but that evening his crew informed us that due to our 'bloody pictures' they had to stay for another day to try and get on board the ship.

As we were leaving the hotel the next day, the skipper of our trawler turned up with the souvenir I had been negotiating for – a life-preserver with the words KOWLOON BRIDGE emblazoned on it. I took this back to London and incorporated it into the goose's pen at the bottom of our garden. It made a great entrance to her hutch. A few months later I was reading a newspaper over breakfast when I gagged on my cup of coffee. The headline read 'Kowloon Bridge in Drug Smuggling Riddle'. It was alleged that the tanker had been loaded to the hilt with opium from a variety of countries. I ran out into the garden brandishing my toast knife, which prompted the goose to squawk loudly and flap her way to safety. I stabbed the life-ring and cut a large gash in the side – nothing.

— 11 —

Honeymoon in the Azores
(July 1986)

Events involving members of the Royal family always seem to bring out the worst in news editors, and the impending marriage of the Prince Andrew and Sarah Ferguson was no exception. ITN was in there with the rest of them, attempting only slightly more up-market and infinitely more sycophantic versions of the *Randy Andy's Ex Reveals All* and *How Big Is Fergie's Bottom?* slant on the proceedings.

I was no stranger to the current epidemic of York-o-mania, being a veteran of Royal press coverage myself. I had spent the whole of 1985 and the best part of 1986 making *In Public In Private* – ITN's documentary film about The Prince and Princess of Wales. While we were making the documentary I met most of the great exponents of round-the-world Royal-chasing (one of the few sports in which the English still lead the world) and saw the ridiculous lengths to which so-called newsmen would go to get a 'Royal scoop'.

About a week before Andy and Fergie's Big Day my regular sound recordist Jonathan Hunt and I were in the ITN newsroom when foreign desk called us over and told us we had been assigned to an 'urgent' story. The two of us, plus journalist Vernon Mann (nick-named 'Vernon Tan – Surf and Sand Correspondent', because he had an uncanny knack of being assigned to news stories which turned out to involve beach resorts) were told to catch a plane leaving for the Azores in just over two hours' time.

We were bound for these Portuguese islands not because there had been a revolution, or a plane crash or a volcanic eruption, but because ITN had it on very good authority that The Happy Couple were going to consummate their marriage on the islands. ITN wanted their cameras to be positioned, if not actually in the bed, somewhere close enough, so that at the appropriate moment the reporter could pop out from underneath the prince-sized duvet and ask the stock reporters' question: 'Excuse me – how does it feel?'

The whole trip started off badly. For the first time in my career I wasn't carrying even one of my three valid passports (a cardinal sin in the eyes of Wells Street where it's the first, and practically the only, rule drummed into every new employee) and our plane was due to leave Gatwick in two and a half hours. Jon and Vernon readied the camera gear while I surreptitiously sloped off home to get a passport or two, leaving two hours in which to get to Gatwick airport from deepest Hackney.

I couldn't get a mini-cab and since rush-hour was approaching I decided to hail a black cab to Victoria station to catch the Gatwick express. One and a quarter hours to go – no problem. I settled down with a copy of *The Daily Shit* to see what our colleagues in the popular press had to say about the state of the world. A Fergie Lookalike Competition, 'Royal Cake: The Currant Fashion' and 'Ten Ways to Conceal a Big Bum' kept me completely engrossed for the first ten minutes.

Some fifteen miles from the airport the train came to a grinding halt and an unusually audible voice came over the loudspeaker system: 'This is the guard speaking. British Rail apologise for a small delay,' he said unapologetically. 'The brakes on this train have seized and caught fire.'

Since this was in the days before serious train crashes became a bi-monthly event, everyone continued to read their papers. 'Will Fergie wear a veil? Twenty top milliners offer their professional advice.'

'It is only a small fire and is being dealt with by British Rail staff. Once again we apologise to passengers for the delay. Please remember, there is no cause for alarm.'

'Oh my God . . . oh no . . . help!'

My fellow passengers were forced to restrain the ITN cameraman from attempting to hang himself from the overhead luggage rack.

I tumbled out on to the platform at Gatwick with twenty minutes left in which to catch the plane. By this time I was in a state of almost uncontrollable panic. I cleared passport control and security and ran to Gate 29 (naturally the furthest gate at Gatwick) only to see the tail of my aircraft turning away at the gate. The worst had happened. I had missed the flight, had missed the story, had missed everything. Why? Because 'Golden Boy' had to go home and get his passport. The humiliation was going to be too much to bear.

There was only one thing left to try and that was to catch the plane up. My original flight to the Azores had a stopover in Lisbon – if I could get there quick enough I might just have a chance of catching it.

Forty-five minutes later I was on a British Airways flight to Lisbon, still a nail-biting bundle of anxiety and shame. At the end of the seemingly interminable three-hour flight I stepped off the plane at Lisbon to hear a member of TAP groundstaff calling my name and felt a burst of relief. The first flight had been delayed on the ground due to a small technical fault and Jon and Vernon had arranged for me to be met on disembarkation and escorted to the VIP lounge at Lisbon airport. The relief on seeing the pair of grinning bastards was fantastic, although it soon became clear I would have to put up with 'Left it at home have you?' jokes for a long time to come.

It wasn't until the next leg of the flight, when the stock of blind-panic-induced adrenaline accumulated over the day had almost evaporated, that we had the opportunity to ruminate at leisure about the assignment. It occurred to us that the Royal couple had not even got married yet. What was the rush? There must be an explanation for this.

On arrival in the Azores, Vernon made a check call to the office to see if anyone there could make any sense out of what seemed to be a patently ludicrous situation. We still cherished the hope that there was a secret that we were going to be let in on – perhaps a pre-arranged rendezvous at a clandestine location. Newsdesk informed us that we knew just as much as they did.

We were now at a complete loss as to what to do. With the initial burst of energy used up in getting to the islands, we now did not know what to do with ourselves. Under the circumstances years of journalistic training prevailed. Since no accommodation had been booked for us, we found a nice little unassuming five-star villa by the beach and started some spectacular investigative journalism –

where was the best place to eat lobster and which bottle of Vinho Verde to have with our meal.

By the second day it was becoming painfully obvious that we were in the wrong location. Another check call was made to the foreign desk. 'We think the honeymoon is there guys – so while you're there, why don't you do a piece on what the Royal couple might see if they did spend their honeymoon in the Azores? In utter disbelief at our good fortune we set about making a mini travelogue, 'The most prolific plant on the island is the rhododendron'. An epic of this magnitude deserved our total dedicated expertise for at least an afternoon. My God it was taxing, the heat, the flies, the lobsters . . . The Azores are the Somme of the lobster world, since they cost about fifty pence each and are the national dish of the islands.

In our travels over the island we found a fabulous hotel at the southern end. Decorated in Art Deco style, it had its own sulphur baths, fantastic wooden panelled rooms, and waiters with their hair greased and parted in the middle.

Despite our luxurious surroundings, an air of desperation was creeping into all three of us. We couldn't fully appreciate the decadence on offer, knowing that we hadn't shot a single frame that was going to be broadcast on any news programme.

Knowing that I had spent a considerable amount of time with Major Ronald Ferguson during the shooting of *In Public In Private*, the foreign desk asked me to see if I could elicit from him his youngest daughter's post-nuptial travel plans. I eventually tracked down the major in his car half way between his home and the Guards' polo club, and with all the diplomacy of a circus elephant I tried to wheedle out the Royal secret.

'Where, Sebastian?'

'The Azores.'

'What are you doing there old boy?'

'Waiting for your daughter.'

'Well you'll have a bloody long wait.'

'You mean they're not coming here then?'

'I never said that.'

'So they might be?'

'Are we going to see you on the polo field this year Sebastian?'

The probe for information was getting me nowhere at all. I said my pleasantries and hung up. We made another check call to the foreign desk. What was going on? Where were we supposed to be? This was getting ridiculous.

'We have heard that the Royal yacht is steaming towards the Azores. Get a boat and try to find her.'

'Are you serious?'

'Yes.'

'Sure?'

'Absolutely.'

The next morning we approached a shark fishing company which specialised in catching these magnificent beasts for the pleasure of boggle-eyed tourists. We hired at reasonable expense a fifty-foot vessel to go and hunt for the Royal yacht *Britannia*. Armed with cameras, fishing rods and Vinho Verde the great white news team hit the Atlantic Ocean with all the fervour a bad hangover would permit. The day was a spectacular success – the catch consisted of two grey sharks apiece. It wasn't until the end of the afternoon that we started to get a small case of the jitters in case the Royal yacht had somehow sneaked in while we were out playing *Jaws*, but as we entered the harbour we saw that the little fishing port was as unruffled as when we had left. There would certainly have been a bit of ballyhoo if anything larger than a matchbox had floated in. Just to make sure our fears were unfounded, Vernon made a phonecall to the local harbourmaster in the form of a casual inquiry about shipping movements. There had been none. And so as the sun set over the veranda of the ITN villa, all was right with the world.

Next day brought us no further news of the blasted *Britannia*, but the early morning bulletin on the World Service reported a lone yachtswoman who had just turned up on a neighbouring island after being on the missing list for several months. Rekindling our earlier enthusiasm we dashed to the airport and caught a flight to the island of St Paul's, where we interviewed a slightly bemused woman aboard her long-lost vessel. I think she genuinely thought that we had come all the way from London. I do not remember telling her anything different. With our little scoopette we headed back to the main island to feed our footage to London by satellite. Finally after four days we had been of some use to our lords and masters, and helped to justify the demise of a great many lobsters.

But someone had been right after all. Eventually, the Royal yacht *Britannia* was spotted off the coast of the Azores. The bad news was that, although they had actually come to the right part of the Atlantic Ocean, the Duke and Duchess had chosen to spend their honeymoon cruising the various islands on board the vessel – far away from the prying lenses of the press. To make matters worse an abortive but ingenious attempt by an Azorian hang-gliding camera-man to get exclusive pictures of the couple rubbing suntan oil over each other had led to the British navy, in conjunction with the Azorian authorities, setting up a five-mile exclusion zone around the yacht.

This posed the working Royal press with a seemingly insur-mountable problem, and the few attempts to get those elusive pictures of the newly weds, cavorting on the bows in bathing suits and in matrimonial bliss, proved fruitless. By this time half of Fleet Street was in the Azores waiting for honeymoon smooch pix, and photographers were busy pulling their hair out, while their corres-pondents chewed the end of their pencils and wore out the Azorian telecommunication systems by ringing their editors with lame excuses about how they couldn't sprout wings and hover over the yacht. News editors back in the office can be very stubborn about the sort of picture they want to see. Whether it is actually physically possible to get that picture bears no relevance, and the best excuses in the world won't get them off your back until you turn in the goods.

Much to our great surprise, in all this time, we still hadn't seen hide nor hair of the Broken Biscuit Company. Maybe, just maybe a brave news editor at the Beeb had said, 'Enough of this minor Royal crap. Let's put our resources into something else.' Whatever the reason it certainly made our lives a bit easier not having to look up from our Lobster Thermidors every couple of minutes to check what the opposition were doing.

Eventually the Royal press office informed the gathered hacks that the Royal Yacht *Britannia* would be docking at the main island at the end of the couple's honeymoon, while they entertained local dignitaries (and I suppose thanked them for their successful efforts in keeping the ratpack at a healthy distance). Our job was now to find the best camera position to film the arrival of the Royal yacht.

Ideally we would have liked to have been at the end of the concrete pier that jutted at least a quarter of a mile into the sea, but the local police were not letting anybody near it, for *security* reasons. Without access to the pier we decided the best vantage point was from a balcony of the biggest hotel on the seafront, so, promising the proprietor that his hotel would be seen on the television sets of over twenty million people, we eventually managed to secure what we thought was the best position in which to see *Britannia* make her entrance.

The Royal yacht appeared over the horizon and steamed gently into the small port guided by a flotilla of tug boats. I got some relatively good pictures, then, hoping that the Royal couple would have a photo call once the yacht had docked, I focused my camera on the end of the pier to film the security police. To my horror instead of the boys in blue I saw through my lens the familiar portly shape of James Whittaker, the *Daily Mirror*'s court correspondent. At the last moment the authorities must have given way under the massive pressure from Fleet Street and allowed the hacks on to the end of the pier.

We dismantled the gear and hurtled at the speed of light in the direction of the pier. By time we got there the yacht had pulled alongside and was preparing to be moored. With just one look into Whittaker's beady eyes, I could tell I was in for something horrible.

'Bloody marvellous pictures Seb. . . . Could you see the Duke and Duchess from wherever you were old boy?'

'Bollocks, shit and piss' I thought, almost audibly. I turned to look at Vernon who even with his outrageous suntan was as white as a ghost. Somehow without losing our cool we had to find out what sort of pictures we had missed.

Whittaker knew he had us by the short and curlies, and he was intending to make me suffer for all the gloating I had done during the year of filming The Prince and Princess of Wales.

'Great snaps Seb,' said a passing photographer. It was patently obvious to everybody that we had been in the wrong location, so a gleeful James Whittaker revealed all. Apparently, as the Royal yacht had rounded the pier, the Royal couple had come out on to the quarter deck and posed for about ten minutes in front of the gathered lenses.

I could feel the blood ebbing from my brain and my heart quickening alarmingly during the telling. 'Bloody Hell James,' I splurted, 'We got all that from the hotel balcony with a long lens. I thought for a moment we had missed something really important.'

As I blatantly lied through my chattering teeth, the glow of victory vanished from James's face, but only for a second, and was soon replaced with a malevolent grin.

'Well old boy, I shall look forward to seeing *those* moving pictures with great interest indeed,' he said, smug in the knowledge that I was clutching at straws, then, turning on his heels he departed with, 'I must be off. Some of us have to file stories you know.'

We had been royally hung, drawn and quartered, and our only consolation was that the BBC, and for that matter any other camera crews were still nowhere to be seen. Rather than lie to the newsdesk we just kept our mouths firmly shut and sent them the best material we could offer, hoping that the stills in the next morning's papers didn't leap off the front page into our foreign news editor's cornflakes.

Through the Royal Press Secretary, we tried to entice the Royal couple back on to the deck, but they weren't having any of it. All that was on offer was a view of the Duke and Duchess as they appeared on deck that evening to greet their guests, and this was an open press facility, not just for us.

— 12 —

Reunion in Vietnam
(February 1988)

Most people would say that I am a lunatic to regret missing something as terrible and destructive as the Vietnam war. Nevertheless I do regret it. Although I haven't the naïveté that many a young American grunt had, I can understand the very beginnings of the heroic notions that fill a young man's heart. The only conception that modern generations of children have of war is a constant diet of John Wayne, Sylvester Stallone, and shells and bullets which seem to hit you only in the shoulder. I always found it very strange that a country which found adulthood in war, and has become peacetime's greatest warring nation, still has generation after generation of young ones who glorify war and all that it entails. Even so, I too have been caught up in the romance of the Vietnam war. Maybe it was reading Michael Herr's *Dispatches* that gave me this peculiar blindspot. Imagining myself part of the Flynn-Page-Herr trio is the romance that fuels my fires of macho camaraderie, and, although recent years have given me the privilege of going to a great many of the world's trouble spots to have the romance literally shot out of me, give me a time-machine and Sean Flynn's whereabouts, and you'll never see me again.

Our flight from Bangkok was uneventful, in reality that is, but I spent the umpteen hours' flight putting myself in the position of the young soldier just coming back from some well-earned R&R in the fleshpots of Bangkok. I began to sweat more than I should have done. Someone else's memories were flooding into my head, or were they put there courtesy of Twentieth-Century-Fox? Clumpf! Our somewhat ageing Tupolev propeller-driven plane landed with, I think, some relief at Pan Son Nhat airfield, Vietnam.

I still remember the first time I saw the cockpit of a Russian airliner. It was on Thatcher's tour of the Soviet Union. I had asked to get some pics from the cockpit and reluctantly the Russian press officer had allowed me. As soon as I walked in, those childhood days of make-believe flooded back to me. How many times had you made an aeroplane fly with a deck-chair, a Fairy Liquid bottle, coat hangers and several pieces of coloured string. Here it all was again, but for real. A steam-driven aeroplane. How do they get men into space?

We passed row after row of Huey bomb-proof hangars as we taxied on the tarmac of what used to be the world's busiest airfield. And still, after all these years, there were burnt-out helicopters and FIII jets discarded all over the place. My mind slipped away again to days of burning Avgas and Cordite and pressure-suited men climbing into their fighting machines, with things written on them like, 'To Hell and Back' and 'No Second Chances'. I craned my neck to catch my first glimpse of Saigon, or should I say Ho Chi Minh City; no, I won't. I was living in dead days, and for some reason wanted to stay there. Saigon – this was the end of my Yellow Brick Road, twenty years too late, but I had reached my Oz.

The reason that we had come to Vietnam was to try and reunite a father with his son. The father, Nguyen Cong Nghiep, had fled with his wife and two children overland to Thailand and then had become one of the famous 'boat people'. Fearing bad weather, pirates, and a multitude of other rather unsavoury ways to die, he had left his eldest boy Hoang behind in Vietnam with his grandmother at their home in the Mekong Delta, in the hope that if he was to perish at sea with the rest of his family, Hoang at least might survive.

Our correspondent, Michael Nicholson, had come across this story purely by chance. Having been ITN's senior correspondent in Vietnam all through the war – or 'limited conflict' as the Americans used to like to call it in the early days – he had been doing some routine research on the present state of Vietnam and had come across an English company who were organising trips back to Vietnam for expatriates. This was a somewhat delicate operation as some of the fare-paying customers had genuine fears that as soon as they set foot back on Vietnamese soil they would, as traitors to the motherland, be whisked away, never to be seen again. I am happy to say that all the passengers we travelled with were greeted cordially and were treated with a great respect as, somewhat nervously, they stepped back on home soil after twenty years or more.

Michael's research eventually uncovered the story of a man who was hoping to return to Vietnam in search of the son he had left there at the end of the war, when he and the rest of his family had fled the country. Nghiep had made it as far as Hong Kong with his wife and two other children – a feat in itself, as a large percentage of boat people never made it at all. Their boat had started to leak badly several miles from Hong Kong and was in danger of sinking, when the British warship *Sabonga* spotted them drifting in high seas. The decision to pick them up and take them all to Hong Kong was at the time a significant political move by the British. Nghiep and his family were later re-located in the United Kingdom, incongruously to the small Welsh seaside town of Colwyn Bay.

The settling down process had been beset with many pitfalls for the family: language, culture, just about everything was alien to them. The only similarity between Colwyn Bay and the Mekong Delta is that they are both on the same planet, but I think at the time, Nghiep even had his doubts about that. He got a job as a watch and clock repairer above a firm of local jeweller's and through the kindness of the people of Colwyn Bay and his friendliness and aptitude for hard work, it was not long before Nghiep was on his way to being accepted into the community. He and his wife even named their new daughter Sabonga, after the British warship that had rescued them. Despite all this, Nghiep's heart was still heavy with the knowledge that his eldest son, whom he had discovered was alive and well, was still thousands of miles away in Vietnam.

Finally, the family received a letter from Nghiep's mother, telling them that – miraculously – the Vietnamese had agreed that he could return to fetch his son and bring him back to their new home in Wales. There were now many questions for Nghiep. Had he the right to bring the boy back to Colwyn Bay and away from everything that he now called home? Was a parent's grief so all-consuming that it overrode the feelings of a child? Hoang had said in letters that he wanted to come to England to be with his parents, but that was in a child's words of make-believe.

The Tupolev was taxiing down the runway and, in a few short

moments, both would be reunited with each other; a son seeing a father he could not remember, and a father with all the hopes and apprehensions you could cram into his head.

We had spent a few days in Colwyn Bay with Nghiep's family, filming their new home and lifestyle, and in the school where Hoang's brother and sister now went. Nghiep's wife had spent days packing and re-packing a case of toys and presents for their long lost son. Every day they managed to find just a little something else to stuff into an already bulging suitcase. At Bangkok airport Nghiep had even bought a model aircraft and assorted goodies. I think it was therapeutic, to ward off rejection.

Anh, Nghiep's wife, had decided she would not go back to Vietnam as it would bring back far too many painful memories; also she would not be able to stand it if anything should go horribly wrong. She would not even agree to come to Gatwick airport on their return as she did not want to make a spectacle of herself.

Both Nghiep's son and his mother were to be at Pan Son Nhat airport to meet him. This gave us a dilemma – should we go before him to jack the camera up and be in the right position, or should we just busk it and shoot from the hip? We had come all this way really for this one shot. The rest of the filming hung in the balance of these pictures. Eventually we decided on the latter option. This was going to be for real.

The plane finally stopped taxiing and Nghiep suddenly had cold feet. Maybe the presence of a film crew would jeopardise the process of winning his son back. We argued that it would help convince the authorities. What a bunch of arseholes we really are! We knew that either way it would be a great story. 'Heartless Commies Refuse To Hand Over Father's Long Lost Son', or, 'Vietnam's Own Glasnost Is Shown To The West'. We couldn't lose.

Old metal stairs, that had seen a thousand American soldiers come down on to the tarmac, scraped up to the aircraft. After what seemed an age, the doors creaked open and two Vietnamese policemen came on board and started scrutinising all the passengers. I could not help thinking that the American troops used to call the Vietnamese military police, 'White Mice'. I saw giant rats looming down the gangway. We were the round eyes behind enemy lines returning with a traitor to the people. They were surely going to single us out and make us an example to everybody else. Was it a slow death, or a single bullet to the base of the skull? The rat laid a large paw on the seat in front of me and smiled. My face was locked in a granite-like stare, determined not to be broken. The rat went past and out of the back of the aircraft. I glanced over to Nghiep who was sitting in a swimming-pool of fear-induced sweat. Whereas my dribbles of perspiration had been the result of playing childish games, poor old Nghiep was genuinely afraid of losing everything.

Just like any other aircraft at any other airport in the world, as soon as you are allowed to stand up and leave the wretched thing, everybody does so at once. We were starting to film in earnest. From now on there were no second chances. For the time being anyway I had to put all the ideas of being Sean Flynn behind me and get on with the job in hand.

Three hours later we were still in baggage reclaim looking for the mountains of steel boxes that seemed to follow us everywhere around the world like demented boomerangs. At the same time we were keeping our eyes on Nghiep who was peering at the faces pressed on the glass on the other side of the customs hall. He had actually found his luggage some one and a half hours before us and was raring to go, but we couldn't take the risk of going through and not being able to return and claim our baggage, so we held up the long-awaited reunion while we waited for the boxes. The customs declaration was predictably funny. Was I concealing any motorbike parts, or a motorbike itself? Next, a customs officer looked me straight in the face and asked me if I was smuggling in a motorbike. I giggled helplessly, being also aware I had to keep a certain amount of decorum so as not to upset any local officer who might have the power to stop us filming at the airport. When we had finally convinced the officials that we were not in the business of setting up a new motorbike showroom in downtown Ho Chi Minh City, we were allowed to leave.

Nghiep was off like a rocket. He had seen his mother but we hadn't. We careered after him bowling over inquisitive onlookers, straw hats sailing to the floor, small children squealing as the gentlemen of the press crushed their small toes. Nghiep had stopped in front of a young lad who looked up at him blankly. Nghiep had recognised his mother, but not the boy with her, and the boy had not recognised the now overweight, crying chap in front of him. A stillness fell over everybody. We waited. The young lad was emotionless, he just stood there looking at his father like someone staring at a banana for the first time. Then it happened. Somewhere in the boy's eyes, memories stirred. For an instant they flickered away from the father and into the camera, then welled with water and burst. He fell into his father's outstretched arms and sobbed softly. I tracked round and round them, filming the moment from here to breakfasttime, not losing a frame, or a snotty back of hand wiping away a tear. I zoomed into the boy's face. His pupils had vanished into whirlpools of salty water, just like the cameraman's.

Nghiep had many things to do in Saigon and, so as not to draw too much attention to the couple, we thought it prudent to let him and Hoang deal with matters by themselves. A priority for Nghiep was to finalise his son's emigration details. We had thought at one point that it would make good pictures to be in on the scene of the Evil Commies begrudgingly handing over one of their populace, but suddenly we couldn't stand the thought of being in any way a hindrance to the proceedings. What nice and considerate chaps we were. Had common decency gotten to us? – Heaven forbid.

In the meantime, Nghiep's mother had gone back up-country to prepare for a great homecoming with all the family who could not make it to Saigon or the airport, so we had a few days in which to film in and around Saigon itself.

We were actually staying in the old Caravelle Hotel, now called The Doc Lap, but to my joy the hotel key rings still had the old tags. Frenzied prying of rusted key rings betrayed me as the filthy capitalist that I am – souvenir one.

I had stepped into my time machine. My room was mouldy and stank of damp, and overhead a fan laboriously tried to push the thick air. I leapt on to the bed and stared up at the fan – choppers, Martin Sheen, Marlon Brando, I loved it. This was one of the hotels that had been mentioned in a hundred books about Vietnam. You could stand on the balcony smoking grass and watch the firefights all round Saigon at night. I was drifting further and further into a dreamworld of my own. I fell into a light sleep of pretty Asian girls and bicycles.

We met in reception the next morning to go and film Saigon and to be shown the sights by Mike. As soon as we left the doors of the hotel we were hit with a barrage of noise: 'You American.' 'You want change money.' 'You want good driver.' 'Me take in best rickshaw,' and so on. After what seemed an eternity we left the rabble behind in our wake. God it was hot. But I wanted to sweat more, smell more, feel more, become part of it all. Mike could sense my childlike excitement and pointed me in all the right directions: the American embassy roof where the Yanks had made their last stand, and the gates of the palace and the dents which the first North Vietnamese tanks made as they triumphantly roared through the city. We went for a stroll down Todo Street, the site of a hundred girlie bars during the war. I relentlessly dragged poor Jon around for hours filming everything that moved or didn't. Eventually we made our way back to the hotel. I threw the movie gear into the room and took up my stills equipment.

Now I was fully immersed in my fantasy. With cameras slung round my neck I was going to photograph the Saigon Sean Flynn never saw. It was as if the war had never ended. Through my view-finder I could see American soldiers on R&R, military vehicles rushing through the streets and I could hear The Four Tops on long-dead jukeboxes.

'You my daddy?'

I spun round to find part of the awful legacy that war had left behind staring me straight in the face.

'You American, you my daddy?'

A group of about ten Amerasian children were waiting for me to answer them. This sad and sorry band had every ethnic group in the United States indelibly printed in their genes; some were quite beautiful and others merely weird looking. My dreamworld ended that afternoon. Somehow, being wounded, getting killed, were bizarrely romantic. But to fuck up the next generation – it sent a cold shiver down my spine.

There is a system nowadays where Americans with guilty consciences can adopt an Amerasian child, pull it up from its already fucked up roots and confuse it a little more. But this little band, for whatever reason, had escaped the net of conscience. Outcasts amongst their own compatriots, they spent their days hanging around the park opposite the old Royal Palace in the vain hope that an American tourist, of which there are now a trickle, may take pity and say the magic words, 'Yes, I am your daddy and I have come to take you home.'

Sad and confused I went back to the hotel. What use would I have been to the Mighty Three if I had crumpled over the sight of some lonely children. They weren't even dead, their bodies weren't burnt by Napalm, limbs weren't missing, Sgt Cally hadn't butchered them. They were just the result of a grunt not able to keep his dick in his trousers.

That night we went out for dinner at an old haunt of Mike's run by an old lady, whose sheer charm and joie de vivre, along with, I suspect, a little courting of both political persuasions, had helped her survive all the ravages of war and stay in business.

Madame Di's place was just a few blocks away from the Hotel Caravelle, set off an old French road, away from prying eyes. The house itself was in the middle of a beautiful secret garden, stocked with all sorts of wonderful plants and trees. On entering, I was reminded more than anything of my granny's front room. Madame Di greeted us like long lost friends. She seemed to remember Mike, or was it the bottle of champagne Mike had brought along that caught the interest of an old lady of definite class and style?

I was staring and gawping like a codfish. The Three had been here. This was no dream of some demented idiot suffering delusions of nonsense. The walls were covered with photographs of them all, with and without Madame. I was in my church, and barely tasted the meal as I sat staring at the walls. Christ, Flynn was a handsome bastard; what had happened to him? He was last seen leaving Saigon on a motorbike to cover a story. There was even a picture of Madame with the great Master of Photography, Larry Burrows.

We left the restaurant more than slightly the worse for wear for cheap Thai champagne and warm beer. I had cornered Madame Di for hours listening to war stories that had been told to her by cameramen and correspondents as they arrived at her establishment still high from reporting the day's war.

The trishaws that had taken us to Madame Di's were still there. I wondered about this for a second and then realised that with us probably being three of just a handful of westerners in town, it was best to wait until the round-eyes had finished their evening's decadence than chance finding another fare somewhere else.

My driver for the ride home went by the name of 'Min'. His real name was probably very beautiful, but he had shortened it for the convenience of the round-eyes:

'You want to change money?'

'No.'

'You want woman?'

'No.'

I asked him to stop the trishaw and explained to him that I did not want any of the pleasures that he was offering but just wanted to be shown around the town at night.

'OK, you Number One, me Number Ten.'

'Stop, listen, let's put a stop to all this One and Ten shit. My name is Sebastian and your name is Min.'

I explained that I was genuinely interested in his town and country and wanted to learn as much as I could.

It transpired that Min, before the war, had been a university lecturer in economics, with a large family to support. He gave me the alternative tour of Saigon: the squalor, the wretched ghettos, and by the end of the evening we had become firm friends. When we reached the hotel, Min looked sad. He confessed that he had originally seen me just as a meal ticket out of Vietnam and asked me please to forgive him. I told him there was nothing to forgive and that, if our roles had been reversed, I would have taken him to the cleaners by now. This seemed to cheer him up somewhat.

The next day we were to be filming in the tunnels of Koo Chi – a whole underground guerrilla network used by the Viet Cong during the war. Complete with schools and hospital these tunnels were now a national monument and kept in very good condition. There was only one problem – they were not illuminated in any way. Jon and I had decided not to bring any lights along on this particular trip, as we thought, wrongly, that they would be more of a nuisance than a help. Panic was now setting in. Where was I to procure a portable film light by ten o'clock the next morning? Min told me not to worry, he would find something. I tried to explain to him that it was rather an exacting piece of equipment and I didn't much rate his chances of finding anything.

'No problem Number One, sorry, Sebastian, I will return.'

I wondered what movies he had been watching recently.

Jon and I spent three hours trying to bluff our way into Vietnamese Television without success. Mind you, try turning up at Vietnamese Television at two in the morning demanding to be let in to steal a hand light! Jon gave up and went to bed while I sat on the stairs of the Caravelle Hotel thinking of black tunnels and bollocking myself.

'I have a light, Mr Sebastian I have a light.'

Out of the gloom Min's trishaw could be seen doing a speed unimaginable for three wheels. He screeched to a halt, almost bowling me over.

'I have a light, I have a light!' His face was fulgent with success and pride.

'Well, where is it?' I said ungraciously. He turned round and rummaged in the back of the trishaw and produced the most enormous domestic light bulb I had ever seen, totally useless to anybody apart from maybe a lighthouse keeper. I took the orb from his hand and studied it. Out of the corner of my eye I could see Min swelling with a sense of achievement, God alone knows what it must have taken to get this extraordinary piece of archaic nonsense in Saigon in the middle of the night. I mustered all the gratitude that I could and thanked him profusely. Clutching Min's prize bulb I dejectedly climbed the stairs to my bedroom. Mike had held a lot by tomorrow morning's pictures and I was going to let him down badly. Maybe, just maybe, I could do something with this piece of glass. What little enthusiasm I could muster for a germ of an idea was quickly dashed, as I noticed that the sodding thing's filament was broken. Unceremoniously I tossed Min's prize into the wastebin whereupon it exploded, and, as if in a final gesture of defiance, showered me in glass. In an uncontrollable rage I picked up the bin and its contents and went to throw them over the balcony. My arms were in mid-air when I spotted Min looking up from below, grinning like a Cheshire cat.

'Good night Mr Sebastian, you sleep well, I be here in morning time.'

Like a child caught in the act of doing something horrible to a small mammal, I turned on my heels with my arms still above my head, clutching the waste-paper bin, and cursed my way back into the bedroom.

At breakfast Mike was getting excited about filming in the tunnels and asked me if everything was all right as far as the lighting was concerned.

'Yeah no problem, sorted that out. All right, let's get to it.'

Jon looked at me in amazement.

We toted the gear to the van, me trying to convince the ever-watchful Min that his precious bulb was now an integral part of our film equipment. Jon, knowing full well that we didn't have a torch, never mind a proper film light, asked me what the fuck I was up to.

'I know, I know,' I snapped, 'I'll think of something.'

'What, smart arse?'

'Gimme a break Jon.'

The journey to the tunnels took over an hour and every second was put to the problem of the light. I had well and truly blown it this time. What the hell was I to do?

'Barrp, barrp.' I was interrupted from my thoughts by a military convoy blaring its horns and flashing their lights in an attempt to get some stubborn oxen off the road.

That was it! I ordered our driver to stop, jumped out and armed with a monkey wrench and screwdriver started to dismantle the front headlights of our truck. Jon instantly knew what I was up to and held back a foaming-at-the-mouth driver. Clutching my prize, I scampered back into the van. Jon was ahead of me and took one of our twelve volt camera batteries and tore the ends off, revealing bare wires. We both held our breaths as Jon touched the ends to the contacts at the back of the headlight. It worked! It bloody-well worked! Actually, a primary school kid could have worked that one out, but it saved the day.

In our preoccupation with higher electronics, we had forgotten about Mike sitting in the front seat – 'Just a little something you thought of last night chaps?'

The Mekong Delta was yet another name that brought memories of old news coverage stampeding into my brain. The Delta had been a free fire zone during the war and had left many villages totally destroyed along its banks.

Nghiep's mother and the rest of their family lived about fifty kilometres up the Delta. This was good news for us as the family could just as easily have turned out to live in an unphotogenic tenement block in downtown Saigon. As it was, we couldn't have asked for a better location.

We left by a small boat from a village which during the war had been a large and very busy American patrol-boat base. It was from here that a lot of search and destroy missions had originated. Now the inhabitants had reverted to the more peaceful activities of growing rice and fishing the ample waters.

As we chugged along the flat, clear river in our small vessel, Nghiep sat with his son in the bows, chatting and smiling, while the boy pointed out new attractions along the riverside. For Nghiep, the river must have held many painful memories, but this was a day of great happiness for the pair of them. They were getting along famously and it was unnecessary for me to corral them into posed positions for the camera.

We stopped at various points along our journey to let other passengers off at their villages. By mid-afternoon I decided it was time to take a break from the filming and soak up some rays. I lay at the stern of the boat dreaming myself into the scene in *Apocalypse Now* where a patrol-boat crew had been patrolling down the Mekong Delta sunbathing and dancing to the Rolling Stones singing 'Jumping Jack Flash'. I was there. I could hear Jagger and smell the suntan oil on the breeze.

'Any chance of filming some of the local colour Seb?' Mike said sarcastically. The Rolling Stones melted away into the sound of our outboard motor. CLICK. I opened my eyes to find my sound recordist Jon Hunt peering over me with his Nikon.

We were approaching our destination – a small inlet on the side of the river where the jungle was so overgrown our boatman had to push away the heavy palm tree leaves with a large hooked pole. Nghiep was now becoming quite excited as he began to recognise familiar sights along the riverbank. News had travelled fast from Saigon. As we passed under a small makeshift bridge, a gaggle of locals cheered and waved at us, then followed us on foot along the creek. Children jumped into the shallow water and grabbed the bows of our boat to help guide us to the shore, while scores of willing hands ferried our gear to the bank. We followed Nghiep and Hoang along a long jungle path, filming as we went. Children climbed trees to get a better view of the return of their long-lost neighbour and his new round-eyed friends.

We rounded a corner in the trail and almost fell over several small mud huts. The cameras were still rolling as Nghiep poked his head into the opening of the first hut. His mother threw her arms around him and held him tightly. Once again moist eyes were the order of the day.

A veritable feast had been laid on and a pig slaughtered especially for the occasion. I filmed just enough to make a decent sequence and then got down to some serious nosebag as friends and guests were devouring the delicious-looking spread at the rate of knots and I was determined not to miss out on some real Vietnamese cooking.

After the banquet Nghiep spent many hours re-acquainting himself with family and friends. Since he had left Vietnam, he had put on quite a bit of weight which caused much laughter amongst his relatives, as, out of breath, he attempted to catch a couple of chickens with his son for the next day's cooking pot. Afterwards they roamed the gardens around his mother's house while I hovered over the pair, filming every moment of their private reunion. Suddenly Nghiep stopped and bent down by an old cactus plant. On one of the cactus leaves, carved all those years ago, was a picture of an American helicopter gunship strafing his village. Another stream of tears fell from the eyes of our emotional father.

We left the happy couple in the village and returned to England. They had a month to get to know each other. There had been no problems with the government and they were free to leave the country unhindered after that time, as the paperwork would by then be complete. Our next stage in the plan, if all went well, was to meet the pair four weeks later at Frankfurt airport and fly with them on the short hop to London.

Nghiep had told us that, in one of his few private moments with his son, the young lad had expressed great reservations about leaving the only place he had ever known, and now Nghiep was

Young girl, Saigon

Hanoi in the rain

deeply distressed that all this effort might have been in vain. It was something that only he could sort out, but we couldn't help thinking it would rather put a damper on the whole story if the son stuck his ground and stayed at home with granny. We shot a last picture of them sitting together on a large log by a small stream, shuffling their feet.

As the giant wheels of the jumbo jet touched down on the rain-soaked runway at Frankfurt airport, we paced the departure lounge like expectant fathers, cameras at the ready to film the instant we boarded the aircraft. We knew through the British Embassy that father and son were both on board. After all, Hoang had decided to travel across the world to be with the family he could barely remember. We found them in the economy section, Hoang with his head on his father's lap, fast asleep. With lights blazing we none too discreetly bowled down the aisle and managed to wake them both from their fitful sleep. Red bleary eyes stared into the camera, a little confused to say the least. After a few seconds a smile of recognition crept over Nghiep's face. We stopped filming and he warmly shook us by the hand. Today he was truly a very happy man. On the last leg of our journey I positioned Hoang by the window to film his first sighting of London. At three hundred feet the visibility was so bad we could not see the end of the wing, at two hundred feet Hoang lost his aeroplane lunch, dinner and breakfast over my feet.

The customs officers at Gatwick were the epitome of good behaviour and the pair cleared immigration faster than you could say 'Anything to declare'. It probably helped having an ITN film crew perched on one of the customs officers' shoulders and a British Airports Authority press officer on the other. Nghiep's wife, Anh, had said she would not come to the airport because she would make a fool of herself, but in the end she couldn't resist it. She had made the journey from Colwyn Bay that morning. As soon as she saw us she ran to her son and clamped her arms around him. The boy just stared embarrassedly into his father's face, looking for some clue as to what the hell was going on. He had no idea who this woman was, and the emotional reunion was definitely a bit lopsided. Nghiep explained to his son who the tearful woman was. The boy stood passively, arms like planks of wood at his side, and allowed himself to be drenched with the emotions of a mother who had not seen her son for nine years.

We raced to Colwyn Bay ahead of Nghiep to film the homecoming. The entire family were assembled in the two-up, two-down in Colwyn Bay, where yet another feast lay at the ready, complete with added little non-Vietnamese tit-bits like Smith's crisps and chocolate fingers. The arrival of the new addition to the household caused much happiness and a great many melted chocolate biscuits. We left the family to enjoy the remainder of the evening without a filthy great camera stuffed up their noses with every glass of lemonade.

The next few days must have been very strange for the young boy, although the people of Colwyn Bay were doing everything in their power to make Hoang feel welcome and Nghiep's boss at the jeweller's even gave him a brand new sports bicycle as a homecoming present. As I filmed Hoang, standing on the seafront, with the younger brother he had never seen, looking out on to a cold but bright morning in Colwyn Bay, I wondered what the hell was going on in that little brain. One minute chasing chickens in the Mekong Delta, the next watching white horses on a cold and windy Welsh sea.

On our final day of filming we went down to the local school, where Hoang was to be introduced to his new teachers and schoolmates. It was a tiny little school run by nuns and boasting the most well-behaved pupils I had ever met. I think the electrician got quite a shock while he was setting up his lights in the assembly hall when a small spotty youth asked 'sir' if he would like a cup of tea.

The whole school had turned out that morning to greet Hoang. The children were busily decorating the hall and putting up a huge welcoming banner, and there was an air of great excitement throughout the whole school. The night before ITN had run the story of the reunion in Vietnam and were ready to edit on sight and microwave-link back to London this final section of the story.

Hoang arrived at the school with his new family, dead on time, looking resplendent, if not a little awkward in his new uniform. His younger brother led him by the hand through the school gates, while children poured out from every doorway to have a look at their new classmate. The headmistress shooed them all into the assembly hall, where they lined up to sing their own special welcome song – the famous Welsh song, 'There'll be a Welcome in the Hillside' re-written by the children to incorporate Hoang's name.

Afterwards Mike and I took father and son down to the beach to get our final closing shot; the opening shot was of Nghiep as he prepared to leave for Vietnam on his own, now with the two of them together it was the perfect ending. Kleenex were going to do good business tonight.

— 13 —

Flooding in the Sudan

(August 1988)

US VERSUS THE BBC

Day One: drought; Day Two: famine; Day Three: a plague of locusts. Any suffering put on this planet by the Almighty in his wisdom can be found in the Sudan. And as with all the other ills of the world this spectacular misfortune is manna from heaven for the press.

This time ITN was sending us out to cover the awful flooding in the region of Khartoum. Over two-thirds of the city was covered by water, and the countryside had not fared any better. We set off on a Wednesday. By our calculations we were well ahead of the BBC in the race for news. If all our connecting flights worked, we would arrive a good twenty-four hours ahead of them, but in Frankfurt we were informed that our connecting flight to Khartoum had been cancelled and would not be running till the following day. However, still no sign of Auntie Beeb, so we settled down to a huge meal in the airport hotel, knowing that it would be the last decent food we would see for a while.

Next morning we arrived at the departure hall to find the BBC waiting for the same flight – and not just any Beeb crew but correspondent Mike Smart and Ian Pritchard – probably the best cameraman they have. Although Ian was a good friend, I knew better than to underestimate the professional rivalry that exists between crews, and especially between ITN and the BBC. I would need to keep a good eye on him once we were in the field. Due to my overconfidence, I had done something that I had never done in the past, and shall never do again, which was to put all the equipment, including the camera, in the hold of the aircraft. Seeing Ian with his camera by his feet didn't do much for crew morale, and I did my very best to appear as unruffled as possible when he asked me where my camera was. The war of attrition had started and I had plainly lost the first round.

As soon as our plane touched down at Khartoum airport we could see that there was a great deal of activity all round the airfield, including several Red Cross planes loading and unloading essential supplies. Needless to say the BBC made much of recording all this, while I pretended that we didn't want to film the comings and goings as it was all old hat, and tried to keep them from hearing my stranded whale impressions. By the time I had rescued my camera from the recesses of the aircraft, everything that needed to be unloaded had been, and the airport was as quiet as Basingstoke on a Sunday afternoon. One nil to the BBC.

In just about every vaguely Marxist state in the world there is the awful Ministry of Information. The Sudanese MOI was the last place we wanted to be, but go we did, as without the proper accreditation, it is not possible to film anywhere in the Sudan, and, believe me, the MOI is quick off the mark if you try it. The first thing you see is a multitude of bureaucrats doing nothing at all. The moment you cross the threshold you are under their control and, if you try to hurry them, or shortcut any of the official procedures, you have had it. We began to work our way through a sheaf of forms the size of a Ph.D. thesis. Without fail the one question they are always interested in is your father's Christian name. What does it matter what your father is or was called? Somewhere in the world there is a training camp for people who make press pass application forms. The coincidence is just far too great.

Eventually we reached the man whose sole task is to staple your photograph on your new press pass. The next target was the chief tea-towel himself – usually a pompous individual who has been given far too much power and takes great pleasure in wielding it, especially over the western journalist. Resplendent in local garb he gestured to us to wait, and didn't look up until he had finished reading or pretending to read some report from one of his hundred and one minions who baked outside in the hot sun. Eventually he raised his head and stared Desmond straight in the eye. I saw a wry smile come over Desmond's face, then the chief raghead shot to his feet and in perfect Oxford English said, 'Desmond, my dear boy –

how on earth are you? Haven't seen you in absolute ages.' Ian Sands (my sound recordist) and I were completely dumbstruck as Desmond and the minister began to chat happily away. Our prejudices and bad experiences in ministries round the world had turned us into little bigots.

Abdulaki was one of the nicest men I have ever had the privilege to meet. It transpired that Desmond and Abdul had both been in the same regiment in the British army. An hour passed as Ian and I lolled in chairs while Desmond and Abdul swapped stories. Through the beaded doorway I was gratified to see that the BBC crew and their correspondent Mike Smart had come into the outer office and were trying unsuccessfully to persuade the man at the desk to let them see our new friend, the Minister of Information. As we swept past them a few minutes later on our way to board Abdul's private helicopter to film some of the worst hit areas, the gentlemen of the BBC were still filling in their fathers' Christian names. One all.

INTERVIEWING THE PRIME MINISTER

We were to do a live interview with the Prime Minister of Sudan. By this time ITN had sent out a small mobile Earth station and we had the capability to broadcast live from anywhere in the Sudan. Anywhere that is that we could lug a ton and a half of satellite dish and other equipment. The temperature that day had risen to an incredible 122 degrees and was even slightly hotter on our chosen location, the roof of the Khartoum Hilton. Why we had selected the roof now escapes me – it seemed like as good a place as any at the time. The satellite dish itself was located in the gardens of the hotel. This meant an enormous cable run to the roof.

When the great man arrived with his entourage, we were up and running, and London was receiving live pictures and audio from us. The Prime Minister plonked himself in front of the camera and Ian put an earpiece into his ear so he could hear John Suchet in London. We had about five minutes to airtime for *News at One* and we were not without our problems. The heat was so intense that it was actually melting vital pieces of technology inside the satellite dish, and we were in real danger of losing the link altogether. A lot of screaming and shouting went on between us and London to get our story moved up the bulletin – not because it was the hardest news story of the day, but because, if they didn't take us at the top of the bulletin, they wouldn't have us at all. So scriptwriters in London furiously set about rewriting the newscaster's lead-in to give our story a bit more oomph and give it the credibility it needed to be story Number One. We now had two minutes to air and the Prime Minister's earpiece kept falling out, so a large piece of camera tape was unceremoniously slapped behind his ear.

At this point we were talking to the foreign desk (not the technicians in master control) where my great pal from the Lebanon Mike Nolan was the duty editor of the day. Coming into the newsroom from another part of the building and seeing our pictures live on his newsdesk monitor, Mike grabbed the two-way intercom, and said in his broadest Aussie, 'Bloody hell mate these are fantastic pics – is that raghead really the Prime Minister of the Sudan?' Desmond and I were stunned into a catatonic state. It had taken a lot of stringpulling to get the Prime Minister in front of our cameras at all. 'Hello blokes', Mike's voice cut into the airwaves once again. 'Jeez he certainly wears all the right gear – look at the sheet on that one.' Desmond lunged for the volume control, while I seriously considered ripping the earpiece, tape and all from the Prime Minister's head. 'Coming to you in twenty seconds,' a disembodied voice announced. 'Can you give us a sound level?'

'Good morning Mr Mike Nolan,' the Prime Minister chirped. 'A fine morning is it not?'

THE PEOPLE WHO LIVE ON TOP OF SHIT

> I am weary of crying, my throat is dry,
> my sight faileth me for waiting so long upon my God.
> (Psalm 69)

Save The Children were setting up a new medical centre in an area just outside Khartoum. I don't know what its real name was – it was only ever referred to as The Dump. The city of Khartoum is surrounded by a big industrial wasteland and at the edge of this is an enormous refuse tip. Before the floods a populace of approximately ten thousand men, women and children lived at the base of this mound, scraping a livelihood out of what they could scavenge from the dump. They had lived for years in the most appalling conditions, but, since the floods, their former existence seemed like abject luxury. The rains had come and had literally forced the whole wretched community to the top of the wastepile, and some pile of shit it is. The mound measures about half a mile in circumference and rises to a height of a hundred feet. The bedrock of the hill is toxic industrial waste and the whole surface is covered in human excreta, in places up to a depth of one metre.

To reach the camp was difficult enough in itself. The first part of the journey was by Land-Rover and then by foot across flooded camps of mud huts. We stopped the Land-Rover about two kilometres away from the base of the dump, and got out and walked through the murky water to the camp. Not one of the mud huts that had made up the shanty town had been left standing by the floodwater, only a few pitiful remains of walls that had once corralled livestock. We had to tread very carefully as a lot of these mud huts had primitive cellars and there was a very real danger of falling into one of these, by now, water-logged, disease-ridden pits. It was hard going and at times we found ourselves wading almost waist-high. Once Desmond stumbled into the brackish water and came up spluttering with the revelation that this was not water at all, but an entire lake of shit and piss. This discovery hurried our previously plodding progress to the foot of the camp. Instantly forgetting the dangers of the cellars, we just wanted the hell out of there.

We finally reached the mound, and, with our equipment strapped to our backs, scrambled and squelched our way to the summit of this thirty-metre-high pile of human misery.

The scene on top was totally shocking – thousands of lost souls clambering about on the top, picking out what could barely be described as an existence. We stopped in our tracks, dry-mouthed and speechless in the face of such mass human suffering. Des and I were lucky to have the latest technology in footwear on our nice little pink feet. Our brothers on the shit pile had only what they were born with, plus a few little additions courtesy of the pile. The first layer of the ground is, as I said, a light crust of human shit. Below this is a layer of softer, wetter faeces and then a nice little surprise –

for when the country decided to go dry, they smashed every single liquor bottle in the land on this tip. The shards of broken glass mixed with toxic waste and metal shavings from our industrial friends made a hideous and lethal concoction. I watched in horrified fascination as a child about four years old made his way over to us. His feet crunched at first through the outer layer of shit then with a muffled squelch into week-old faeces. When the little feet came out of this obscene mess they were inevitably torn and bleeding, no doubt with the most awful infections instantly running rampant. In the midst of all this the aid workers were miraculously able to set up a makeshift first aid centre. There were six of them altogether, including a doctor and three nurses, one of whom had only arrived from Belfast that morning. Their brief was to deal with the worst cases of infection. To us there didn't seem to be degrees of infection; just one – terrible. It soon became apparent that we would be of more use as part of the medical team than as a film crew, and we started to help as best we could. It was frightening that as soon as we put the camera equipment down and stepped into our new roles as medics, an instantaneous queue formed in front of each of us, dozens of people with hideous disorders of every kind. We tried with our limited medical knowledge to sort out the worst cases for the immediate attention of the aid workers, and ourselves set about orally rehydrating small babies. By placing tubes down their noses and into their stomachs we could get some life-saving rehydration salts into their system. If a novice medic tried to insert a tube up the nose of a healthy two-year-old they would probably get kicked to shreds – but handling a little dot who has not seen food or water for possibly days is like holding something as limp and passive as a dead chicken, and Des and I were able to administer the simple mixture of water, glucose and salt which has saved the lives of thousands of children all across Africa and the Third World.

An old man came into our makeshift surgery with a bandage on his left leg, limping quite badly. I gestured to him to sit down, while one of the nurses finished treating another patient. The temperature in the tent was by now over 100 degrees. It was stifling. Desmond, who had been suffering from a raving dose of the shits, was taking a turn for the worse and was on the verge of fainting. The old man was gesticulating to his leg and by now moaning quite loudly. As the head nurse started to unwrap the filthy, pussy bandage, the smell of the rotting flesh underneath was surprisingly sickly sweet. She suddenly reared back gagging and holding her hand to her mouth. I looked up from treating a small child with minor abrasions to see straight into the old man's wound. It was moving and shifting independently from the rest of his leg. The entire terrible gash in his thigh was alive with bloated maggots, some in the final stage of pupation with young flies trying to take to the wing. Like the young nurse, I recoiled violently, my hands involuntarily flying up to cover my face. Desmond had had enough, and rushed outside the tent to add the contents of his stomach to the shitpile.

— 14 —

Armenian Earthquake
(December 1988)

I was working in West Belfast on a dreary wet morning. We were filming a background story on Michael Stone – the lunatic who threw six grenades into a crowd of mourners at Milltown cemetery and then fired at them with a handgun, killing a total of 3 people, and wounding 150. Now his case was about to come to trial. We were filming Stone's family house when we were pounced on by some local thugs who didn't seem to like what we were doing. I was negotiating for the safety of my teeth when my bleep went off. 'Sorry chaps, we'd love to continue this stimulating conversation, but duty calls.'

We hurriedly got into our camera car and drove out of the area as fast as we could. The bleep was the foreign desk, who wanted me to go to Russia as soon as physically possible. Apparently there had been a large earthquake in Armenia and they wanted me to cover it, not because of my incredible talent as a news cameraman, but because I was the only one with a valid Soviet visa. I flew from Aldergrove to London, managed a quick stop-off at home to see my wife and children, and six hours later I was Moscow bound.

The weather in Moscow was a staggering fifteen degrees below zero. I am told it usually gets a lot colder in mid-winter, God forbid. On arrival I found the Moscow bureau crew and correspondent Ian Glover James doing a valiant job of covering the Armenian earthquake from Moscow, using only Soviet telly pictures. This was not an unusual procedure, as covering any story outside Moscow requires the most hideous amount of red-tape cutting. They told me there was no chance of reaching Armenia, and I was to do Christmas cover relief for the bureau cameraman. Not a welcome suggestion at all, and with much muttering I left the bureau and went to spend the night in the vast Kosmos – possibly the world's ugliest and noisiest hotel. The next morning, in a downcast mood, I made my way back to the bureau. The thought of doing stand-uppers and interviews all day in Moscow depressed me no end and I spent most of the twenty-minute cab ride from the Kosmos to the bureau dreaming up fictitious diseases to try to get me back home where I would miraculously recover in time for another more congenial assignment.

The constant chatter of the wire machines in the bureau can drive you to absolute distraction. Four teleprinters constantly churn out news from around the world and, with a splash or two of vodka still swimming round the brain, it's like listening to pneumatic drills. If you can't beat them join them. I shuffled over to watch computer print paper spew on to the floor. The scale of the disaster was only just beginning to unfold: twenty more children discovered dead under a collapsed school, chatter chatter; an old woman discovered alive in a crushed block of flats in the Armenian city of Spitak, chatter chatter; a Tass spokesman says this is the worst earthquake ever recorded in this area, chatter chatter; the world's money markets are stable, chatter chatter; the Dow Jones index closed at . . . the Nikki Dow closed at . . . chunter chunter; the British Prime Minister said today in Question Time in a reply to an accusation by opposition leader Neil Kinnock . . . chatter chatter; a team of doctors from Manchester calling themselves SMART (South Man-chester Accident Resuscitation Team) chunter chunter, are flying with a number of British firemen, chunter chunter, on a special Air Europe flight to Yerevan to assist in medical help for the Armenian earthquake victims. This flight is to stop at Moscow en route, chunter chunter end file.

The idea was simplicity itself. Get on the connecting aircraft on the final leg of its journey with the doctors and firemen. What could be easier?

My peers dismissed the idea as typical Rich lunacy. Anyway, they didn't want to upset the Soviet authorities by smuggling people on board aircraft without the right documentation. I argued that as I wasn't part of the official Moscow bureau any skullduggery on my part wouldn't necessarily reflect on them.

'Come on – I'll drive you to the airport.' Bureau chief Ian Glover James was as desperate to get a camera out there as I was.

Gaining entry to the VIP transit lounge where the doctors and firemen were waiting for their connecting flight was the easy part. I acted like a noisy latecomer calling out to my bewildered compatriots on the other side of the door as though I had always been one of the Team. These antics got me into the VIP lounge, but I still had the problem of tickets, boarding cards and the reams of paperwork necessary for travelling from one part of the Soviet Union to another. The doctors offered to smuggle me in their cases and the firemen wanted to dress me up as one of their own – a childhood fantasy I declined for the time being.

As well as smuggling me on board there was the further problem of my equipment. I did not have the one-man-band equipment, but the old two-man gear, which is heavy enough even with a sound recordist to help lug it. In order to get all the equipment into my two rucksacks I had had to abandon virtually all my cold weather clothes. Since I fully expected to be back at the Kosmos that evening, I hadn't been unduly concerned.

We were coming up with more and more outlandish schemes when the Soviets suddenly announced that the connecting flight was going to be delayed by at least six hours, so could all the firemen and doctors collect a new boarding pass at the door of the VIP lounge, to enable them to leave the lounge and have something to eat in the airport cafeteria. I lined up and took a boarding pass out of the hand of an unsuspecting security guard.

Hardly able to contain myself with excitement, I sat down to the longest dinner in the world. Even when we had actually boarded the plane I was on tenterhooks, sure that any moment the KGB would be on to me and hoick me out of the Tupolev aircraft and attach electrodes to my bollocks. I had been reading Gerry Seymour's new novel *Archangel* on the way over to Moscow and my imagination was running riot.

Finally the Tupolev took to the air – I had got away with it. The doctors were looking forward to getting down to work as soon as possible and the talk was mainly about amputation and crush syndrome – the latter being the most prevalent in this sort of disaster. While the firemen discussed the merits of their heat image intensifying camera systems, I reassembled my camera and recorder and filmed everything that moved or talked aboard the aircraft. In my excitement at having an exclusive, I nearly blew it all at the last minute by asking the captain if I could film our approach into Yerevan through the cockpit windows. He politely declined. If he thought it was peculiar that a doctor should be carrying so much film equipment, he was gracious enough not to say so.

The approach to Yerevan airport is difficult at the best of times, and, since the earthquake, the number of planes landing there daily had risen from thirteen to a staggering two hundred and fifty, including many of the giant Antonov cargo planes. Only two days before a Yugoslav plane had crashed on its approach killing all the flight crew and many passengers and losing all its valuable aid cargo. The pilot had seen people walking on to the runway as he was landing and had tried to gain altitude and bank, but too late. The day before that, fifty-five Russian soldiers had died when a Soviet troop-carrying helicopter had crashed trying to avoid another aircraft.

I started to scan the skies anxiously. All seemed to be clear and we made a perfect landing. The airfield was awash with movement – every possible type of aircraft seemed to be here loading or unloading its cargo, and the noise level was almost unbearable. The Armenian Red Cross had laid on two very old and dilapidated buses for the doctors and their equipment; we were destined for the city of Leninakan and had nearly 130 kilometres to cover before nightfall. A quick glimpse of the capital Yerevan reminded me that just before the earthquake Armenia had had its own internal problems in the form of nationalistic riots and demonstrations, for the whole town was under curfew with APCs trundling through the city centre.

As we left Yerevan the countryside unfolded into sharp contrasts of mountains and lowlands. The doctors were still in good humour, excitedly chuntering on about limbs and plasma and cutting tools. As the journey progressed the traffic that had been with us all but disappeared while the oncoming traffic increased. The most unnerving thing was that it was mostly open trucks full of coffins, not nicely varnished, brass-handled affairs either, but hundreds of very plain plywood caskets. I couldn't help wondering where they had got them from in such a short space of time. Perhaps there was a special government department that swung into action at this sort of disaster. The sunlight was failing fast as we hit the outskirts of Leninakan, where we became ensnared in a vast traffic jam. It was chaos – like some awful living web. Caught up with military vehicles of all shapes and sizes were hundreds of refugees leaving the city. Terrible gaunt faces peered out of the windows of passing trucks, and horses pulled carts full of entire families, clutching what little was left of their household contents. It started to rain.

As our two dilapidated buses slowly drew nearer the city, the scale of the disaster shocked us all into stunned silence. We saw piles of rubble some ten metres high which just days ago had been highrise blocks of flats. Whole streets had been gobbled up, entire districts totally devastated. And the coffins, hundreds more on every street corner, and on the pavements rows of corpses lying face up in the rain as they awaited the arrival of yet more plywood boxes. At four minutes to four on 7th December 1988 four-fifths of a city the size of Southampton had been destroyed in a few minutes.

We ground to a halt in what was once the central square of Leninakan city. Soldiers and civilians shared the warmth of enormous bonfires and there were large numbers of people milling around aimlessly, either crying into their hands or standing rocking to and fro as they stared up at the night sky.

I had never seen so many people gazing so vacantly into nothing, not seeing the moon or the clouds or the flames of the bonfire, but something far more disturbing. Most had lost their homes, their friends, members of their family, everything. They never saw me thrusting my camera into their grief.

I felt utterly useless. There I was with thirty thousand quids' worth of equipment on my shoulder, and I couldn't heal, provide shelter, or dig through rubble with it. I'd have been more use with a packet of Disprin. I left the doctors to finish setting up camp, and went off to film what I could. Every street corner provided its own terrible view of hell – so many bonfires, dead bodies and coffins, collapsed buildings and crying and screaming – where else could I be?

I knelt down on one knee, not to pray, but to get a better shot of a young couple hugging each other by a bonfire, and to get a pile of coffins to feature prominently in the foreground.

'Fantastic pictures!' I could imagine the reaction back in London. I gently put a young girl's arm back into its casket, so many coffins.

The pictures in this news editor's dream weren't going to vanish overnight, so I decided to return to see how the British doctors were faring.

On my way back it started to rain again, romantic notions of some clumsy god trying to clean up after some cosmic cock-up were short-lived. There weren't many people who believed in God that night.

I had nearly reached the camp when a young soldier blocked my way and started shouting at me in Russian. In any language I knew exactly what he was babbling on about – he wanted to see my papers, my accreditation, my permission to film. 'I'm sorry I didn't have time to pick up my press pass and ticket for the three-forty earthquake you fucking moron,' I snapped and pushed him aside. It all seemed so utterly stupid. Who gave a damn about who I was in the middle of this nightmare. Anyway, it was obvious – once again I was the vulture, the fly on the piece of shit, programmed to feed off the misfortunes of others, just like this soldier was programmed to ask for paperwork. I turned round, walked straight up to him, kissed him gently on the cheek and left without saying another word.

The Brits were not having a lot of luck organising themselves. During the fifty minutes or so which had passed since I had left them in the square trying to get their act together, what was left of the local authorities had arrived on the scene and told them to move their camp to Leninakan airstrip where an American aid group were already established.

When we arrived there we found the Americans well settled in. We had just begun to unload all the equipment for a second time, when someone rushed up to our interpreter and explained that they could hear children's voices coming from a collapsed apartment block. We left half the team to continue setting up camp, while five firemen with the heat-seeking cameras and two of the surgeons set off in a smaller truck to find the building in question. There was enormous enthusiasm all round. The thought of rescue was terribly exciting and being part of it was making me feel slightly less of a parasite. Our good spirits were short-lived, however, for as we rounded a street corner to arrive at our location, we found ourselves looking at a nine-storey apartment block which had been reduced to an eight-metre pile of concrete slabs, lying quite neatly packed like a discarded game of cards.

The by-now inevitable bonfires were burning at the base of what was left of the block of flats, while some of the former occupants huddled around to keep warm. The temperature had by now dropped to somewhere around twelve to fourteen degrees below zero. The impossibility of the situation hit us instantly. Even if you managed to locate someone, how the hell would you get them out of this concrete tomb?

A light flurry of snow started to fall, and I remembered that it was only two weeks till Christmas. Even this light covering of snow was beginning to warp my perception of my surroundings, as my brain tried to romanticise the scene before me. The ITN machine once more whirred into action: sad faces in the snow, reflections of orange flame in their hollow eyes; pan right . . . fireman scrabbling up the wreckage; pan left . . . doctors comforting local children; zoom into old man's face – he seems to be looking for someone or something – it doesn't matter what, it will cut beautifully. Even better, an American dog handler comes across from another site to lend us a hand. Good for British consumption, the dog shot. Close up of dog sniffing through rubble, zoom out to dog handler.

The chief fireman called for quiet. The image-intensifying cameras were not able to pick up anything, so they were using sophisticated listening devices.

A fireman's hand shot up to indicate that he had heard something and everyone immediately stopped what they were doing and strained to catch a sound from inside the rubble. The fireman beckoned me over and handed me the earpiece. 'What does this sound like to you Sebastian?' he asked eagerly, as if wanting confirmation. I held the earphones to my ears and listened intently.

Sure enough I could hear the unmistakable sound of a human voice. Fantastic! We had found someone alive in this mess, but wait a minute, what was that background noise? It sounded like music –

a radio! Someone had left a radio on; underneath all this rubble, a sodding radio was still playing.

Everyone was plunged into instant gloom until our firemen pointed out that since there was no electricity to this building, nor could batteries be left on for this length of time without running flat, someone must be turning the set on and off. With new-found vigour we all began to claw away at the ungiving rubble. Had we had some heavy lifting gear we might at least have had a fighting chance, but as it was the task was impossible. The old man I had filmed earlier came to my side and pointed to something lodged beneath a slab of concrete. He bent forward and grabbed a blue plastic bag full of washing, then burst into tears as if the discovery of the laundry had confirmed his worst fears. I learnt later that this old man had lost his wife, daughter, son-in-law and his two grandchildren in this apartment block. Now he was clutching the ground, sobbing and softly moaning into the blue plastic bag, the side of his face covered by a pair of pink baby's leggings. A terrible guilty embarrassment swept over me and I backed away from him as if his terrible anguish was a contagious disease.

At three in the morning, some twelve hours after arriving in Armenia, we were still scrabbling away at the rubble. It was hopeless. Even if there was a living person in there, it would take heavy earth-moving equipment or a miracle to shift any of the awful mess in which they were entombed. Since neither was forthcoming, a decision was made to call it a night. We climbed dejectedly back into our bus and the driver started the engine and grated an ancient gearbox into forward motion.

As we pulled slowly away I looked up to see Grandpa screaming and waving his arms on top of the pile of rubble and I asked our translator to tell me what he was saying. He threw back the window and the freezing night air brought the old man's voice into the bus.

'It is not good for you to hear.'

'Tell me,' I insisted.

'He wants you to come back and dig out his family. He will pay you with his life.'

A doctor closed the window and we drove on, arriving back at the airfield to find that the remainder of the team had put up camp with the Americans and we now had a tent of our own. The temperature had dropped a further five degrees, and this made it somewhere between 'freezing' and 'fucking freezing'. My lack of cold weather clothes was beginning to tell. By now I was shivering convulsively and had lost all feeling in my extremities. The doctors gave me all the spare clothes they could and, wrapped up like a mummy, I crept into my sleeping bag. A despondent mood had settled over the occupants of our tent. It was becoming increasingly obvious to the doctors that they had arrived far too late – the dead were dead and the most seriously injured had already been airlifted to Moscow hospitals for treatment.

I woke up early and filmed the doctors as they woke, dressed and made coffee on a stove in the clear morning light. There was talk of pulling out of Leninakan and returning to Yerevan as it seemed they could not be of any use here. If I couldn't get pictures of them saving lives I was determined at least to get one of them putting on a bandage, so I left for town with Denis Edwards, the director of the intensive care unit at Manchester Royal Infirmary. Denis was completely depressed at having travelled all this way for nothing, and kept saying that the only good that had come out of this fiasco was that it had been a worthwhile exercise, and that they would be quicker off the mark next time. We arrived at what was left of Leninakan's central hospital to find most of the wards practically empty. We finally stumbled upon a doctor trying to insert a drip into the arm of an injured man. The poor man's arm was a mass of welts and bloody lesions. Denis, who was visibly appalled at the poor conditions and dreadful lack of hygiene, immediately offered assistance which was gratefully accepted. We found out that this doctor was a junior intern and that most of the other staff had been killed. This was his fifty-second attempt to get this needle into his patient's arm, and it was this, not the earthquake, which had caused the terrible welts. I filmed Denis as he efficiently inserted a fresh needle, but this completed, he could find no one else in need of his expertise. We thanked the doctor and a nurse who was half-asleep in a doorway, and left the hospital. Back in the street Death was everywhere. Somehow the cover of darkness and the snow had made it seem like a giant film set, but now it was very real. The early

morning sunlight showed the extent of the disaster all too clearly –
crushed cars littered the streets, some with their occupants trapped
and rotting inside. Children played in water from burst mains, and
large brown rats scuttled in and out of little holes in the rubble. I
tried not to think about what they were feasting upon.

'Excuse me, do you speak English?' I turned round to find an
unshaven youth of about twenty-five at my elbow. He introduced
himself as Vortek and offered to help me with any translation I
might need and to show me around what was left of Leninakan.
Vortek turned out to be a student at Yerevan University who had
come to search for his girlfriend in the ruins of Leninakan. Local
knowledge combined with spoken English, his presence was a
godsend. We toured the broken streets and Vortek pointed out what
used to be, every now and then pausing to weep on his coatsleeve. I
asked him if he had managed to find his girlfriend, and as he looked
at me through red eyes, I knew the answer before he spoke a single
word. Apparently she had died just a few hours before we met, in
the remains of her parents' home in the centre of Leninakan. In the
town centre we found that a bread van had arrived and was in the
process of being torn apart for its contents. Troops had started to
try to clear some of the main streets to allow essential supplies
through, but without much success. The earthquake had happened
at four minutes to four, four minutes before school finished for the
day, so a lot of the dead were children. Desperate parents stood in
small groups outside the remains of schools waiting for what
seemed to be inevitable news. Every now and then there would be a
scream as another tiny, squashed body was brought out of the
rubble.

Vortek, Denis and I cruised around filming one horror after
another. Through Vortek we could now talk to the local people. In
the face of competition from other news crews, I would doubtless
have had few scruples about thrusting my camera into the faces of
grieving parents, but since, remarkably, I seemed to be the only
cameraman or journalist in town, I could afford to be more re-
strained and try to tell the story in a different way. By this time
Denis was anxious to return to base camp and report back to his
group. His recommendation was that they pull out immediately and

regroup in Yerevan. We went to the Central Committee headquarters where Vortek convinced one of his friends to drive us to the
airfield.

On the way we passed a huge crowd of people gathered in front of
a collapsed building. Vortek told us that this was the site of a
cinema, which had been packed full of people at the time of the
earthquake. We got out of the car and went to have a look. The
cinema had been completely sliced in half with a cut so clean that it
resembled an architect's model. The whole of one side of the
building was completely missing, revealing rows of seats, many
with their occupants still in them. The grisly task of the workmen
and the army was to remove them and lower the bodies to relatives
for identification. There were row upon row of coffins in the street
outside the cinema. We watched as people went from coffin to
coffin, lifting the lids in the hope of finding their loved ones. Their
faces were a terrible mixture of emotions as they lifted each lid and
pulled at the clothing – disappointment, relief that this corpse was
not friend or family, apprehension about the next body. I realised
that the one thing I had not filmed yet was close-ups of dead bodies.
There has always been debate in news coverage about whether
events should be sanitised for the viewer, or if accurate reporting
demands uncensored pictures. Although I don't think TV screens
should be awash with torn flesh and blood, sometimes a little more
graphic detail is necessary to bring home the true horror of a
situation.

For once all the bodies were in caskets. I walked along the line of
boxes trying to find one that was open so that I could film it.
Eventually I came across one that had the lid resting by the side;
inside was the body of an elderly gentleman with half his head caved
in. As I started to film a gust of wind blew his shirt over his face. I
bent down to pull back the cloth, but, with the unaccustomed weight
of the recorder around my neck, I lost my balance and tumbled
headlong into the coffin. As I struggled to break my fall, I put my
one free hand straight through what remained of the old chap's
head.

Resembling some nightmare farce, I flayed around like an up-
turned turtle until helping hands pulled me free, covered in brains
and embarrassment. I looked up to see dozens of faces staring

straight at me. It was the first time in two days I had seen anyone look at anything but vacant space.

Vortek helped me gather my composure and we were heading back to the car when, out of the corner of my eye, I spotted a very familiar sight, a cameraman and his sound recordist, and then another and another, all spilling out of a bus. I realised instantly that these were the official pool crews from Moscow being given a guided tour by the Soviets. I ran to the car. Now the only important thing was to get the pictures to Yerevan as soon as possible. The pool crews had just started what I would imagine to be at least four or five hours' official filming, so if I could somehow get on a plane back to Yerevan where the nearest satellite station was, I could still get my story back before theirs.

So far I hadn't thought about getting back at all. To all intents and purposes I was here illegally, so going through any official channels was immediately ruled out.

'Drive to the airfield as quick as you can please,' I said to Vortek's friend. About two hundred metres from our campsite at the airfield we were stopped by an army roadblock and asked for identification. Vortek convinced them that Denis and I were both very important doctors needed in Yerevan as soon as possible, implying that they might be in a spot of bother if they hindered our progress.

As we approached our campsite, something about the tent line-up looked wrong. Denis suddenly let out a small grunt from somewhere deep in his throat: 'They've gone, they have bloody well left without me, the sods!' We found some of the American doctors who told us that the doctors had left on a Soviet cargo plane bound for Yerevan. Since these flights were very rare indeed, they had decided to grab it, assuming that Denis and I would somehow make it back. 'Shit.' Another few hours and, in news terms, my pictures would be old hat. To my utter surprise the army guard at the airfield checkpoint spoke good English. I gave him a melodramatic description of how we had become separated from our team of fellow doctors and it was now a matter of life and death that we rejoin them in Yerevan as soon as possible. This Red Guardsman appeared to be slightly brighter than most of the military personnel we had so far encountered, and asked what a doctor was doing with TV camera equipment. I explained that although I was indeed a doctor, I was also filming the team to show other doctors at hospitals in the UK how the aid work was getting on.

He stared long and hard at my passport, laughed, then slapped it shut and pointed to a small Soviet military cargo aircraft. Not quite believing our good luck we started to walk briskly, but not with too much obvious excitement, towards the aircraft.

'STOP!'

It was the army guardsman. I felt like the character in all those terrible war movies who is called back at the last moment by the SS and my heart sank to the floor.

'Sign this please.' He waved an indemnity form at us.

Jesus Christ get me out of here, I thought. We signed and walked back towards the aircraft.

'STOP!' His voice boomed out yet again.

'Bloody hell now what?' I muttered under my breath.

'Not that aircraft – that one over there.' The soldier had a huge grin on his face.

We walked up the loading ramp of what looked like a miniature Hercules C130 aircraft. Sitting in the corner was a Soviet major.

He barked something unfriendly at us in Russian.

'And a good morning to you,' I replied.

'It is not morning it is now afternoon,' he retorted in perfect English. 'What are you doing here on board this aircraft?'

We went through the, by now, slightly worn repertoire.

'Well, I don't know who gave you permission, but I am afraid there is no room on this aircraft to . . .'

He broke off in mid-sentence as three stretchers bearing critically injured people were rushed on board, accompanied by one young medic. Denis immediately switched into working mode and began to examine the injured. Our chances were beginning to look good when the major turned on me: 'If you are a doctor, look after these people.' He indicated the stretcher cases. Denis shot me a concerned look, and I started to take pulses and blood pressures and make reassuring noises to those in obvious distress while Denis and the medic did all the real work. At last the major vanished up to the flight deck and I was about to grab my camera when one of the patients grabbed my hand and started talking to me in a soft, earnest voice. I asked Vortek what she was saying. 'She is saying thank you for coming to our country and taking care of our people.' I don't think I had ever felt so ashamed.

Denis, meanwhile, was doing a fantastic job. The Soviet medic was just about to inject a woman when Denis's hand shot out and stopped him. He had seen the label on the ampoule and to his horror realised that the young medic was about to administer an almost certainly lethal dosage of this drug. The engines roared and the hydraulic loading ramp hissed shut behind us.

Two minutes later we were in the air. As we banked my passport fell out of my rucksack on to the floor. It had fallen open at the page with the photo on it. I picked it up. Maybe the soldier had been laughing at this ridiculous old picture. Directly opposite the photo was clearly printed, Occupation: film cameraman.

At Yerevan airport, Denis, Vortek and I ran as fast as we could into the terminal building. I was in hyperdrive by now and the only thought in my mind was to get to the TV station as soon as possible and get a satellite booked, up and running. Vortek went to look for a cab to take us to ATV. Denis wanted to look for his companions, but I was having none of it. I think he saw the change in my character, and decided it was probably best to tag along and keep quiet until this madman had finished his task. We dived into the cab Vortek had procured and set off for the station which was on top of a high hill. The others had now been caught up in my frenzy, and were shouting at the cab driver to go faster. I looked at my watch. With the time difference in our favour I had just an hour before *News at One*.

The cab came to a screeching halt outside the TV station, where we were stopped by two burly soldiers. The usual questions started. We had no time for this sort of nonsense, but to argue would have taken much longer, and we finally got through the gates and were ushered into the master control room. I was spinning at a hundred miles an hour. Not only had I got the first western TV pictures out of the disaster area, but since I did not have a journalist to lay down the voice track I would have to do it myself. When I told the station controller I was from ITN and would like to book a satellite to feed pictures and sound to London, I was flabbergasted to be told that this had already been done. Had ITN been booking every available satellite in the hope that I would surface sooner or later? 'What time is the bird?' I asked. The answer was a terrifying, 'In fifteen minutes.'

I had to get the package together incredibly fast. I didn't even have time to ring London to tell them what was going on, but I was secretly pleased, as it gave them no choice but to run the piece with my commentary. I had just started to write my script when I heard English voices in the corridor. Was it the BBC? Please no, not after all this hard work.

ITN's Peter Sharp walked round the corner and greeted me with an enormous grin. He and his crew had boarded a Soviet cargo plane at London airport and had just arrived. The cameraman was one of my very best friends, but I was torn between giving him a big hug and telling them all to get lost, since now my first chance to voice my own pictures had just vanished.

Instantly we all became a team and co-ordinated the satellite feed to London while Peter wrote a new script.

Soon it seemed as though the entire world's Press had descended on the Armenian capital of Yerevan, including the BBC reporter Kate Adie. This was one of the few times Kate had completely missed the boat. To escape the problems of getting to Armenia via Moscow and the Soviet authorities, she had come overland by truck through Turkey and then over the border to Armenia. When she burst through the hotel doors, she discovered not only that she was the last hack to get there, but that the rest of us had been there sending out stories for some considerable time. Kate being Kate, she wore that one on the chin and it was not long before she caught up with the rest of the pack.

By now, reporting from Leninakan and Spitak was becoming an everyday event. The initial difficulties of getting back and forth from the capital had been overcome with the roadblocks being lifted to allow food and aid through, and to some extent to make the journalists' lives slightly easier. The government were grateful for any kind of assistance, and our pictures were certainly helping to bring the plight of the Armenian people to the attention of the west.

Two weeks had passed since the initial shock of the earthquake and London was just beginning to be a trifle bored with the story. It began to drop rapidly down the bulletin as back at home a Pan Am Jumbo exploded in mid-air and British Rail started to plough their trains into each other.

We had heard from the office that French Television were to bring an Earth station to Leninakan overland from Paris in an articulated truck. No mean feat, but it was bound to prove very lucrative for French Television as networks from round the world had booked satellite time on the thing in an attempt to be the first to broadcast live from the centre of an earthquake zone.

The night the French station was due to arrive, I, Mike Inglis, another ITN cameraman, and sound recordist Ray Cheeseman were despatched down to Leninakan to gather fresh footage to butt up with our live spot with Ian Glover James. The rendezvous for the ground station was to be the courtyard of the local hospital. At about four-thirty in the afternoon the artic roared into the hospital grounds, the back doors flew open and revealed the TV equivalent of an Aladdin's Cave. Laden with the very latest technology, it included two small studios, two edit booths and the capability of doing a multi-camera outside broadcast. In the middle of all this death and destruction, it was all a little bit vulgar.

While the French set up their gadgetry, we negotiated with a nurse for somewhere to spend the night, as the hospital, or rather what was left of the hospital, was deserted. We were guaranteed two beds in the doctors' quarters when we had finished working that evening. Two beds for three big chaps – that should prove interesting.

The French were now ready to beam pictures to anywhere in the world, on behalf of any network with the required amount of cash. One of the many gadgets they possessed were two Marasat telephone systems. For the first time since we had arrived, I was now able to talk to the office direct from the scene of the disaster. It took only twenty seconds or so for the novelty of telephoning from the middle of a devastated city to wear off and we were soon talking about booking satellite feeds and gossip.

Ian Glover James arrived about three hours before *News at Ten* and put together a superb first live piece from the scene. Ian was wearing an expensive full-length, black, cashmere Crombie over-coat, and this, combined with the fact that he is always a few kilos underweight, had the effect of making him look like the local undertaker. Rather apt on this occasion, I thought.

We were the first of a great stream of hacks from all over the world giving their own versions of the disaster. We watched in fascination the different ways you could position journalists in front of coffins and rubble: the French would stand slightly side-on; the Brits would stand head-on, invariably to the left of the screen, while the star system of the American networks decreed that the background was irrelevant and that the talent should be firmly embedded in the centre screen, definitely establishing a presence at the scene of the disaster. The sight of a twenty-eight-year-old blonde bimbo painting her face and spraying a disgusting mixture of sticky hairspray and Chanel No. 5 over herself really was the pits, and we were all momentarily ashamed of our chosen profession.

A wretched family slowly traipsed into the background, seemingly not going anywhere, just shuffling around as so many other people in Leninakan appeared to be doing. Just as the bimbo was about to go live to New York, she managed to corral the distressed young mother and her two drastically underclothed children to become part of the early morning breakfast fiasco that was about to spew into the kitchens of millions of Americans. They pathetically stood bolt-upright to the left of Lucrezia Borgia.

'Can't someone tell them to look more sad or something? They were great a minute ago,' the bimbo said.

It was time for me to go for a walk before I ripped the silly bitch's throat out. Without a camera I just walked and walked for hours in the rubble and devastation. Even though I had filmed all this over the last couple of days, I had not really absorbed the total destruction around me. I had been viewing the whole mess through my own little TV screen in my camera.

It's a curious phenomenon. I find that every time I film something, it ceases to seem real, and if I really want to see it I have to put my camera down. So when someone asks me what something was like on a certain location, I tend to remember not the images I have filmed, but those I have seen with my naked eyes.

— 15 —

The Incredible Mr McGinty
(and Other Aquatic Mammals)
(1989)

'The sunken fleet of what?' an incredulous senior news editor said to me early one Monday morning. I had been trying to convince a bemused Nigel Hancock that we should cover the anniversary of the sinking, during the First World War, of the entire German fleet in Scapa Flow in the Orkneys. Nigel's eyes were getting wider and wider as I unfolded my tale; but it was not that I had him spellbound by a great piece of television journalism, it was more in disbelief that anyone could really be trying to flog a seventy-year-old story.

Over the years ITN had covered anniversaries of many great historic moments, but I think this one probably deserved to stay in the history books. Nigel listened patiently, trying not to look too bored, as I tried to explain that, with today's underwater technology, I could offer very clear pictures of the wrecks. This, I insisted, when combined with a couple of filmed interviews with survivors of the German fleet and one with an English naval captain who was a rating at the time, would make a very interesting film package.

I was rapidly losing ground. Nigel was starting to look over his shoulder as I was speaking to him. I had to gain back his interest fast or this venture would see the bin in about two more seconds. I had a brainstorm. My mouth suddenly sprang into life without me giving it any instructions to do so. I heard a voice say: 'I can give you a reporter walking on one of the wrecks and talking at the same time.'

Nigel's eyes sprang back to meet mine. 'How much will all that cost?' he said accusingly.

I had done it. I had aroused his curiosity, but I could not believe what I had just said. This was excess bullshit, even for me.

'I will have to do some costings and get back to you,' I said somewhat nervously.

'If it's at the right price, go for it, it sounds great,' an excited Nigel blurted out. He spun on his heels and shot across the newsroom at great speed, more than likely grateful to be out of earshot of a complete lunatic.

One of the first big feature films I worked on as a camera assistant was called *Seven Cities to Atlantis* and starred Doug McClure and Cyd Charisse of the legendary pins. I got the job through a well-known cameraman at Pinewood studios who phoned up one day to ask if I would act as clapper boy and camera assistant to the second unit action team. One catch – the second unit was the underwater unit.

'You are a diver aren't you, Sebastian?'

'Yes of course,' I replied unhesitatingly.

'Good – I'll see you at the harbour in Gozo in two days' time.'

I hung up and put my head in my hands in desperation. What the hell was I going to do? I had never dived in my life.

I decided the only thing to do was to read as much about diving as I could over the next two days, then watch the other divers when I got there and pray to God that on the day I would not blow it.

On arrival at the location I was terrified. There was a mass of very complicated-looking diving gear and underwater cameras everywhere.

'Seb, put the arri in its housing would you, and check the O-ring seals.'

What the hell was he talking about? Bullshit had finally got the better of me, I was bound to be sent home in disgrace. A tap on the shoulder brought me out of my panic-induced trance.

'You haven't got a clue have you, Seb?' It was my boss, the lighting cameraman.

Fortunately for me, shooting on the picture had been set back a couple of days and the lighting cameraman was willing to teach me to dive to try to make me into a useful member of the camera team. I worked like crazy every second of the day and learnt everything I possibly could. The end-result was happiness all round. The producers were none the wiser, and I discovered a passion for diving which was never to leave me. Years and many diving qualifications later, I persuaded the powers that be to let me form ITN's 'underwater unit', but sadly I had as yet had little opportunity to put it to the test.

I left the newsroom and collected my thoughts on the fire exit stairwell. What the hell was I to do? I really had got myself into complete cack this time – a walking, talking reporter underwater. Jesus Christ!

I rang my great diving buddy Mike Sears and explained what I had done. As ever, a calm and nonplussed voice said, 'So, what's the problem?' This was one of the reasons Mike and I got on so well together. We both had the habit of saying yes to anything and sorting the problems out afterwards. Mike assured me that we could put this together. Some time ago the BBC had made a programme called *Reefwatch* in which they had a presenter walking and talking from the bottom of the Red Sea in Israel. She had been wearing a very elaborate diving suit with a bubble helmet enabling the viewer to see her talk underwater. This lady also just happened to be a marine biologist and a very experienced diver, none of which we had on the reporters' roster at ITN.

I left Mike with the job of tracking down the equipment and putting together some sort of diving budget. Although I was now marginally more confident of turning this crazy idea into a reality, I still had the task of finding an ITN reporter with the right credentials. Not only did the volunteer have to be reasonably fearless and have a taste for the unusual, but it was also looking more and more likely that Mike and I would be teaching whoever it might be to dive from scratch. I had bitten off more than I could chew. I went to see Lawrence McGinty, our science correspondent, to bounce the idea off him and also to see if he was interested in getting himself involved in any of the topside filming. Not only was he delighted to be involved, but he wanted to do the underwater stint as well. I looked at Lawrence in astonishment. I had to admire his pluck as he was more than a few pounds overweight, smoked like a chimney and the deepest he had ever dived was to the bottom of a pint glass. I was just about to back-pedal diplomatically when I thought, Why not? He is after all the science correspondent, who else is better qualified to do the piece and, anyway, what else can you do when faced with such enthusiasm and boyish grins?

With the help of Nigel's delightfully cunning assistant Gilly Blake, we managed to make the budget look vaguely acceptable. Christ knows how, but with a little jiggery-pokery and pushing it under Nigel's nose when he was at his busiest, I sneaked away with budget approval for the tests.

Mike had done a magnificent job of tracking down the equipment and personnel to do the job. All that was left to do was to teach Lawrence how to dive in his spacesuit, and walk and talk under-water. Lawrence was under strict instructions to cut down on the amount of light ales and ciggies if he was to stand any chance whatsoever of staying alive, so with new purpose he set off to do some serious lunchtime training in the Green Man.

Before going to the Orkneys, we were planning to do film tests with Lawrence in a flooded dry dock in Greenwich. Two days before commencing the tests, Nigel Hancock called me into his office.

Oh God, I thought, he's been looking too closely at that bloody budget.

'Are you sure you've picked the right journo for the job, Sebastian?'

I left Nigel with the impression that a new and fantastically fit Lawrence McGinty was the next best thing to Jacques Cousteau, but I still had one problem. Quite rightly, Nigel wanted to see the results of the test shoot before making his final decision whether to pour money into the final phase. So he had seen the budget after all.

On an incredibly cold, dark and grey Saturday morning, Lawrence and I, with a slightly larger than usual ITN crew, arrived at the dry dock in Greenwich. To make all this work the crew consisted of eight men: I was the underwater cameraman; Jon Hunt, the sound recordist, was to be the link between the seabed and the surface, and to monitor the video feed from my camera; Mike Sears was dive supervisor – his job was to teach Lawrence how to dive, also to make sure that everyone was observing their decompression tables and to coordinate the numerous dives and divers it would take to make the whole thing work; Russell Padwick, electrician, was in charge of all the underwater lighting and the most respected man on the test unit as no one else had fancied the risk of being turned into so much battered cod and chips with the flick of the wrong switch; Jock Stewart was in charge of the dive suit and bubble helmet, and was also to act as Lawrence's right-hand man; Malcolm Weaver, stunt man and underwater electrician was to give Jock back up if Lawrence's suit were to fail and we had to bring him up from depth. On the test and shoot he would also assist me in the placing of the film lights underwater. Jon Johnson, designer and manufacturer of the underwater camera housing, joined us on the tests only, to see if we had any problems that occurred in the test filming that could be rectified before we went to the Orkneys to do the real thing. Finally, there was Lawrence himself who had just won his wings as a novice diver. Mike had given him a crash course the week before the tests and was very happy with the way he had handled himself.

This was the first time that Lawrence had actually clamped eyes on the bubble suit and I thought that I detected just a glimmer of apprehension in his eyes. Mind you, who could blame him? The suit lay on the floor like some deflated Michelin Man, ready to suffocate anyone who was foolish enough to set foot in it. The suit itself is fairly simple – made out of one piece of eight millimetre neoprene, it enables the wearer to withstand extreme cold for some considerable time. At the neck is a rather cumbersome metal collar which the helmet is attached to, not unlike the space helmets we all got used to seeing in the early days of manned space flight. The only difference was that to keep buoyancy, this helmet had a filthy great lead weight on the back of it. Without this chunk of lead the diver would find it almost impossible to descend. In the normal way compressed air is attached to the diver by means of twin tanks strapped to his back. There is, of course, no visible demand valve, as this would defeat the purpose of having our man speaking underwater. In the absence of a mouthpiece, the air is brought into the helmet by means of a supersensitive valve located behind the wearer's head at the base of the helmet, out of sight of the cameras. The air flows into the helmet on demand from the diver: as he inhales, the air pressure changes within the helmet, causing the special valve to release compressed air into the bubble.

Jock and Malcolm levered Lawrence into the suit while the rest of the crew and I became familiar with the bits and bobs that made up a huge tangle of cables and wires. The water was crystal clear in the

Malcolm Weaver (lights), Sebastian Rich (camera), Lawrence McGinty (reporter) diving on the scuttled German fleet, Scapa Flow, Orkney (*photo: Mike Sears*)

Above: A Mujahadin look-out near Kandahar airport, Afghanistan
Below: A Mujahadin herb garden, bordered by live shells. Tia Khan's
secret hideout, Afghanistan, summer 1989

dock, but unfortunately the water temperature was more favourable to polar bears than *homo sapiens*. Mike and I lowered the camera into the water and tested it for neutral buoyancy. A quick test dive showed us that all the controls were working smoothly and, most important of all, that we had no leaks anywhere.

The only component not as yet tested was Lawrence himself. Sitting at the side of the dock with his legs dangling in the water, Lawrence waited for Jock to lower the helmet into position. Malcolm guided Lawrence down the steps into the water and held him in place while Jock, with a menacing Scots grin, bore down on Lawrence. With a final loud click, the helmet was in place. Jon Hunt asked Lawrence if he could give him a sound check. It was perfect. The hard work that ITN's sound maintenance department had put into the communication rig had paid off and Jon was picking up Lawrence loud and clear.

Mike and I descended to about ten feet and waited for Jock and Malcolm to bring down our star turn. I looked up to see Lawrence's large form looming towards us. All of a sudden his feet vanished from view and were replaced by his head. In all the preparations we had forgotten to put the lead weights on his feet to give him stability. He had completely turned turtle and was now thrashing about like a demented sperm whale. Mike and Malcolm instantly grabbed hold of him, righted him and then brought him up to the surface.

Jock gingerly lifted the helmet off to be met with, 'Fuck that for a game of soldiers!' from Lawrence.

Without giving him time to think, weights were strapped to his feet, the helmet snapped on and as quick as a flash he was unceremoniously dumped back into the water. Once he had landed on the granite floor of the dock, it took Lawrence a little while to find his footing with all the unaccustomed weight encasing his body. After a few minutes of falling and sliding all over the place he was soon waddling around quite confidently. I checked his air pressure gauge – in his strange surroundings he was breathing very heavily and using up air at quite an alarming rate.

It was time to get on with the test. I gave Lawrence the universal divers' sign for OK which he returned with a stupid grin on his face. Someone had put an old rowing boat on the bottom of the dock; this chunk of wood was to take the place of the entire German fleet for the time being. Lawrence rested one hand on the rowing boat with a confidence that said: I've been here for hours, where the fuck have you lot been? I gave him the cue to start talking. 'As you can see . . . ARRRRRRGHSSSS . . . this . . . AAARRRRGHHSS . . . wreck . . . has . . . AAARRRRGHHSSS . . . been on the . . . AARRGGSSSSS . . . seabed for some seventy . . . AAARRGGHHHHSSS . . . years.' The exertion of getting kitted up and turning turtle had taken its toll on Lawrence. He was breathing far too erratically and in such a laboured fashion as to be virtually incomprehensible. We sat on the bottom twiddling our thumbs, waiting for Flipper to get his breath back while Mike kept a watchful eye on an ever-decreasing air pressure gauge.

A sceptical Nigel Hancock and a bemused Stewart Purvis, editor in chief of ITN, were called into an edit suite in the main newsroom to view the test results of our folly. Miraculously, the duff takes had vanished the night before with some clandestine editing, and the remaining pictures flashed on to the monitors. The clear water in the dock and the eventual clarity of Lawrence's speech made for a stunning and fun ten minutes of rushes. There he was walking and talking underwater as if it were the most natural thing in the world for him to do. Our press-ganged audience had never before seen anything like it adapted to suit news coverage. Their first reaction was to burst out into hysterical laughter. The sight of Lawrence in his Michelin Man suit wobbling about underwater was very amusing, but along with the laughter there was genuine interest as the possibilities of such a technique opened up a new and as yet unused sphere of news coverage.

It was therefore with full budget approval that we set off for the Orkneys. It was one thing doing the dive in the controlled environment of a deep water tank but it was going to be another kettle of fish doing it in the open sea in the infamous changeable weather of the Orkneys. Apparently it was not uncommon to have all four seasons three times a day.

Our first task was to find a reliable boat to use as a dive platform and, even more important, a skipper with a good knowledge of the locations of all the wrecks. While the rest of the crew were sorting out their equipment, Mike and I went on the hunt for just such an old sea dog. After enquiring in several boatyards in Kirkwall, we were recommended to seek out a certain Captain Terry. He was to be found at his house in the town of Stromness. We couldn't miss him, we were told, because he was just about the skinniest person on the island.

A tiny lady wearing a woollen bobble hat and an infectious smile answered the door. I asked if Captain Terry was in. A voice from the next room bellowed, 'Come on in, don't stand out there all bloody day.' An enormous man weighing in at least twenty-two stone pressed a hand the size of a shovel around mine. As he slowly crushed just about every bone in my hand to dust, he said, with a twinkle in his mischievous little piggy eyes, 'So it's Captain Terry you're looking for is it lads?'

Another old sea dog sat in the corner of the kitchen cleaning an old gas cooker. I thought, Well that can't be our man, he certainly doesn't fit the description given by the men in the Kirkwall boatyard.

'And what would you be wanting from our Terry then?' the enormous man said.

I said who we were and that we wanted a captain and a boat for about three to four days.

'And you would pay good money for this would you?' as he started to rub his giant shovel-like hands together. By this time I was getting pissed off with this fat bastard's interrogation. I said that I would discuss that with Captain Terry if he could just tell me where to find him. He grabbed my hand again and said, 'Glad to meet you, Terry's the name, be only too glad to help you mate.'

'But, but . . .' I started to squawk.

'I know, I know. They told you I was the skinniest man on the island. Bit of an old joke that I'm afraid.'

Terry showed us his pride and joy in the small port – a renovated fishing trawler named the *Girl Mina* which now spent its life taking sportsdivers to the numerous wrecks in Scapa Flow. He assured us that the boat was ideal for our purposes and would be ready for us the next day complete with provisions, a compressor and also a generator to run our underwater lighting. Mike made a general enquiry about the overall condition of the vessel. He told us with great pride that the *Girl Mina* had sunk only once before, but that he had successfully retrieved her from Davy Jones's locker, and she was now as fit as a fiddle. Mike and I looked at each other in mild horror, hoping that this was just another example of the Orkney sense of humour. Much against our better judgement, but due to the fact that it was getting late and we needed to find a boat and skipper by the end of the day, we agreed a price and left for our hotel with mixed feelings about the skinniest man on the island.

On the way we were joined by another member of the crew, an electrician, Martin Harrow. A freelance lighting man whom I had used on many occasions, Martin was a very competent technician with the same dreadful say-yes-and-worry-about-it-later habit as Mike Sears and myself. A small man, resembling one of Snow White's seven dwarfs, his character was definitely Happy's. He never seemed to tire of my requests for lights to be positioned in some of the most awkward and ridiculous places on the seabed. This, combined with a seemingly bottomless well of painfully funny anecdotes and a silly elfin grin, made him one of the most popular people in the crew.

Back at the hotel we told the rest of the crew the good news about Captain Terry and the *Girl Mina*, carefully omitting the part about the miraculous resurrection of the boat.

We arrived at Stromness harbour at seven-thirty the next morning with twenty-nine large metal cases, plus all our diving equipment. Terry's eyes were like saucers. He had seen many dive groups before, but none such as this, and I'm sure he now regretted his original quote. The first mate, Jim, helped us load up, giving us several withering looks as if to say, 'Have you got nothing else better to spend your money on then?' His job on the unit was to make sure that all the divers' air tanks were constantly full and that the compressor was maintained correctly, a job he did without fault all the way through the trip. Even so, I couldn't help thinking that at times he wished we would all jump in with empty tanks.

The diminutive smiling lady who had opened the door to Terry's house the day before turned out to be Terry's wife, Mo. Since she was about five foot nothing and weighed no more than six and a half stone, it gave the crew much enjoyment trying to work out how on earth she and Terry ever got it together in the sack. Mo turned out to be a complete star. With her never-ending cups of hot tea and doorstep sandwiches, she managed to keep the elements at bay and us in constant good humour.

The *Girl Mina* bobbed gently in the early morning slack water. Terry and Jim had expertly brought us directly over the German wreck the SMS *Bremse*. She was in the perfect location for our purposes, sitting, at low tide, in no more than twenty metres of water. The SMS *Bremse* was a destroyer and we were assured by our sea dogs that the main bow gun was still intact on the deck. The plan was to position Lawrence just in front of what remained of the fourteen-inch-thick steel gun-housing. The steel plating on the wreck of the German fleet had a unique quality; because the ships had been sunk before the advent of the nuclear bomb the steel was free of any background radiation, which made it a very valuable commodity to scientific laboratories. Over the years large chunks of the plating had been looted, and some had even found its way on to some of the space shuttle missions.

Mike and I descended into the clear but very cold waters. Our drysuits kept most of the cold at bay, but, because we had to work, our gloves were only three-millimetre neoprene. This made it very easy to operate the camera, but it was only a matter of minutes before the cold turned one's fingers into little watery stalagmites. Divers often piss in their wetsuits to keep themselves warm and I had to keep reminding myself I was wearing a drysuit and must refrain.

We had chosen this time of the year to film – six months before the actual anniversary of the scuttling – because the algae were not so abundant in the sea, and the water was therefore much clearer. Although the visibility was good for the first few metres of our descent, after about five metres it suddenly became quite dark. This was an indication that the weather was once again on the move and we could only guess what it would be like when we surfaced.

I began to relax. The quiet of the undersea world always gave me great comfort; no sound could be heard apart from our own breathing or the odd noise from the anchor chain as it rolled across the silty bottom. This was my favourite place to be, where no one could bother me with any problems and my bank manager couldn't pester me about my overdraft.

'Scrackeesh . . . Can you hear me, Seb?' I nearly jumped out of my drysuit. I had forgotten that I was wearing a special mask normally worn by police divers which allowed you to talk to the surface and vice-versa. My silent world vanished as Jon Hunt tested out the communications systems.

'Yes, I can hear you loud and clear,' I replied somewhat curtly.

Mike swam up beside me and tapped me on the shoulder. I turned round to see the enormous bow gun looming out of the gloom. It was more impressive than I could have hoped for – the bow of the destroyer was almost intact and, looking at my depth gauge, I could see that the location for Lawrence was only nineteen metres. At this depth not only was it relatively safe for Lawrence with his minimal diving experience, but it also meant we could work for long periods of time without the hassle of decompressing.

I looked up to see Malcolm coming straight towards me, the underwater lights trailing behind him. Malcolm was wearing a set of prescription goggles and the effect of the water refraction made him look like a giant illuminated frog. I giggled as best I could through my demand valve. I called to the surface to say all was ready and it was time to send Lawrence down. Jon told me that it would take about fifteen minutes for Lawrence to descend as he was having problems clearing his ears. For some technical reason I was only getting every other word through my headset, so we decided not to communicate any further with the surface for the time being, as it would probably only make matters worse. The only thing we could do was wait. I turned on the camera to check everything was OK and to my dismay the low battery warning light was blinking furiously at me. 'Shit,' I thought; there was Lawrence psyching himself to do probably the most dangerous thing he had ever done in his entire life and my camera battery was running flat. I turned the camera back on in the vain hope that it was an intermittent fault. No such bloody luck, the nasty little red light was blinking at me with an accusing eye.

My earpiece burst into life again, 'He's on his way, Seb, on his way.'

I had no option but to abort his descent. By the time he arrived at the seabed the camera battery would almost certainly be flat and there was, as yet, no way of changing one underwater. I reluctantly told the boat crew to hold Lawrence where he was and that we would be surfacing in a few minutes. At the surface the camera immediately loses its neutral buoyancy and becomes a twenty-five kilo monster with a mind of its own. The wind had crept up even in the short space of time the first dive had taken. Martin threw over a strong rope and as I struggled to keep myself and camera somewhere near the hull of the *Girl Mina*, the rope whiplashed me in the face. Mike, who had been supporting the camera from underneath, surfaced to see what the hell was going on. He grabbed the end of the rope and expertly tied a bowline on to the handle of the camera. Martin and Jon struggled to pull the camera the three metres or so up the topsides. As it neared the handrail Terry's shovel-like hand appeared from nowhere and effortlessly plucked it to safety. I had no one else but myself to blame for the condition of the camera battery, but nevertheless it put me in a stinking mood and, unfairly, I took it out on the rest of the crew.

Lawrence was having his own set of special problems. While we had been messing about on the sea floor, Lawrence had actually descended to the great depth of three metres, but he had not been able to clear his ears. Normally you would clear your ears by holding your nose and blowing, but having his head totally encased in Perspex made this impossible. There was a small rubber block at the base of the helmet for just such a purpose but Lawrence was having difficulty reaching it. It was imperative that he clear his ears, otherwise they would, to put it technically, burst. Eventually Lawrence devised his own unique way of clearing his ears. He had obtained from somewhere a noseclip and a piece of string; he would blow as hard as he could and on achieving the desired effect he would then chew the piece of string until it pulled the clip from his nose.

Once again we kitted up and went back down to the wreck to await Lawrence's arrival. My communication headset was proving more of a hindrance than a help and I was starting to scream at the topside crew as their messages made less and less sense. They could hear me perfectly and see the pictures I was sending them, but all I seemed to be getting was, 'Pictures . . . zzhhassh . . . colour . . . zzhhasshh . . . receivsshhh . . .' and I would reply, 'What? What? For fuck's sake what?' After ten minutes of this abuse the surface crew thought it better to leave well alone and only pass on the most vital of messages like, 'Lawrence is dead,' or, 'We are sinking.' After what seemed an age I received a garbled message to surface as there was a problem up top. I gestured to Mike and Malcolm to ascend. Mike put his hands on his hips and looked at me as if to say, 'What now for chrissake?'

As we broke the surface we saw it was snowing and chucking down hailstones the size of pennies. We had gone under in brilliant sunshine and now there was a raging blizzard. We dreaded to think what it was going to do next. The problem topside was that Lawrence had descended to five or six metres and had sprung a leak in the seal between his helmet and the suit which had quite rightly put the wind up him. I could see that Lawrence was on the verge of packing it all in and putting the whole thing down as a bad joke. Although we still had a few hours of good daylight left, we decided the wiser course was to call it a day, get back to the hotel for a few light ales and start afresh tomorrow.

At six o'clock the next morning the rain hammered against my bedroom window. No sooner had my heart sunk at the sight than the rain came to an abrupt halt and was replaced by a beautiful sunrise. I was finding it very wearing trying to keep up with this weather. Full of cornflakes and hot tea we set out into a slightly choppy sea. Everyone was in good spirits as they busied themselves with their various tasks, but at the same time we all kept a watchful eye on the heavens.

The dive crew had kitted up and, in a brief patch of warm sunshine, we lounged on the foredeck like beached, multi-coloured seals, while we waited for Lawrence to be suited and booted. Both Lawrence and Jock were in a good frame of mind. Jock was humming some obscure tune while Lawrence grinned happily as he cleaned his Perspex bubble helmet. I think that we had all tried to move a bit too quickly on the first day and a great many problems had cropped up. We now all knew what to expect in just about every type of weather condition, and I suspect that Jock had had a confidence-boosting chat with Lawrence somewhere in the small hours over a wee dram of Scotch Mist.

'Ready when you are chaps,' Lawrence piped up. We decided we'd all accompany him down to the wreck as this might give him some moral support. It would also help us to gauge how long it would take before he actually started to descend and would enable us to conserve our own air supply and not waste it on the sea floor waiting for him to arrive. The descent was faultless and even the communication with the surface was marginally more comprehensible. Lawrence gently bumped his way on to the deck of the old destroyer kicking up a fine layer of silt. He started to lose his balance but grabbed hold of the huge gun just in time. As he looked up to gather in his surroundings he smiled the biggest smile I had ever seen on a human being. He had totally forgotten there was a job of work to be done and was now completely overwhelmed with the sights and sounds of his new and exciting undersea world.

'Zhaaarassssee.' The headset rasped in my right ear. 'Ready when you are, Seb . . . zhaaarassssee . . . looks great from up . . . zhaarassee . . . here,' chirruped an excited Jon Hunt. Malcolm positioned himself next to the camera with his hand lamp and lit up Lawrence. It looked fantastic – the sunshine topside was blazing away, giving us plenty of light to work with, and with our own lighting as well it all looked wonderfully surreal. All the worries and doubts I had had from the onset of this ridiculous venture were instantly dispelled and my toes were curling with sheer pleasure in my drysuit. Lawrence leaned up against the barrel of the gun and fell perfectly into the role of the well-seasoned marine correspondent: 'Blah blah blah blah Lawrence McGinty, News at Ten, in the Scapa Flow.'

— 16 —

Sri Lanka
(July 1989)

He was young, he was fit, he was scared shitless, he had thirty minutes to live. I knew the terrified man in front of my lens was a dead man, and I knew the haunting image of his live-dead-man face would make great television. What it would make me was another question.

ITN had been commissioned at short notice by Channel 4 to make a documentary for the series *Dispatches* on the political climate in the war-torn jewel of an island, Sri Lanka. Accordingly Desmond Hamill and I suddenly found ourselves in the most devastatingly beautiful place I have ever been to, fantastic beaches, a lovely climate, great cooking and so it goes on: a holiday brochure photographer's dream, but with one unfortunate drawback – Sri Lanka, formerly Ceylon, is now home to ten different armed factions all trying to kill each other.

Two years before the Sri Lankan government had invited the Indian army into the country in a bid to stop the Tamils and the Sinhalese from slaughtering each other. They have since become, like the British army in Northern Ireland, an army of occupation, an army trying to do a policeman's job. Even though the government of Sri Lanka has now asked the so-called 'Indian Peace Keeping Force' to leave its shores, the Indians, for their own colonial reasons, have refused. The result is total confusion. A branch of the Tamil Tigers, calling themselves the EPRLF, have thrown in their lot with the Indian Peace Keeping Force while, remarkably, the remaining majority of the Tamil Tigers have gone over to their old enemy – the Sri Lankan government. When the Sri Lankan Foreign Minister, Ranjan Wijeratne, was asked his views on the terrorist force, the Tamil Tigers, he replied: 'Anyone who can fight the might of the Indian army is an ally indeed.'

Meanwhile the most powerful and sinister bunch of nasties are the Janatha Vimukti Peramuna (People's Liberation Front), with over two thousand deaths attributed to them in just the first half of 1989. Marxist in ideology, scumbags of the first order in reality, the extent of their influence is staggering. While we were in Colombo the JVP put up just ten average-sized posters around Colombo city proclaiming a daytime curfew. The posters loosely translated said, 'If you go to work tomorrow or walk in the streets you will be shot'. The following day, Colombo ground to a halt. I had never heard of a daytime curfew imposed by a terrorist group, but the fear the JVP inspire is so profound that nothing moved that day and a city of 683,000 people and twice as many vehicles was utterly silent. The true power base of the country had flexed its muscles and there was nothing any of the politicians could do about it.

We spent two weeks travelling around the country, filming the president Ranasinghe Premadasa at a religious ceremony and interviewing some of the inhabitants of Sri Lanka and representatives of most of the groups involved in this very complex and destructive drama.

The last group we met were the students of Colombo University. The students invited us to interview their leaders and to view photographs of atrocities committed against them by the Government Security Forces. On their grassy campus we filmed a group of students standing under the palm trees, their faces masked with red scarves. They then produced some of the most disgusting photographs of tortured and mutilated bodies I had ever seen. The students told us that most of the killings had been carried out by death squads run by the police or militiamen sympathetic to the fragile government. It seemed no one had been spared; men, women and children had all come under the executioner's gaze.

The next morning we received a phonecall from a contact who told us that the students had captured three police informers in the campus grounds and had tied them to trees. After weeks of recording hearsay and rumour, this was just what we needed to bring our film to life – some tangible evidence, seen with our own eyes and filmed with our own cameras. We scrambled out of the hotel, and hurried down to the university, fearful that it was all a wind-up, or even worse that whatever was happening would be over by the time we got there.

When we arrived at the campus everything looked utterly normal. The place was teeming with students, girls in pigtails laughing, young men running to their next class clutching books under their arms, the Buddhist students in their saffron robes sitting and chatting on the grass.

We strolled through the campus, relaxed but slightly pissed off that this looked as though it had been a wild goose chase. I stopped a student, and felt slightly silly as I said: 'Excuse me, but have you seen anyone hanging from a tree around here?'

The reply was shocking in its simplicity.

'Yes sure – just over there by the canteen. You must have walked straight past them, go back about thirty yards and they are on your right.'

It was like being given directions to Sainsbury's.

'Thanks.'

Sure enough, on the right by the canteen there were three young men tied tightly to palm trees. A large crowd had gathered by now, and was staring at these hapless chaps. The two nearest me had their heads lowered to the ground and were completely silent, the third was in a terrible state. His face was very swollen and puffy, he was swaying and crying and every now and then he would dry-retch. Desmond went to question the student leaders to try to find out exactly what was going on and returned with the information that for several days these three men had been spotted talking to people on the campus, although they were obviously not students themselves. We still couldn't understand why that had led to this sort of extreme action, and began to wonder if maybe this was some sort of complex stunt for our benefit. Just then a student appeared, waving what appeared to be some sort of diary. He claimed they had found it on the scared and crying man. When we had examined the book I realised why the scared man was so scared. If this was truly his diary, he was without doubt going to die.

The diary contained long lists of police station telephone numbers and a contact name in each station, but the most damning thing of all was an entry outlining in some considerable detail the execution of a student. I filmed the diary and its contents and then went over to the terrified man. There was a strange fascination, knowing this poor bastard was going to die. I stuck my lens in his face and recorded his last vomit, his last tears, but definitely not his last screams.

The students told Desmond that they would hand over the hostages to the Vice-Chancellor. He wasn't expected for at least an hour, so the only thing to do was to sit and wait. We sat under a palm tree, staring at the three hostages and wondering when other film crews would turn up. Having the whole story to ourselves seemed too good to be true. An hour passed – still no Vice-Chancellor. Des was getting edgy – he had set up meetings with various party leaders that he was now in danger of missing, so I suggested that he get on with the day while I stuck this one out on my own. After all, the only shots left were the arrival of the VC and the release of the three men. Des left in our car and I once more took up my relaxed position under the palm tree. The students mean-while began to hold a meeting in the campus grounds. I was only allowed to film the backs of their heads for fear of identification and subsequent reprisals for the abduction of the informants. The meet-ing was conducted entirely in Sinhalese and I began to drift in and out of a light doze, wondering fleetingly at my ability to sleep with such a strange scenario only twenty feet in front of me.

A frenzied holler and a loud screech of brakes pulled me back to reality. I looked up to see several armed men running towards the hostages. I jumped up and fumbled around getting the camera running. I was so fazed to be witnessing a real live rescue attempt that my reaction time was twice as long as it should have been. One man kept the crowd of students at bay with a large handgun, as his colleagues went to untie the hostages. I wondered briefly why the students were making so little attempt to stop the would-be res-cuers, but, when the gun was waved in my direction, I saw that it was indeed a pretty effective deterrent.

I quickly decided that it was wisest to concentrate on filming one set of events rather than trying to pan around and risk missing everything, so I trained my lens on the scared hostage. Two men untied him from the tree and yanked him to his feet. While the gunman still held the crowd at a comfortable distance, they started to run towards the university gates, the hostage between them, his hands still bound securely behind his back. I plucked up what little courage I had and ran after them. Strangely, no one tried to stop me, and I followed them as they ran, unhindered, across the campus and through the university gates.

As I attempted to follow, the gates were slammed shut in front of me. I could see the group through the railings, so I squeezed the lens through the gap and zoomed in to get a close-up of the men's faces. To my surprise the rescued hostage wore an expression not of relief but if anything even greater terror than he had displayed earlier. Something was terribly wrong, but I was damned if I could work out what it was. Behind me a car engine started up and the crowd parted to let the vehicle through. It was the same one that had brought the gunmen, yet the students appeared to be making no attempts to stop it. When it reached the gates they were opened just long enough to let it through. Outside the car doors flew open and the scared hostage (I never saw what happened to the other two) and his rescuers piled in. A hand blocked the camera lens.

'You must not film any more,' an angry student shouted at me. As the car roared off, the crowd cheered. What the hell was going on? I tried again to pass through the gates but again my way was barred.

'It is too dangerous for you to go out right now. Those men rescuing their comrades were members of the Green Tigers' (a branch of the Sri Lankan police force).

So I did as I was told and waited until about five minutes later, when a student arrived to tell me that it was now safe to leave and there was a taxi waiting just outside the gates. I jumped in the cab eager both to get the hell out of whatever it was I was in and panting to show Desmond my precious footage.

Desmond was ecstatic when he saw what we had got. This story would lift the whole film. It gave you the feel of what was going on here, a feeling of drama, and behind the white beaches and colourful markets, a picture of intrigue, danger and bravery.

That evening we received a phonecall to tell us that the hostage had been found dead. We had been duped by the students who had contrived the entire set-up, rescue and all. Obviously intending to kill the hostage all along, they hadn't wanted to be seen to have done it themselves, and what better for their purposes than an eager and gullible cameraman? I had been filming a piece of theatre in which the only true participant was the terrified man, and, whatever his crimes, he had never had a chance in hell of standing before a court of law. These nice hard-working boys and girls bent on education and social reform had peeled the flesh off his head like a grape and then shot him in the back of the head.

— 17 —

Afghanistan
(Summer 1989)

By the time I got to Afghanistan both Sandy Gall and the Russians had been gone a good two months. Much to the news media's surprise and annoyance, the Muj had not come screaming down from the mountains slaughtering everything in their wake and tearing the heads off terrified children. It was not another Saigon as a lot of journos would lead us to believe. 'Russia's Vietnam' was their favourite epithet, something the great unwashed could get to grips with. The Russians had trained the government forces well. They had always maintained that if the Muj had not taken a major city in the six months after they had withdrawn, then it was to be a true victory for the Soviet Union. And so a stalemate had fallen over the entire country, the Muj holding the countryside while the government held the cities.

The city that looked as if it could be the first to fall was the city of Kandahar, famous for its dazzling blue mosques. By June the Muj had the city surrounded and were poised to take the strategic civilian and military airfields. Kabul by this stage was looking more secure than it had done for some time. The news desk was bored with pictures of the horrendous food queues in the capital and was looking for something a bit more dramatic. It had dawned on several editors at ITN that in all the coverage since the Soviet withdrawal we had not seen any actual fighting. The brave BBC had stomped over stunning snow-capped mountains that dipped into awesome sunsets, and ITN had done the 'day in the life' of every-body in Kabul. Every form of live two-way satellite hop had been exhausted, the circus had left town. Our brief, if you could call it that, was to come home with some action footage.

In a world now dominated by the accountants, it was a brave news editor who sent two men into the field with no more of a brief than 'Go on ya buggers, go and get the goodies.' In effect he was only doing what any decent news editor would have done before the money-men strangled 'following a hunch'. Nowadays it's wait for a piece to crop up in the Sunday pops just to make sure someone else is spending some money, and then send a crew and reporter to turn an old story into moving pictures. Mind you the money men were not far behind us. The new working practices at ITN had just come into effect, and for the first time I was officially to be cameraman, soundman, and spark all rolled into one. That was fine as long as the technology held up; if not, I was going to be completely scuppered. I was a film cameraman before the bright new era of 'EJ' – electronic journalism, as the Americans called it – came into being, and if I take off the side panel of my camera, it's like looking into the Control Centre at Houston launch pad. As far as fixing anything is concerned, forget it. Still, this form of crewing kept the cost down on our foreign coverage, and if that meant covering more stories like this, so be it.

The plan was to fly to Pakistan's Islamabad airport where I would meet up with Terry Lloyd, who had been there for three weeks already. I was looking forward to seeing him as we went back a long way, and I had not worked with him for some months. Although we were very different personalities, we gelled well in the field, and our luck for falling on to a good tale had not let us down yet. Unfortunately this good luck over the years made the desk feel confident that we would turn in the goods. Although this was very flattering it was an enormous pressure to carry.

I had been longing to go to Afghanistan, ever since the Russian invasion of ten years ago. Having missed Vietnam I was not about to miss this war as well, but the gods were not with me. I could not get a look in edgeways, and when, finally, I was asked to cover the Soviet withdrawal, I was on my first holiday with my family in five years, and another cameraman jumped into my shoes before I could say 'Kalashnikov'.

As I flew into Pakistan, I was determined not to be wound up. I was going all out to have fun and games, stomping around the countryside of Afghanistan waiting for people to kill each other. It sounds callous, but that is what this was all about. Anything less was just not going to make the air waves.

Terry met me at Islamabad airport with a dead badger stuck to his smiling face. 'Bloody hell, not you as well Tel,' I said. Just about anyone who had been to Afghanistan had grown the obligatory beard. It was the silent way of telling everybody where you had been when you got back to the London newsroom. The jokes about beards were so rife in London that when I went to draw some videotapes from the stores department, the storeman, seeing the location on the chit, asked me what colour beard I would want drawn out of stores. The newsroom had the idea that we would blend in with the local populace a bit better if we had all this ridiculous fungus around our chops. It wasn't so bad on my darker skinned colleagues but on a blondie such as myself it was absurd.

At Islamabad airport I found that the crew who had been with Terry up until my arrival were going back to London on the plane which I had just arrived on. They had already checked through customs, so I had not even had a handover of any sort – just a rucksack full of useful bits and bobs, ie. chocolate, Cuppasoup and condoms. The Cuppasoup was great. Terry was in his element away from London and working on a decent story. Keep him cooped up on the reporters' desk back home for more than thirty seconds and he turns into a homicidal maniac. Maybe that's why we get on so well. He was bursting to start straight away and wanted to get down to Quetta, a dust town in the west of Pakistan, to establish contacts and get across the border to Afghanistan. Being a gentleman, Terry gave me just enough time to have breakfast before setting off for the internal flight to Quetta. I had not slept at all on the long flight from London and felt dreadful. The *man* thing had started; I couldn't even show my tiredness to one of my best pals.

'You tired Seb?'

'Not at all mate, let's go.' Jesus Christ, I thought, what I wouldn't give for a bed.

On arrival at Quetta airport, the sun dried my eyeballs and an already dehydrated tongue. Every movement made me gush with sweat, enough to have a bath in. Our hotel was something quite magical, owned by the Aga Khan. It was heaven in the midst of filth. Pure white marble floors with highly polished oak surrounds, it oozed style and tranquillity. Something told me to make the most of this luxury while it lasted.

One of our first jobs was to make contact with our Mujahadin guides. This was not so easy as it at first seemed. The commander of the unit which we were to be with had gone 'up country' and would not be back for some days. In his absence he had jacked up another trip to be led by his second-in-command, but we were to wait in the hotel for a couple of days to be contacted. This suited me fine. I could finally get some proper sleep.

Feeling pretty refreshed the next day, we went into town to pick up a few essential supplies. Quetta was a bustling community of street traders, cripples, gunmen and, best of all, tailors for the well-dressed journo to have all his ethnic wardrobe catered for. We were to buy local wear, once again in an attempt to blend in with the crowd. To me it looked exactly what it was, white men in fancy dress; but I got a kick out of dealing with the tailors, one of whom originated from Bradford and whose brother had a shop in Hackney. He had decided, however, that he could make more money in Quetta supplying guns and shirts to the Mujahadin, and charging outrageous prices to journalists and camera crews who had more money than sense. The next stop was to one of the many chemists in town. In fact there was a whole street dedicated to chemists. How they made any money, I don't know, all being in the same location. I needed those little extras that were not included in the ITN medical kit. Like most Third World countries, prescriptions were not needed for even the most powerful of drugs: a junkie's haven. We needed slightly more powerful pain-killers than Panadol. Ever tried to stop the pain of a bullet wound with an aspirin? I can assure you if you tried to give it to a wounded man, your patient just might not have much confidence in you. The pharmacist did not flinch when I asked him for a selection of the most powerful pain-killers available. I got some Valium for myself. I always like to travel with a supply, not for calming the nerves, but to use on long-haul flights as a sleeping pill. With most sleeping pills you feel as if you're fumbling around in a giant marshmallow for hours after you wake up. Valium relaxes me just enough for a good sleep but I can still wake up instantly if need be. I had been caught out before on a long-haul flight. (Once, when I boarded a flight to the States, I had immediately taken two strong sleepers, only to be shaken awake half an hour later by a strong-armed air hostess who informed me there was a technical problem and we had returned to Heathrow.) The pharmacist unashamedly handed over enough Valium to sedate a herd of wildebeest.

On our way back to the hotel we passed a sports shop. In the window was the finest collection of polo sticks I had ever seen, bundles and bundles of them. On enquiry I found that they were all hand-made on the premises. I was almost afraid to ask the price, as a good stick in London costs over seventy pounds. To my great pleasure these fine examples cost the princely sum of two pounds fifty each. I bought twelve instantly with a promise to return and buy the lot. I hadn't yet worked out what the hell I was going to do with them. It was the beginning of the trip and this sort of decadence was normally reserved for the end of a particularly successful assignment.

Terry's contacts came good on the third day of our stay in Quetta. We were told to be ready at nine o'clock the next morning, when we would be taken to the local Mujahadin HQ, and our onward transport would be arranged. It sounded good in theory, but we both had our doubts. However, when we arrived at the HQ, to our utter amazement, there was a four-ton truck waiting for us. This was too good to be true. Just behind the truck I could see a small crowd gathering. This was not unusual as the sight of white men in fancy dress always drew an audience. Then it dawned on us that this was not an ordinary gathering of rubberneckers, but the other passengers on our journey. About thirty assorted Muj were waiting to get into any space that became available. On a given signal from an unknown source, they scampered on board leaving Terry and me staring at each other in frustration. Our equipment was unceremoniously thrown into the back of the truck, followed by three of the biggest Muj I had seen, instantly crushing and rendering totally useless our solar panels – our only means of charging the camera batteries for the whole trip. Who knew when or if we would ever come across a power point. My hysterical screams of anger were only met with expressions of laughing bemusement.

I was shown to the front of the truck with my camera and told to get in the cab. To my horror, there were five or six people already in a space only designed for three, never mind half a dozen Muj fighters and their weapons, plus a white man and his bulky camera.

My protests went unheard. Through a very bad interpreter I learned that I had to be in front where it was easy to hide me since I was the only one likely to be spotted. Maybe I should have grown that bloody beard. I asked how long it would take to reach the border, and was told only one and a half hours, so I meekly crawled under several rather ripe gentlemen to start our journey. How I envied Terry on his luxurious ammo crate at the rear. Six hours later I was still in a foetal position with my nose sampling the fragrance of Muj armpit. Where the hell were we? We had passed through several checkpoints already. What was going on? It transpired there had been a small problem with some of the local police, so they had decided to take the long way round, and the checkpoints had been nothing more than local district borders. Jesus, we were still in Pakistan. When I asked how much longer to the border, I was told another six hours at least. I slumped as far as I could, which was nowhere at all, but my spirits slumped for me and ended in the bottom of my boots with my now rancid toe-jam. Every bump jarred into me, and the weight of the camera had taken on elephantine proportions. The smoothest ride you could give the camera was to put it on your lap, but it did nothing for your love life.

Three hours later with no border in sight, I had had enough. We were in the middle of a desert in the boiling heat of mid-afternoon. I screamed at the driver to stop. He slammed on the brakes as if he had come across an invisible wall. I fought my way over my travelling companions and fell out of the passenger door on to the desert floor to more sloppy grins and raucous laughter. It was good to be able to move one's body more than a couple of centimetres in either direction. Terry grinned at me from his perch on top of the ammo crate and told me that it was 'no picnic up here either'. We both rubbed our various grazes and bumps while our companions took the opportunity to pray. We were arriving in Afghanistan at the time of Ramadan and the Muj could not eat or drink until seven-fifteen in the evening, which made us feel like lepers each time we stuck a handful of peanuts in our mouths or drank from our canteens. No way was I going to continue our journey in the front of that thing! Sod being spotted, I could hide under something at the back if it came to it. I was ready for a fight to get into the back but, to my total amazement, no one said a word. In fact they all helped me into the back and slapped me on the back and offered me cigarettes. So what was all that cloak-and-dagger nonsense of the last nine hours? I sat in the back fuming and avoiding the inquisitive stares of the Muj.

As dusk began to fall the scenery was breathtaking. The sky was turning the deepest shade of purple, butting itself up to the orange floor of the desert, and the mountains were absorbing the last vestiges of daylight, giving them an almost metallic blue sheen. Then, with an unnerving swiftness it was dark. The only point of reference was the lighted cigarette-ends of our fellow travellers; the tips were dancing frantically like children holding sparklers, and every now and then a face would be illuminated as hidden lips sucked hard. Sooner or later we must surely reach the border. The cramp was becoming unbearable and I was fast losing all enthusiasm for our *Boys' Own* adventure.

The route grew even bumpier. Christ, it did not seem possible. We were now scrambling along an old mountain road, using the four-tonner more like a giant stick-insect than a truck. A voice said to me, 'Where do you come from mister?' His name was Ali, what else, I thought. The lighted ciggy told me he was a stinger-missile operator and he had killed many Russians. He paused, waiting for me to react. 'How many?' I asked. 'How many hairs on a dog's back?' he replied proudly. Ali had learnt English at school and turned out to be a pleasant travelling companion, apart from a rather unnerving line of conversation about how we were travelling with very bad men, and must be very careful. Apparently he was not with this particular group of Muj, and had only come for the ride to his home town.

At last we came to a halt. We had stopped outside what looked like a deserted farmhouse in the middle of the desert. 'We eat,' a voice in the gloom said. A giant, filth-encrusted cloth was thrown on the floor. An old man appeared out of the doorway with much hand-waving, shouting, and back-slapping. I twigged that this was a restaurant. Two young boys rushed out of the house with bubbling cauldrons, into which our companions buried themselves up to the elbows, and pulled out the most disgusting stringy meat.

'You eat,' the Muj next to me said. 'You eat.' With great diplomacy, Terry and I anounced that we were life-long vegetarians and that we were very sorry we could not partake in their great hospitality. We chewed lightly on some pitta bread which I presumed was made of something vaguely edible. Recalling the seven-foot-long tapeworm I had contracted in Africa from eating dodgy meat, I was not about to go through that nightmare again.

'Where the fuck are we?' Terry said miserably.

'Oh, just about three miles from the B27 which connects to the A12. How the fuck do I know Terry?'

We laughed and drank rather delicious green tea, remembered we had no deadlines to meet, and decided to relax a bit and flow with the tide, a decision that was to tax our patience to the extreme.

All of a sudden, the truck stopped with a lurch, and we were thrown to the front with a crunch of bones and painful poking of Kalashnikovs. What was it now? Gul Rackman, our totally useless interpreter, was trying to tell us that this was as far as we would go this evening.

'Why?' was the immediate question. What had brought about this very definite decision, a move not usually accredited to the Muj. Still no answer. We had arrived outside what appeared to be a very large mud hut, its entrance barred with big corrugated iron doors. Our driver started to flash his lights and blare his horn. No reply from the gates. One Muj jumped down from the truck and started to bang frantically against the gates with the butt of his rifle. I glanced at my watch. It was two-thirty in the morning. The home guard was probably in the Land of Nod.

Eventually there was a stirring from behind the gates, followed by much grumbling and scraping. A chain was pulled and one side of the gates fell open. Our headlights revealed an elderly fighter who, under a deluge of abuse from the younger men, begrudgingly opened the remaining gate. Once inside the courtyard we were told that we were to spend the night here.

'Where?' I asked.

'There,' one of the Muj replied, pointing into a dark recess in the corner of the yard. It was five-star luxury — a ten-foot square, roasting, mud box, but by this time I could have slept anywhere.

Having refused the invitation of our comrades to share their food earlier, we were now starving hungry. I inspected my rucksack; the supplies had taken their toll after a day of Muj jumping up and down on them. One water bottle had burst and had soaked everything into a sodden pulp. We salvaged two packets of drinking chocolate, lit our portable stove and drank as if we had never tasted anything so good. Then without bothering to wash the day's grime from our very smelly bodies, we fell into a deep and grateful sleep. No sooner had we managed to doze off, when the most dreadful noises erupted from outside our oven. The Muj had started praying. It was four-thirty in the morning! But the body had had enough and wasn't going to take much notice, so I went back to sleep with the sound of 'God is great' ringing in my ears and a squadron of flies using my nose as a ski slope.

A single shaft of sunlight burst into my left eyeball. I hurrumphed and angrily turned over, which seemed to be the cue for an army of oversized cockroaches to march over my neck. I leapt to my feet, which was no mean feat with all the zips still firmly done up on my sleeping-bag, and I promptly nose-dived on to the dust floor. Terry had managed to sleep through my early morning machinations and was busily snoring in his bivvy bag with his legs twitching every now and then, like a dog dreaming of chasing rabbits. Time for tea, I thought. There was no reason for Terry to wake, I just wasn't going to let him sleep if I couldn't. Nice friend eh? I unzipped his sleeping-bag and thrust a boiling cup of green tea under his nose.

'Morning Tel.'

'Fuck off!' was the predictable reply.

The flies had risen early as well and now started having their early morning jog around the top of our mugs of tea.

A noisy delegation of Muj arrived in our 'bedroom' and sat at the end of Terry's sleeping-bag. We were informed that the river ahead had swollen with the rains and it was impossible to proceed any further. What rain, I thought. It had been, on average, a hundred and ten degrees every day. The conversation painfully lumbered on through our one-sentence-of-English interpreter. Something was very wrong. Then through the babble of Farsi, we heard the magic word 'dollars'. We were to witness a magic show. If we handed over a thousand dollars, the river would vanish and we would be able to cross. Terry sat bolt upright and flung a stream of abuse at Gul

Rackman, the interpreter. Luckily no one understood a word of Terry's outburst, not even me at some points, but the inflection was unmistakable. I had never seen him so angry. He insisted that we were immediately taken back to Quetta where we could express our extreme displeasure to Jamait HQ. This unexpected change in our travel arrangements would cost us a few hundred dollars, but it was going to be money well spent, as it was becoming apparent that we were in the company of nothing more than not very accomplished bandits. Terry and I agreed that we would keep up this verbal attack and act of aggressiveness, as the ferocity of Terry's initial outburst had taken them by surprise, and to show any sign of weakness now would almost certainly be our undoing.

My friend Ali, the stinger-missile operator, told me he was ashamed at his comrades' obvious corruption, but that he could do nothing to help, as he was only a soldier and could not do anything behind his commander's back. To do so would bring severe punishment. He assured me that not all the Muj were like this, and please not to judge them too harshly. I needed convincing of that.

I was desperate to wash and clean up but, looking around, I could see no water or any facilities whatsoever, and the Muj, at this moment in time, were not the people to ask. Mr Stinger looked at me sympathetically and beckoned me to follow him through the maze of mud huts that made up the town of Jonghi. We stopped at a slightly larger hovel where a man sat at the door collecting money. My new friend handed him some coins and we were shown inside. To my utter amazement it was a bath house with private cubicles in which to do one's ablutions. In the middle of all this shit, flies and poverty there was this little haven of cleanliness. In each little mud cubicle, there was a tap at floor level (why it could not have been put just above head height I'll never know) and a small steel bowl with a rather grubby bar of much-used soap. I hurriedly removed all my clothes, filled the bowl with water and threw it over my filthy body. Half a dozen fleas were disturbed from their nibblings and unceremoniously flushed away. I emerged a new man ready to do battle with anybody. Terry followed suit and we readied ourselves for the long journey back, having achieved absolutely nothing. To our surprise, Gul Rackman decided to return to Quetta with us, knowing that we were livid with rage and were bound to report him to his commanders.

After much negotiation, and without the interference of Gul, we were the proud hirers of a very beaten-up Toyota pick-up truck, in a bad condition even by Muj standards. Keeping up our momentum, we hurried our belongings on board and let out a string of obscenities at every possible moment. As we were about to leave with our driver, Gul informed us that we had to wait for the permission of the local commander before we could leave. I was just about to express my annoyance when Terry said in his broad northern accent, 'Bollocks,' and pushed me into the truck.

'You coming or not you slimy bastard?' Terry said to a, by now, slightly jumpy Gul Rackman. The aged Toyota sprang into life and we tore into the desert.

As we rattled on in the searing heat, Gul dropped the sham of being ashamed and was now trying to be the comedian.

'Terry my dear, why do you have a face so full of anger?' Gul asked, smiling.

Wrong, I thought.

'Anger, you bastard? We have travelled a total of forty-eight hours in stinking lorries, eaten shit, slept in shit, been bitten to death and survived a vain attempt at robbery, and it might also have escaped your notice that we have not shot a single frame of film you prick.'

Gul was not fazed at all. 'Well at least you will have a warm bed tonight Mr Terry.'

I had to stop Terry from strangling Gul. For reasons of his own, Gul was very pleased to be going back to Quetta. Maybe he had some undiscriminating Quettaran crumpet awaiting his triumphant return from the wars. Who knows? The only thing I was sure of was that at every turn Gul had been trying to make our lives as difficult as humanly possible.

The rest of our journey passed without incident, except for one puncture and a near-collision with a herd of wild camels which had strayed into the desert road. Gul sat by the driver, humming a merry tune, while Terry sat in the back emanating hate and loathing and devising new forms of testicular torture. The first phase of our trip had been a total failure, but it had taught me a lesson in patience and a better understanding of the Arabic '*Enshalla*' – 'If it is God's will. . . .'

Our second attempt to get back into Afghanistan was proving equally chaotic. Although we had had some satisfaction in seeing the hideous Gul Rackman being verbally chastised by his superiors, at the time we would have much preferred to have seen him hanging from a gibbet with his entrails pouring on to the floor.

Nevertheless, with fresh verve, we embarked on the seemingly endless rounds of green tea drinking and hollow smiles to achieve entry into the cursed land. Our aim was to reach the town of Kandahar to film the fighting at the international airport. Kandahar was securely held by the government forces, but the Muj were a threat to any incoming aircraft, as they occupied extremely close positions – about three hundred yards from the end of the airport runway – and were keeping the Afghan army busy with their RPG attacks and sniper fire. After a few days of sipping tea and rabbiting to local 'representatives', we managed to secure the services of a fresh bunch of Muj guides and, best of all, a newish jeep. Then, for the second time, we set off in the quest for action.

A terrible feeling of *déjà vu* crept over me as darkness fell in the back of yet another cramped and smelly jeep.

It seemed that we had finally reached a point near the Afghan border, as through another incompetent interpreter and much muttering and stabbing of fingers in my direction, we gathered that it was time for me to disappear under the heaving mass of Muj bodies in the back of the jeep. At least it gave me the chance to move my legs which felt as if they had been on loan to somebody else for the day. The relief of movement was short-lived, as a number of very heavy Muj made a great deal of commotion in trying to hide me; the final result was me being pinned to the floor of the jeep far more securely than in the first place. Several-days-old Muj armpit sweat was definitely not Chanel No 5, and with a grenade jostling for position with my Adam's apple and a Kalashnikov digging into my ribs, we lurched off in the direction of the fabled border. If their calculations were wrong in reaching as far as this point, how long would I be travelling in this awful position? Soon, however, we came to another ball-grinding halt; this time an ammo crate squashed me between a smelly Muj bottom and a toe-jam-encrusted foot. Whilst eyeing the toe with a great deal of apprehension, I heard a babble of voices and saw a light shining through the filthy layers of dirty rags that were trying to hide me. The foot looked even more revolting with a bit of backlight. More babbling from the disembodied voices and then blackness as the border policemen's torches retreated. My eyes had not adjusted to the inky blackness yet and I was less concerned with whether the Pakistani border guards would discover us than the whereabouts of the hideous foot.

The sound of first gear engaging was followed by high-speed forward momentum, causing an as yet unseen ammunition crate to bury itself deep into my thighs.

'That's enough,' I thought, and was on the point of throwing all the bodies and the rags off me, when a voice came through the darkness.

'Mister, it is Afghanistan. We are home, it is Afghanistan. Mister, look!'

Hoo bloody ray, I thought, and was about to look when the hideous foot finally found its target on my right eyeball.

We drove on for a few more minutes and came to a stop by a large mud hut. This was the Muj's forward command base for the area, and was to be home for the night. We had a meagre meal of green tea and nan bread followed by several slabs of good old Cadbury's chocolate. The heat inside the mud hut was too much to bear, so we decided to spend tonight *al fresco*. We only realised what a foolish notion this had been at about three-thirty in the morning when a light frost began to form over the entire length of our flimsy summer sleeping-bags.

Later, along with our equipment and a few extra Muj we piled into two rather dilapidated jeeps and drove off into a seemingly endless desert. The morning light was crisp and sharp and we felt a certain amount of satisfaction in the knowledge that we had finally crossed the border. We were making our way to a village just on the outskirts of Kandahar, to meet Commander Tia Khan, a man of some considerable influence in the area.

After several hours of driving we arrived at a small village, just in time for our escorts to partake of the Morning Prayer. The entire village had been turned into an enormous ammunition dump for every type of ordnance from handgun to stinger missiles and, under camouflage, even some heavy artillery pieces. It was disturbing to watch small boys kicking around live shells in the absence of any footballs. When they had finished their devotions, our companions loaded yet more guns on to our already heavily laden jeeps, and we were once again on our way.

We were travelling in the lowlands, to the left and right of us we could see huge blue-coloured mountains. We drove on and on, one hour melting gradually into another, until eventually it began to grow dark. I was just about to ask the futile question, 'How long till we get there?' when the jeep turned abruptly off the desert tracks on to a path leading into an enclosure hiding several vehicles and some rather tatty mud huts. Much to my surprise, we had arrived at our destination – Tia Khan's secret hideout.

The great man himself was not there this evening but was expected early the next morning. Terry and I were shown to a small residence in the far corner of this tiny hamlet. Well, at least we had a roof over our heads, and the hut was surprisingly warm. We laid out our sleeping-bags and prepared for a well-needed sleep. As we were faffing around organising ourselves, two young fighters came into the hut carrying bowls of steaming brown rice, nan bread and of course green tea. This was gratefully received, even though we felt awkward eating under the close scrutiny of our curious waiters, who lingered in the hut staring at every movement we made. We were not well-versed in the art of eating with our fingers and were making just a little bit of a mess. Finally we managed to shoo the audience out of our hut, drank our tea and curled up into our sleeping-bags for a fitful night's sleep.

They relentlessly dive-bombed us all night. The only cover offered was the inside of our sleeping-bags. The roar of the wind passing over tiny wings seemed to fill every space in the still night air. Mosquitoes! First you hear that nasty little whizzing noise right by your ear, then silence, and you know that somewhere on that pale body of yours that sharp-nosed winged bastard is having its dinner. By five-thirty in the morning I couldn't stand it any longer, so with a cliché or two in mind, I set off to film the sunrise. Terry work an hour and a half later to the sounds of Rich trying desperately to boil some water on our little stove. Having eventually made and drunk something vaguely resembling tea, the pair of us readied ourselves for the day's rigours. We were to be taken by road to a small village outside Kandahar and then continue by foot to a small mountain range from which hopefully we would be able to witness the battle for the airport.

Since it was nightfall when we had arrived, I hadn't had the opportunity to take in my surroundings that closely. As we walked through the small hamlet I noticed some delightful herb gardens being tended to by green-fingered Mujahadin. It seemed slightly incongruous that these hard fighting men were looking after a garden. As I passed him, a young fighter stuck a newly cut rose under my nose. It smelled unbelievably fresh amidst the dust and early morning human excreta. The borders of the herb gardens were of an interesting nature. The Muj had made ingenious use of the materials at hand. Never had I seen such a perfect use for ordnance – the cardamom plot was bordered with an intricate design of BM12 shells buried nose first into the ground, while the rosemary was hemmed in with a slightly smaller calibre shell. It was only on closer examination that I realised that a large proportion of these shells were live. I didn't dare to speculate on the means of embedding them into the ground. At the entrance to the herb garden were two enormous missile casings cut in half, with their rear stabilising wings holding them upright, explosives long gone and replaced with a wonderful display of rhododendrons. As I mused over this bizarre Chelsea Flower Show, I noticed two vapour trails in the sky. But there were no commercial flights in this area, and two brilliantly clear white lines reminded me abruptly that this was a country still at war.

Terry and I piled ourselves and our kit into yet another dilapidated jeep, this time of Russian origin, and riddled with bullet holes from battles gone by. With a wary eye at the sky we set off in the direction of Kandahar. The main road to Kandahar was half in Mujahadin hands and half in government hands, so guessing that sooner or later we were going to have to leave the comfort of the tarmacked road, I took off my jacket and put it underneath my bum.

The road out of the village was strewn with the remains of a Russian tank convoy. This made very eerie pictures: great lifeless

Behemoths turtled at the side of the road, with turreted guns poking at the bright blue sky, and nothing more to do than act as playgrounds for the local children, or feed the picture-hungry lenses of news crews. We could hear the sound of distant shelling and with every passing kilometre it grew louder. 'Here we go again,' I thought, 'going in the wrong bloody direction.' As predicted, we soon turned off the main road on to a dusty track, leading across countless shell-pocked rice fields. Suddenly, there was a great whooshing noise.

'Shit incoming,' Terry said, rather matter-of-factly.

The shells exploded about five hundred metres from our jeep, a long way by the Muj's reckoning, but close enough for my sphincter to do a small fandango.

We eventually came to a stop in a small dusty village about six to seven kilometres from Kandahar airport. It was about one-thirty in the afternoon and we were eager to film the fighting and get the hell out before nightfall. But oh no, as usual, the Muj had other ideas. In good trade union tradition, they insisted on a tea break and nosebag before going any further. That was the final straw for Terry. He started screaming abuse at everyone who came within spitting distance. For at least ten minutes everyone was a 'lazy fucking wanker' or a 'good for nothing shithead'.

After this initial outburst failed to elicit any response, we tried another tack and started to cajole and flatter the Mujahadin fighters, and after a quick green tea and nan bread break, we were allowed to start on the slow trek to the mountain range. As we progressed across long-dead rice fields, the youngest of the fighters started dancing up and down with delight, pointing at the ground. He pulled a long sharp-looking knife from under his jacket, deftly plunged it into the ground and lifted out something metal. To our utter horror it was a land mine. The young fighter extracted the knife from his prize and gesticulated all around him. He was trying to tell us that we had been walking for the last half an hour in a minefield and that they were still all around us. This was too much for me and I screamed nose to nose at this 'fucking idiot' that we were not in the business of being turned into hamburger for the sake of a few minutes' film. These arseholes were supposed to be our guides and escorts not our undertakers. With a sneer that could have turned gold into shit, he spat a great splot of snot over my shoulder and stomped off towards the mountain. Terry and I looked at each other briefly and fell quickly into the footprints of 'Snotface'.

The noise of war was intensifying with every footstep we took towards the mountain, but we could not see the action. I considered running away from the noise, but that would mean running back on my own through an uncharted minefield, and half of me still wanted to see what was going on on the other side of that mountain. Who knows what we would be walking into over there? As we came out of the minefield at the base of the mountain, I suddenly realised that the sun was unbearably hot. The fear of treading on anything bigger than a cornflake had occupied all my thoughts and I was now sweating my cods off. We sat down for a brief rest at the side of an old Russian water well. I noticed that my hands were shaking slightly, so I quickly sat on them. I didn't want the Muj to see that the cameraman had been cacking himself.

As we climbed the small but tricky mountain, our guides, who now seemed just a little bit more interested in our safety, showed us the nastier inhabitants of the slopes. Lengths of earth-coloured wires criss-crossed the entire mountainside; the Russians had left booby traps all over the place. So discovering a new-found gracefulness, we picked our way to the summit. The débris of a fierce battle lay before us. Russian posts, hurriedly deserted or taken in the heat of battle, now stared silently at Kandahar airport to the right and Kandahar itself to the left. The brilliant blue roof of Kandahar's great mosque could be seen quite clearly, glinting in the late afternoon sunshine. As we took in the view a great chunk of field shot up into the air, as a shell fell just short of a farmhouse in the suburbs.

I made a good camera position out of one of the old Russian dugouts and focused up on the airport. Afghan army APCs raced up and down the perimeter fencing, dodging the incoming fire from a lone Muj armed with an RPG launcher. We could quite clearly see his position just on our right at the base of the mountain. He was re-loading at his leisure, not seeming to be taking any incoming fire whatsoever. To the left of the airport we could see the Muj combat troops darting in and out of half-destroyed buildings, returning

Above: Mujahadin horsemen, Hindu Kush, Afghanistan
Below: Sound recordist Russell Padwick riding through snowy pass on
Mujahadin arms trail through the Hindu Kush, winter 1989

Above: The coldest ride of the trip, Hindu Kush, Afghanistan

Left: The end of a long day's ride. Reporter Sandy Gall and Sebastian Rich in a *chai karna* near Robot, Afghanistan *(photo: Russell Padwick)*

small arms fire with the Afghan army who were hidden in the recesses of the airport passenger terminals.

It was an almost perfect camera position, being able to see the shelling of Kandahar city and the fighting at the airport at the same time. Terry was just about to do a stand-upper when a stray shell landed nearby with a thunderous crash, sending Terry and me to our knees, which in turn caused our Muj escorts to burst into hysterical laughter.

We had just scrambled to our feet when two ageing Soviet built MiG 25 fighter aircraft dropped out of the sky from about 800 metres at a forty-five degree angle, throttles at full power, stretching the limits of the old airframes. They unleashed four bombs apiece on the Mujahadin positions to the west of the airport. As sheets of pure orange flame licked the crystal blue sky, I was once again sanitising war through my camera lens. The contrast of colours was fantastic and seemed to have nothing to do with the fact that several people had probably been killed in that one instant.

The aircraft pulled up through balls of smoke and headed back to airfields unknown. Terry made a second attempt at his stand-upper only to be stopped in his tracks by the most revolting noise we had ever heard. One of the Muj had a terrible cold and chose this moment to empty the entire contents of his sinuses at Terry's feet. Once again the air was alive with a bit more than hot ordnance. Our snot-ridden Muj could not understand why he was the target of so much abuse from the white men, and went to pick up a large rock to hurl at us. Fortunately, an elderly Muj saw the ramifications of splattered foreign journos, and held him at bay while we finished off Terry's statement to camera.

It was growing dark and we were eager to return to Tia Khan's base at least by midnight. We had very good action pictures and now wanted to be on our way back to London as soon as possible. So, with a last clichéed shot of Kandahar's blue mosques merging into yet another magnificent sunset, we stomped back down the mountainside, happy that we had filmed some actual fighting; but not so cocksure as to forget the array of booby traps in our homeward path. The journey back to the jeep seemed to pass very quickly, and as we arrived back at our battered craft, the last vestiges of daylight were to be seen scampering for cover as the early night sky was lit up with tracer rounds. Tracers are used for about every third or fourth round to enable the firer to see what he is firing at. To be able to see the trajectory of the bullets is like watching a fire burn in a hearth: it somehow hypnotises you to the spot. It also has the optical effect of slowing down the speeding bullet which, in fact, is travelling faster than the speed of sound and is totally imperceptible in daylight.

The journey back was a little scary as tracers and bullets periodically crossed the path of our truck. We arrived at Tia Khan's camp at around midnight to find the great man had arrived while we had been away filming. He spoke good English and we chatted into the small hours. I had one request. I pointed out that we had some very good action footage but most of it was the Muj getting three bales knocked out of them by fighter bombers. I didn't have that much of Muj returning fire. He stopped me in mid-sentence and said, 'No problem, tomorrow we shall be giving the government breakfast. You are invited to join us,' and with a smile he went off to bed.

Early next morning we were woken to sounds of much panting and groaning. We looked out from our mud hut to see several large Muj pushing a great Stalin organ across the herb gardens.

Tia Khan appeared and said, 'Come, it is Breakfast Time.'

I was slightly worried about all this and asked if he was going to do this even if we weren't here. He assured me that this was a daily occurrence and not to worry, this was not being done for our benefit. I still had my doubts, but if they were going to go ahead with it anyway, who was I to look a gift Stalin organ in the mouth. I readied the camera while two rather sleepy Muj pored over supposed coordinates of the government position. After much fiddling about they pronounced that they were ready to fire. 'That's got nothing to do with me,' I said. 'Don't you bloody well dare fire the fucking thing from my command. You told me that you were doing this anyway, you fire it when you need to.' They all stuck their fingers in their ears, and a second later there was a terrific whoosh and sheets of flame shot out of six of the twelve barrels. The government troops would be having breakfast in about ten seconds.

I tried not to ponder on the ins and outs or the rights and wrongs of what I had just witnessed – it did fill the much-needed gap in our combat footage.

As we returned to our Muj hut to gather our belongings, a young Muj on a captured Russian motorbike roared into the base to deliver a message to Tia Khan. I eyed the bike with some interest. Although it did not resemble anything we had in the west, it might be fun for a joyride. I bribed the young Muj with a packet of ciggies and leapt on to the antique. I had gone only twenty metres or so out of the compound when I came across two young men walking towards me. No sooner had they acknowledged me with a friendly wave than they threw themselves to the ground and held their hands tightly over their ears. What was going on? Was there some custom I had missed over the last few days? Did Ramadan insist that you threw yourself into the path of an oncoming motorcycle at certain times of the day? My questions were answered as three loud explosions went off directly behind me. I turned round to see three sheets of flame erupt from just outside the herb gardens. I turned the bike around and gave it full throttle back to the mud hut. It did not take Albert Einstein to work out what had happened. The government troops were very obviously not happy with the first course of breakfast and were slinging it back with a vengeance. I skidded the bike and dropped it with the engine still running. Outside the mud hut the force of the shells had sent clouds of dust into the air, cutting visibility to about three feet. Where was Terry and where was the camera? I had left it just outside the hut. As these thoughts went spinning through my head, I heard three distant bangs then a fierce whooshing noise. Breakfast with all the trimmings. Suddenly the last thing on my mind was finding the camera, and I ran for cover in the opposite direction. Three more ear-splitting explosions shattered the tiny hamlet. The Afghan troops certainly had our positions well worked out. The Russians had trained those boys well.

I saw a dusty figure staggering towards me. It was Terry rubbing the dirt out of his eyes. 'Thank God,' I thought. We grabbed hold of each other and ran to a makeshift air-raid shelter with other Mujahadin. As we ran hell for leather past the mud hut, Terry stopped and yelled 'Where's the camera?' I informed him that maybe this was not the best time in the world to be looking for it, and I continued on towards the relative safety of the hole in the ground. I looked behind me and Terry was nowhere to be seen. I leapt into the opening of the shelter as another rasher of bacon exploded just outside, its blast pushing me further into the recesses of the shelter. Had Terry been caught in that? I was sure he had.

'Christ, the silly bugger went back for the camera,' I said to a non-plussed Muj in the shelter.

'This, I believe dear boy, is yours,' Terry said with a smirk on his face, as he stumbled out of the gloom clutching my camera.

We stood in the dark shelter waiting for more incoming, but that appeared to be that for the time being. We tentatively stuck our heads out of the hole to see our Muj guides calmly loading our kit on to the back of a jeep ready for our homeward journey. Does nothing faze these buggers? I thought. We said rather hurried goodbyes to our hosts, jumped into the jeep and got the hell out of there.

— 18 —

Damp Squib in Iran
(October 1989)

Hopes were raised when the Iranian government invited representatives of the world's press to (in their own words) 'A Very Important Press Conference' with the new Iranian President Ali Akbar Hashemi Rafsanjani. 'Hostage Release' was on the tip of every news editor's tongue. Terry Waite had now been incarcerated for 1,013 days, John McCarthy 1,290 days and Brian Keenan 1,296 days. Perhaps, as a token of goodwill to the west, the new administration would put pressure on the Hisbullah to free them. At the very least the press conference might signify the release of Roger Cooper, the British businessman who was imprisoned in 1985 for allegedly spying in Iran.

Was this the story we had all been waiting for? I was certainly hoping it was, not, for once, to boost the ratings of ITN, but out of a genuine concern for anybody taken hostage. I could only use as a yardstick my own experiences of being kidnapped in the Lebanon a few years before, when it was uncommon to intern somebody for years on end. My ordeal had only been for a few hours and that had had a profound effect on me. What would be the state of the hostages' minds and bodies after all this time?

And so it was with great excitement that I set off with Paul Dickie, my sound recordist, and reporter Terry Lloyd for Teheran. The last time I had been to Iran was as a freelance cameraman working for the American ABC network, and after my experience of the country I had vowed never to return. In the early days after the revolution Iran was a difficult place to work. The people of Teheran were caught up in a revolutionary fundamentalist fervour which cast every white man as a spy or, even worse, an American spy. The fact that I was working for an American network at the time didn't help.

Still, ten years had passed since the American hostage siege of 1979 – maybe life had changed.

We arrived at Teheran's Mehrabad airport at about four-thirty in the morning, and as we filed into the arrivals hall to have our passports checked, memories of the old Iran came flooding back to me. Here were the queues again – a Jumbo Jet full of people and they were hand-checking everybody. But there was one factor missing when I finally arrived at the booth to have my papers checked. Gone were the hard faces and the suspicious stares that I had grown accustomed to in the Iran of ten years ago. In broken English the immigration official looked up at me and said, 'Good morning Mr Rich, and how are you?' before his face erupted into an enormous toothless grin. A forced smile crept across my face. I had landed in another country, not Iran.

'Welcome to our country, please enjoy,' the official said. I looked over my shoulder to make sure he was not talking to someone with a diplomatic passport.

'Thank you,' I said, and walked away a little confused.

The same sort of behaviour was dished out at customs. A charming and helpful gentleman assisted us with our mountain of silver boxes and signed our camera list in record time. Paul and I looked at each other in disbelief. You don't get this sort of treatment in any country.

We scrambled into a fleet of clapped-out old taxis, silver boxes were crammed into just about every available space. Well at least the taxi-drivers hadn't changed; they were still as dead against the revolution as they had been at the beginning. My driver was resplendent in a Lacoste T-shirt and Rolex watch. As he helped me into his cab a waft of Polo cologne forced its way up my nose. Taxi-drivers are the same all over the world, all that differs is the currency and the choice of aftershave.

'What do you think of the Ayatollah mister?' the driver said, probing none too gently.

'The Ayatollah? I think he's dead,' I replied.

We stopped at the Lhala Continental hotel, formerly the Intercontinental.

I remembered the days just after the revolution when the management of the hotel could not make up their minds whether to go dry, in accordance with the New Order, or to serve you booze with your food. Some nights wine and beer would flow freely, on others they would serve only gut-rotting cola drinks.

We presented ourselves at the check-in desk, only to be informed that we didn't have rooms. It was now five-thirty in the morning and Terry was getting just a little agitated, so Paul and I backed off to let him deal with the management. Half an hour later and after a lot of screaming and shouting we were shown to our rooms.

When I awoke the sun was already hot through the double-glazed windows. A noise like trumpeting elephants reminded me that I was sharing a room with Paul, a champion snorer. I sat and watched the back of his throat for a few seconds wondering where in the human body was the organ responsible for such a racket.

The press conference was scheduled for the following day, but we had to report with our cameras to the Presidential Palace at ten o'clock that morning, so that all the equipment could be checked for explosives. This meant that we would then have to leave the cameras there overnight, so that they could not be tampered with. We were all a little nervous – thirty cameramen parted from their cameras for twenty-four hours; I dreaded to think how we'd react if anything were to happen overnight.

Next we had to get some more passport-sized photos done for special security passes for the press conference. Our driver took us downtown to a local photographic shop. I had never seen the streets of Teheran bathed in sunlight before. On my last visit winter was setting in and the sky had been a monotonous charcoal grey. For the first time I noticed the many types of trees and the large and rather pretty park right next to the hotel. As we walked along the street I realised that the people whom we passed were smiling either to us or their friends. I really could not remember a single smiling face from the trip before.

We teamed up with Tony Birtley and his cameraman from TV-AM for dinner and more speculation about what this presser was going to reveal. Tony Birtley had a contact in Beirut who had confirmed the rumour that this press conference was very important indeed, and so confident were ITN that something big was going to break that they had sent a crew to Cyprus in case the hostages were released there, and Brent Sadler and crew were on standby in Beirut.

The one strange thing about all this was that there were no rumours at all on the streets of Teheran. Not even the Polo-drenched taxi-drivers had a morsel for us to chew on. We went to bed completely sober and no better informed.

At nine o'clock the next morning we were herded into two coaches and taken back to the Presidential Palace where we picked up our camera gear at reception before being led into the old ballroom. The ex-Shah may have been a shit but he had great taste in interior decoration. The room was at least thirty metres long and illuminated by a single, central chandelier. The cream walls were decorated with intricate wood panelling and a marble stair-case swept up twenty feet to a gallery which ran around the entire circumference of the room. Several armed guards leant against the carved mahogany balustrades surveying the milling throng of journalists.

The first coach had arrived a few minutes before us and the early crews were already jostling for position. We managed to squeeze in between ABC and the BBC. Paul and I had brought along two cameras just in case, one camera to film the press conference and the other to leap around with if one of the hostages were suddenly to appear. If a British hostage was to be wheeled on stage we weren't intending to give any quarter to another network. We had already worked out our plan. Paul was to operate the presser camera, while Terry and I made ourselves scarce. Then at the relevant moment we would leap out in front of all the other cameras and put in the first question for the hostage to answer – that was our plan anyway. Having set Paul up with all the gadgetry, Terry and I shifted to the sidelines. A single, rather ornate chair had been put in the middle of the stage. Surely they would have put more out if there was to be a release of some sort? Rafsanjani appeared to our left, flanked by four plainclothed bodyguards. He took up his position in the velvet-covered chair. A hush fell over the two-hundred-odd members of the press. Like static electricity in the air you could feel the expectations in the gathered throng and you could almost hear their thoughts in unison – 'Where's the nearest telephone?'

Rafsanjani adjusted his dress and spoke quietly. All eyes turned to the interpreter's lips.

'We welcome you to this press conference.'

The suspense was becoming unbearable as we waited for the President to begin his statement. Rafsanjani again spoke and the interpreter leaned towards the mike.

'Are there any questions?'

These words fell from the President's lips on to the assembled press like a shower of cold water. It was suddenly apparent to everyone that Rafsanjani had summoned us here for no other reason than to establish his own position internationally. Most senior journalists were either too flabbergasted to ask any searching questions about the hostages, or were already worrying about keeping their accreditation for the next and possibly genuinely important press conference, so most of the questions asked were along the lines of 'How do you like your new job, sir?' and 'What are your hopes for the future?'

Tony Birtley asked Rafsanjani if we would be allowed to visit Roger Cooper while we were in Iran, and the President agreed, but every subsequent attempt on our part to do this was diplomatically blocked, and, instead, we spent our last two days in the country on an official tour of some oil refineries.

— 19 —

Afghanistan Again: A Diary
(October/November 1989)

October 31st

I returned from Iran to be informed that I had one day in which to recover from the trip, see my family, and assemble everything I need for a month in Afghanistan. There are again rumours of a big push by the Mujahadin forces and I am to supposed to be accompanying Sandy Gall (who is already out in Pakistan) on an undercover foray across the Afghan border. Once we are there we will be unable to communicate with anyone for several weeks.

November 1st

I leave London with my sound recordist Russell Padwick, a big, good-natured man with an extraordinary photographic memory for facts and figures. I have a restocked survival kit, which includes portable dentist's equipment, and, with the publisher's deadline [for *People I Have Shot*] only a month away, a tiny lap-top word processor. We fly British Airways to Copenhagen, then PIA to Islamabad, then catch an internal flight to Peshawar.

Sandy meets us at Peshawar airport and takes us to the Continental hotel for lunch and some sleep before setting off for the border at five o'clock the next morning. We have a twelve-hour drive over some of the most inhospitable terrain in Pakistan, including the heavily snowed-in Malakand and Lourie Passes. This is rather worrying as in London we were told to expect 'autumnal' weather, and I have brought little in the way of cold weather clothes.

I book an alarm call for four o'clock in the morning, to be ready by five. At four-thirty the phone rings and it is Sandy to tell us there is a problem with our escorts and we won't be ready to leave till eight-thirty at the least. Having already been up and dressed it is difficult to return to bed and try and catch up on sleep, but we do and oversleep till eight forty-five.

Our first destination is the border town of Chitral, the closest point to the Afghani border. There is actually an internal flight to Chitral but we cannot take this for fear of discovery by the authorities. It seems that things have tightened up since we travelled last earlier in the year. Our truck ride starts pleasantly enough with everyone in high spirits, but the lack of physical exercise sends everyone one by one into a fitful sleep. The sound of Russell's head banging hard on the window is a great source of amusement to one of our guides Sabat, who has just returned from selling hotdogs in California!

Dusk starts to fall as we start up the first pass. The snows have come early this year and we are soon in deep winter. Our truck manoeuvres through the most dangerous tracks up the pass. It takes some hours to reach the top which is nearly 3,200 metres above sea level. The air is fresh and very clear and is a pleasure to breathe, but you wouldn't want to be out in it for very long. We pass through many provincial checkpoints without hindrance, but at one we are stopped and looked at a little closer. Our driver barks at the border policeman and hands him a piece of paper which he reads and pushes back to him very quickly and sends us on our way.

Hashim, our driver, turns round to Sabat and laughs, 'You boys didn't know you were rich men.'

Apparently the back of the truck contains not only our equipment but also two hundred million Afghan rupees, about two hundred thousand pounds sterling. We all laugh loudly, if somewhat nervously. I look back at our equipment in a new light.

We arrive in Chitral slightly ahead of time – it only took ten and a half hours! We are greeted by John Mohamed, an old friend of Sandy's, a great big lovable chap, with a smile that would melt steel. However he is most definitely in charge and I suspect that behind that soft face he has the strength to put your lights out very quickly. We sit down to green tea and good conversation.

This is proving very different to my last trip. These guys have their act together. Our mission is to team up with Masoud, the legendary fighter and leader who was going to let us in on the last of the fighting before the winter sets in. All of the men we are with have close connections with Masoud and I am feeling confident, so far!

We hid at a safe house in Chitral for the night, and ate the obligatory nan bread and kebabs, followed by masses of hot green tea. We are to sneak across the border tomorrow evening. A new checkpoint has been installed, with apparently uncorruptible Pakistani border guards. Also, I gather that another reason things have tightened up is that Masoud has upset the Pakistani government in some way and they are now making life more difficult for him and his men. Masoud has not received any ammunition at all this year – the Pakistanis have seen to that. But he has been stockpiling ammunition by ambushing Afghan convoys on the Salang highway. The harassment by the Pakistanis also includes stopping western journalists reaching Masoud to report on his progress.

We all fell into a deep sleep and woke to a splendid clear morning in the mountains. Our safe house is sitting deep in the valley surrounded by the most magnificent snow-capped mountains. The early morning air was quite cold but the day soon warms up very pleasantly. The light is superb, the brightest and clearest I have seen for a long time. For the time being, it's the most beautiful place in the world. We're not to be allowed to leave the house and its gardens for fear of discovery, so we settle down to a day of relaxation and hot green tea.

Left John Mohamed's house midnight November 3rd in back of pick-up covered in sleeping-bags destined for the Muj in Afghanistan. I sit with Russell. We are both six-footers, both claustrophobic. Pass through all checkpoints with little or no checks by the Pakistani border police. After six hours the truck stops and we are let out of our confines. Oh, by the way, Sandy is strapped to the roof hidden under a tarpaulin. We are now in the middle of a snow-capped mountain range – the Hindu Kush. The border is on the highest point between the two countries. We have to walk, or stagger the last 150 metres. On reaching the summit, we suffer from awful altitude sickness – this takes the form of acute motion sickness plus a desire to pass out, and severe headaches. It's a real accomplishment to film anything at all. It takes five hours to get down the mountain to the first base camp. Sickness getting worse even though we're now descending. On the way we pass dead horses, some killed by old Russian mines, others don't make it because of the cold and the rigours of the mountains. We reach our first stop, a camp called Topkana and promptly pass out.

Revived by delicious green tea. We are separated from our gear and it is a freezing stay of twenty-four hours before the gear turns up. Our interpreter finally arrives with the gear but is very sick and cannot continue.

Evening of November 4th
I am in a mud hut at the base of the Wishti valley with all the equipment plus about forty Muj, having dinner on the floor. It is total chaos, people treading over everything.

November 5th
We get horses for the first time – it's a seven-hour ride to the first stop. Temperature well below zero. No saddle, no stirrups, we just sit on top of gear. Fantastic scenery, but fucking cold. We have to go the long way to the town of Phiau because the easy way is government-held. Already saddle-sore. The novelty is wearing thin, especially when we realise there's another three days of this – if the weather holds out.

First night falls – it's very eerie riding in the dark. My clothes aren't standing up to this extreme cold and I am now in great pain. Finally reach first teahouse or *Chai karna* 'Tangal Magmawole'. A Muj grabs hold of me and keeps me near the fire to thaw out. Spend the night screaming with the most severe headaches I've ever had in my life. Want to go home please. Broken sleep disturbed at about four-thirty due to wakening Muj using me as sidewalk. Breakfast of nan and green *chai*. Horsemen ready the horses. I don't want to get back in the saddle. One of the horses is now lame – still, only eight hours to do today!

Am filthy dirty and have found a nit in my hair. Body falling to pieces. Also have been filming from the saddle – good polo practice I suppose.

November 6th

Start trek. We have to lead our horses across the mountain range as the track is too small for us to ride. We are now in the middle of the Hindu Kush. On one side of us is the mountain, on the other a drop of 5,000 metres. We film a great stand-upper from Sandy. I am getting used to the trek and starting to enjoy the countryside which is vast and magical. We have good Muj guides – personal aides to Masoud.

Second night spent at ROBOT, an old Russian air base and the dirtiest, filthiest, dustiest place in the world.

We are offered a place in the kitchen – I use the term very loosely. It consists of a giant boiler used to brew gallons of steaming green or black tea. Everything is covered in dust as there is never any flooring – just the dirt ground. Decide to refuse hospitality of the kitchen as this is always the command centre for every Muj decision from having a shit to winning the war. We sleep this night in the grain store, so much dust your bogies are the shape and size of your nostrils in the morning.

We still have not washed body or clothes or in fact changed clothes. Most of the time it's too cold to bother. I can hear the squeaking of rats all night long.

November 7th

We start off at six-thirty, still not washed. This is getting me down, the filth. Russ has some eye drops – a life-saver. Today is a ten-hour ride to the bottom of the Wishti Pass. The worst is yet to come, I am told by a wise old Muj. Well, that's the interpretation I put on a thumbs-down signal and a forefinger up your nose.

All is right with the world, though I'm very saddle-sore. Things are looking good and we got great pictures today. One of the commanders who are travelling with us is trying to learn English from a terrible book that he reads constantly – even while riding his horse. He is also trying in vain to teach me the basics of Farsi.

NAN	bread	BURRA	sugar
GARM	warm	ABI	hot
AOW	water	PILOA	rice
KARNA	house	CHAI KARNA	teahouse
CHAI	tea	ASP	horse
KOSHTE	goat	MOI	fish
MARISE	sick	SABAD	tomorrow
NIA	no	PANGE	five
OOBAHS	good	PISCE	to pay, or money
SARD . . . . hours, or watch as in wrist watch		TASHAKOR . . . . thank you	

Once again, we arrive at today's destination in the dark, after we were promised we would not! This makes all the difference as none of these places have any form of electricity, and of course, due to bad planning on my behalf, there is only one torch; and to make matters worse, only one set of batteries for the thing, so you cannot keep a check on your bags etc or get yourself together for ano terrible night's sleep. Finally we get another hovel allocated to u. and we bed down.

November 8th

The day starts badly when we have to climb the first part of the Wishti, which takes at least two hours. After this we get back on the horses for a spectacular four hours of the most breathtaking mountain scenery imaginable. We climb to a height of at least twelve thousand feet when altitude sickness hits again, but not quite as bad as before. We have to dismount as the horses cannot cope with the altitude or the steep climb. A novel way of climbing is to grab hold of the horse's tail. We reach the top very tired but with a great feeling of elation and personal achievement, which is soon to be knocked out of us as the downward trek is to prove harder than the up.

Carrying the camera and the other bits and bobs, we fall and slide down to the bottom of the pass. This takes some five hours. Now very cold and wet, we are supposed to reach the town of Phiau tonight, but once again darkness is falling, and it is now starting to snow. I should have learnt by now that you should never ask how long to the next stop-over. The answer is always 'Enshalla' – whatever is God's will. It is now inky black as the moonlight cannot penetrate the snow clouds. Depression is the worst it has been so far, and we are still a long way from our destination. We turn up at a *chai karna* that has run out of everything including a shit house to sleep in and are told the next stop will have to be Phiau itself. We snap. We cannot go any further tonight as it is getting ridiculously dangerous on the mountain passes in the snow and ice. The horses are beginning to lose their footing.

We dismount while the commander goes into the *chai karna* to negotiate for food and a bed. Meanwhile, the snow is falling harder. Note on these *chai karnas*, they are made of mud and water and straw and have been set up by the Muj as flop houses for travellers. The most basic of services are laid on, i.e., a roof, no floor, and the outside world is the toilet. All you get, if you are lucky, is a place near the boiler with your sleeping-bag.

The commander says we can stay the night here, not inside, but under a covering that has no walls and is made for supplies. But we can come in for a cup of tea. On entering the *chai karna*, over a hundred faces look up at us from a space of barely more than two square metres. This is too much for me. I run back into the snow and start to make a bonfire by the covering. While the guys drink the tea in the asylum, I try to make the covering as comfortable as possible. The snow is coming down even harder now. The scene is very picturesque as I look out from under my sleeping-bag to see a Muj guard silhouetted by our fire, with the snowflakes sparkling across his Kalashnikov. The magic is soon to turn to shit as the snow on the roof starts to melt and pours through the makeshift branch roof. We try to ignore it for a while but this becomes impossible, and at about four-thirty give it up as a bad joke and sit round the fire with our guard and the horsemen.

November 9th

First light breaks at about five-thirty. Depression even worse, and everything is going wrong. Cannot even boil water and cut my hand on Swiss army knife. Snow is falling even harder. I fall off my horse trying to mount and walk off into the forest to collect my thoughts, near to tears.

It should be only two hours to Phiau. Weather is very bad now. Cannot see hand in front of my face for snow branches smashing into my face. Lose my temper completely – smash horse on top of his head and leap off and walk to Phiau.
Note: have been treating Sandy's various cuts and bruises. When the Muj see my medical kit there always seems to be some small ailment to be treated; these tough bastards are like little kids when it comes to headaches and splinters.

We finally reach Phiau and are the guests of the local commander. Because, needless to say, the transport arranged by the Muj has pissed off because we were so many days late. Finally, we have the opportunity to wash. Bliss, even though the mountain stream is just above freezing point. My hair is completely matted with filth so I totally immerse my head in freezing water – and nearly pass out with the shock.

The local commander's hospitality is second to none, even though it is very basic. There are children in the village and we have fun trying to teach each other different languages. I have arranged to ride the head man's prize *Bastachi* horses tomorrow. This is the first time we have stopped in the middle of the day. It is fantastic to relax and dry out our gear and to take stock. The commander's guest hovel is warm and dry.

We are now waiting for the transport to be contacted and for it to return and pick us up, and take us to Masoud, wherever that might be. The really depressing thing about all this is that we are still only one-third of our way into the trip and we have to return the same way. Anyway, time to keep warm and get some hot tea and see what tomorrow brings.

November 10th
Last night was fantastic. All the commander's children came into

the hovel and sang revolutionary songs about Masoud and the cause. We drew pictures of cats and dogs and aeroplanes and then went on to basic entertainments like shadow creatures. I showed them pictures of my kids. Dinner arrives – superb food. We never see the women who cook all this as we are still in the Dark Ages when it comes to women. The food is served by a servant: saffron rice with chicken, stone ground nan bread, chilli peppers, and chicken soup, followed by the biggest water melon I have ever seen. It is cut into two halves and we all dig in. It must be a special treat as the children are allowed to dig in as well.

Through our interpreter we chat for ages about war, *Bastachi* and polo. The boiler is throwing out an immense amount of heat. I take a Valium and a sneaky swig of brandy and fall into the first proper sleep for six days.

Note: I have been given a great drawing of a chicken signed by all the children. One of them is a girl who even at this age of about five is not allowed in the presence of men. A beautiful child with enormous eyes and a smile that is tearing us all apart. In a few short years she will be destined for life under a sheet, serving saffron rice to weary travellers like ourselves, but never to be seen again.

Our transport still has not arrived and it is now ten-thirty in the morning. This is the first time I have seen Sandy agitated at all. We have now been a total of ten days away from base and we still have not met up with Masoud or even filmed anything relevant to the story. But we do have a good tale of journos in adverse conditions. We passed a very old jeep the day before – about four kilometres further back from Phiau, so our guide, Commander Ismail, has gone to negotiate the hire of it. We were also told yesterday when we passed it that the brakes did not work.

Ismail has worked wonders. He has returned with the jeep plus a driver in an old Russian uniform top.

We had not gone two kilometres when the bloody jeep came to a grinding halt. Our driver leapt out and achieved precisely fuck all. With a limited mechanical knowledge I could see that the carb was flooding badly, so with a few turns of a screwdriver I managed to impress everybody with my vast knowledge of the internal combustion engine. This happened a few more times over a distance of about fifty kilometres. Finally, to cap it all we hit a small ridge at a fairly low speed but the impact was enough to knock off the front wheel.

We are now in the middle of a vast plain with night about to fall once again. Russell and I endeavour to light a fire as we can see that we could be here for the rest of the night, and to cap it all, it now starts to piss down with rain. The wheel is beyond repair. Ismail takes it all in his stride while we are losing our cool. He takes the opportunity to have some target practice with his Kalashnikov while Russ and I struggle unsuccessfully to light green sodden twigs.

As luck would have it a truck stops and offers us a lift to the next village. All of us have to squeeze into the front cab and we suffer extreme discomfort for another hour until we reach a small town called Chaman. We have to spend the night as this is as far as our transport can take us. This turns out to be rather fortunate as this is one of the communication bases of the Muj, and they put us up in beds for the first time in six days.

We have managed to get a message to Masoud to say that we are still on our way, even though we are a few days late. This trip is turning out to be one of the hardest I have ever done.

November 11th
We wake in the ex-government station of Chaman at, would you believe, a staggering seven-thirty – a lie-in! We also take our first proper wash since being on the road (nine days). They have an outhouse – a boiler affair with about six gallons of hot water in it, a concrete floor with channels cut into the side to let the water run away. It might not be the most sophisticated in the world, but after all this time it is heaven to wash your bollocks in warm, soapy water. Then breakfast of scrambled eggs and nan bread and, of course, green tea. As I look out of the window, scoffing my scrambled eggs, I see a beautiful horse being exercised. On enquiry it turns out to be none other than Masoud's. I tentatively ask if I might have a ride. The answer is yes, to my mixed feelings. The most fantastic animal I have ever seen, and pretty damned wild. The

groom (a prisoner of war) tacked him up for me with the traditional wooden saddle. Trying to appear full of confidence, I trotted off and then, even more tentatively, I cantered, then galloped for a short distance – fantastic!

We are now waiting for a jeep to arrive from wherever, to take us to our final destination – Taleqan. Meanwhile, lunch has arrived. Chicken and chips. And, of course, green tea. In all the hanging about today I have also learnt how to strip and reassemble a Chinese Kalashnikov – really useful that.

Our jeep has arrived – it is two-thirty in the afternoon. This is another old Russian jeep but in a lot better condition than the last. Mind you, it still wouldn't be allowed on the road in the UK. We pile in, seven of us, and all our gear, Taleqan bound. It takes another three and a half hours to reach Taleqan and en route our heads are filled with the promises of hot baths and beds by the new interpreter we picked up in Chaman. He speaks perfect English, with an American accent. His name is Haroun. On the way, we pass the scene of a tremendous battle that occurred three years ago. Dead tanks still litter the road. This is the first time in all our travels that we have come across a tarmac road. It feels very exposed and I would be a lot happier with the cover of the mountains.

On arrival at Taleqan, Sandy is very ill with what looks like 'flu, so we decide not to see Masoud tonight. A mistake as we are shown to a house with little or no facilities. When does it get better? I'm beginning to think it never will. So it's sleeping-bags once again, and green tea, and we see Masoud tomorrow to find out what was so important to bring us all this horrendous way.

November 12th

We are still waiting for word from Masoud to come and see him. In the meantime we have breakfast of nan bread and BLACK tea and the remnants of Sandy's peanut butter. We have asked the owner of the house to show us to a bath-house. It is a very primitive affair but effective – about four and a half square metres, full of steam and glorious hot water. We wallow for about half an hour, then get back to the house in case one of Masoud's men has been around with any information. On the way back we spot a primitive barber's shop and I am given a cut-throat shave by an extremely competent young man before being dabbed down with old Russian aftershave. When we arrive back at the house there is still no word of our meeting with Masoud – it is now eleven o'clock in the morning.

The day passes very lazily, but with a wary eye on the sky as we have just been told that the Afghan airforce bombed the shit out of this town just seven days ago. The airforce have adopted new bombing tactics; they have converted transport planes that fly at very high altitude and drop their payload a safe distance from the Muj's stinger ground-to-air missiles, which have a range of about 2,000 metres.

We have been told we are to be moved to another house sometime this afternoon and we are now twiddling our thumbs. At five-thirty, the great man himself arrives, out of the blue. Masoud greets Sandy like an old friend. They sit and chat and Sandy gives him gifts of Maxwell House coffee and Cadbury's chocolate. Masoud is a handsome, charismatic bugger – he instantly reminded me of all those old Che posters.

After we move house, we are to be collected by Masoud's driver and taken to dinner with him. Our new house, needless to say, is no different from the last one except that the floor is slightly less dusty, and there is a diesel stove. We go to join Masoud for dinner which is a truly elaborate affair by Afghan standards. Eggplant, pumpkins, spinach, meatballs, rice, nan bread and, of course, green tea. We interview Masoud at great length to find out how he is faring and what his military plans are for the next few weeks and if there is anything we can go and join him on. He is going away for the next three days on some recce or other and has organised us a driver and jeep. We decide that when it turns up we will film the town.

November 13th
Have got a dose of the shits. I've been up half the night squatting over a hole in the ground and have severe stomach cramps. Anyway, the jeep and escort never arrived as predicted.

We went and filmed the town on our own, a lively place of about 100,000 people. There is plenty of fruit produce in the markets. Meat and clothing are abundant, and surprisingly, the few pharmacies that are here are well-stocked. In fact the town is a normal trading market town with even its own jugglers and conjurors. It's nice to find a story about the Muj that's something other than fighting. This town is the only example of a provincial capital functioning under a Mujahadin administration.

Ninety-nine per cent of the people here have not seen a white man, never mind a television camera, so every time we stop to film anything at all a crowd of a couple of hundred forms in a matter of seconds. The novelty soon wears off for me and I get claustrophobic in the middle of the city. We also film in an old Russian base, now a hospital, where we meet a young Uzbeki lad of thirteen who lost his left hand by playing with a live Russian grenade. His name is John Mahoumad. I still have the raging shits and am rushing to the nearest gutter whenever I can. As night falls, we go to shoot the sunset and the camera starts playing up, the picture in the viewfinder wobbling.

Disaster has struck, our main camera has finally given up the ghost and the spare camera has also packed up, so we are fucked totally. But we think we already have enough good pictures to put together two cracking pieces.

Something is really wrong with my gut. One-fifteen a.m., feeling very poorly indeed. Sandy is feeding me yoghourt as it seems to be a local remedy and everything else has failed. We shall see.
Note: The Farsi translation of Taleqan is 'The Whirlpool of Blood'!

We cannot get to see Masoud again until he returns from wherever he has gone, and that won't be for a couple of days yet, so once again we have to sit and twiddle our thumbs. I don't think I have ever had so many emotional ups and downs in one trip. I feel totally surplus to requirements without my camera, and I am now seriously debating with myself whether I shall do any more of these difficult, dangerous, macho trips. It's about time I did some soft ones. Still, I suppose I have made my bed over the years and will have to lie in it a little longer.

November 15th

It gets worse. I have been hit with amoebic dysentery very badly. Spewing blood and shitting blood. Time to call it quits. Broken camera and broken cameraman. We must make plans to get the hell out of here.

November 16th

I spent all day yesterday in my sleeping-bag only getting up to be sick. I vomited blood all over Russell which gave him a bit of a fright. It frightened me as well. The doctor has been and confirmed amoebic dysentery. He doesn't want me to travel for another six to nine days. Bullshit, we are making plans to leave today. I would rather get weaker on the road leading to civilisation than turn into an even bigger pile of shit here in the middle of 'The Whirlpool of Blood'. How aptly named. If the bullets don't get you, the bugs will.

We eventually get a roadworthy jeep and set off back to Phiau. One small bit of luck is that Commander Masoud is in Phiau, so at least Sandy can have another chat with him before we leave for Pakistan. Also, we have been told that there will be six horses for us ready to take us on first thing in the morning. The seven-hour journey is bright and sunny, but I am too preoccupied with keeping all my orifices firmly shut to notice the scenery. On arrival, I give myself a Vitamin B1, B6, B12 jab in an attempt to get myself better.

November 17th

Of course the bloody horses have not turned up. They have only two, which are tacked up all wrong, and it will take another day to get four more! Well, at least I am feeling a little better today although I have pissed a little blood.

November 23rd

Back in Chitral. The journey back was so absolutely shattering that I did not have either the energy or the motivation to keep up the diary. The awful cold weather and the dysentery has made this the hardest and most miserable trip I have ever done. We have ridden for five days, two of them through driving snow on horses in a state of near-collapse. I unsaddled my mount one night to find that the awful stench I had been smelling all day emanated from an open gangrenous wound covering half his back.

Today we started off for Peshawar in two jeeps from the Afghan Aid Workers house in Chitral. We had driven for several hours when we were turned back at the pass by snow and ice. Also, a truck had overturned blocking the pass so, even if we had got over the ice, we couldn't have got through. I cannot believe that these drivers don't have chains for their tyres. So, we are now back at the Afghan Aid house. We have tried bribing the airfield police for some places on the old boxkite that flies between Chitral and Peshawar. We have to be at the airfield at seven-thirty with a handful of dollars. Well, we'll see what happens. Plan B is to send another car from Peshawar to meet us at the top of the pass. ENSHALLA! Sooner or later our luck has to change. Christ, I hope so.

November 24th

We were to try and cross the Lourie Pass again today but our escort knows an airport policeman who is bribable, so there is a possibility of catching an internal flight to Peshawar. There are three flights a day, but our bad luck is keeping pace with us and the first two are cancelled, so we debate whether to try the pass once again. Our minds are made up for us with the sound of an incoming aeroplane. We race to the airfield to meet our paid-off policeman, and to our surprise, yes, we can get on the plane. Has our luck finally decided to change? But oh no, at the last minute we are informed that there are places for only two passengers, not three. Sandy, who is not in favour with the Pakistani authorities, must go, and I, by chance, have all the rushes in my shoulder-bag. So Russell, who has braved hundreds of kilometres on foot and horseback, has to be left behind. He does not grumble a jot but mutters under his breath 'Fucking Enshalla . . .'

The short flight from Chitral to Peshawar was a bit of a culture shock to people who have seen nothing but mountains and shit for nearly a month. The ISI – the Pakistani secret police – are keeping a close eye on Sandy, so we have to be a little careful of what we say and do in Peshawar. Fortunately all the film is absolutely fine and we are both delighted with the results. But dear old Russell is still rotting in Chitral. Hopefully he will be on the next flight in tomorrow and I shall be there to meet him with a big, wet kiss . . .

On arrival at the hotel we find that ENSHALLA is keeping pace with us. There is a seminar going on and there are no rooms to be had . . . but Sandy knows the manager and we have two people thrown out of their rooms. The first sit-down bath in a month is something else. Even after an hour of soaking, I still feel dirty; but an ice-cold Murray beer sorts out the rough edges. It's good to be back.

November 25th

All flights from Chitral have been cancelled today and it's proving impossible to find when the next one will be . . . Russell must be going potty by now. I know I would be tearing my hair out. All our movements for shipping our film out, and Sandy, revolve around Russell's eventual arrival. We are trying not to send Sandy and the film together back to London as the Pakistani secret police are on the lookout for him. We don't think it's anything too serious, but the thought of possibly losing all that hard-earned footage is too much to bear. I have talked to my wife and children for the first time in a month and it's a very strange sensation indeed. As Penny put it, quite bluntly, I have become someone she knows and talks about at dinner parties, rather than a husband. She tells me that Bobby in particular has missed me very much this trip.

It is now five-thirty in the afternoon and still no sign of Russ. I must admit to a little feeling of unease about this situation, but I am sure he will be all right.

We just heard the news on the World Service. Mass demonstrations in East Berlin, and vast political changes forecast. Eastern Europe is the place to be right now, not bloody Afghanistan.

November 26th

Russell back safe and sound after a twelve-hour drive over the snowbound Lourie Pass. As well as being held up by snow, he and his escort were caught in the middle of some warring tribal factions. This is his first major foreign trip and yet he is ten times more buoyant and cheerful than well-seasoned hacks like Sandy and me. More news from abroad: the Berlin Wall is coming down. Why aren't I there?

Index